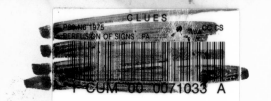

A PERFUSION OF SIGNS

Contributors

Diana Agrest
*The Institute for Architecture
and Urban Studies*

Paul Bouissac
University of Toronto

Mario Gandelsonas
*The Institute for Architecture
and Urban Studies*

Henry Hiż
University of Pennsylvania

James D. Meltzer
The Roosevelt Hospital

Jean-Jacques Nattiez
University of Montreal

Erik Schwimmer
Laval University

Thomas A. Sebeok
Indiana University

Harley C. Shands
The Roosevelt Hospital

Edward Stankiewicz
Yale University

Rulon S. Wells
Yale University

J. Jay Zeman
University of Florida

ADVANCES IN SEMIOTICS
General Editor, Thomas A. Sebeok

A
PERFUSION
OF
SIGNS

Edited by
Thomas A. Sebeok

Indiana University Press • Bloomington and London

Copyright © 1977 by Indiana University Press

Published in Canada by Fitzhenry & Whiteside Limited, Don Mills, Ontario

Manufactured in the United States of America

Library of Congress Cataloging in Publication Data

North American Semiotics Colloquium, 1st, University
   of South Florida, 1975.
   A perfusion of signs.

   (Advances in semiotics)
   1. Semiotics—Congresses. I. Sebeok, Thomas
Albert, 1920–   II. Title. III. Series.
P99.N6 1975   149'.94   76-29318
ISBN 0-253-34352-6

1   2   3   4   5   81   80   79   78   77

It seems a strange thing, when one comes to ponder over it, that a sign should leave its interpreter to supply a part of its meaning; but the explanation of the phenomenon lies in the fact that the entire universe—not merely the universe of existents, but all that wider universe, embracing the universe of existents as a part, the universe which we are all accustomed to refer to as "the truth"— that all this universe is perfused with signs, if it is not composed exclusively of signs.

—Charles Sanders Peirce

Contents

PREFACE

In his twilight years, in the course of a discussion about two kinds of indeterminacy—indefiniteness and generality—Charles Peirce explained that the former "consists in the sign's not sufficiently expressing itself to allow of an indubitable determinate interpretation," since, as he had written somewhat earlier (1906), for a sign to fulfill its office, "to actualize its potency," it must be compelled (he meant in a purely physiological manner) by its object. The latter, generality, he held, "turns over to the interpreter the right to complete the determination as he please." These observations, which have a direct bearing upon the question of pragmaticism, and much else—in particular, the notion of duality—besides, are immediately followed by a singularly haunting passage. The title for this volume builds upon this bedazzling sentence, one that Peirce himself might have characterized as exceedingly simple yet for that very reason most difficult to grasp: "It seems a strange thing, when one comes to ponder over it, that a sign should leave its interpreter to supply a part of its meaning; but the explanation of the phenomenon lies in the fact that the entire universe—not merely the universe of existents, but all that wider universe, embracing the universe of existents as a part, the universe which we are all accustomed to refer to as 'the truth'—that all this universe is perfused with signs, if it is not composed exclusively of signs."

It fell to Jakob von Uexküll and his successors to eventually provide the theoretical biological underpinning for Peirce's view, which is tantamount to the assertion that in man, as in all other animals, semiosis has its source in the regulatory circuits that equilibrate and thus unify every living system (Cannon's principle of homeostasis), as well as establishes and maintains networks of stable relationships among diverse organisms (in Jacob's ascending hierarchy of integrons). Semiosis must, of course, conform to the universal laws of thermodynamics, as René Thom—who was strongly influenced by both Peirce and von Uexküll—has lately shown in several landmark contributions, rooted in topology, that surely betoken the most consequential turning point in the history of semiotics since Peirce.

In 1962, a conference was convened at Indiana University for a consideration of the twin topics of "paralinguistics" and "kinesics," the results of which were published two years afterwards under the prescient title *Approaches to Semiotics*. (The whimsical circumstances that led to this *ex post facto* relabeling are related—or rationalized—in my 1976 book, *Contributions to the Doctrine of Signs,* pp. 21–22 and 51–52.) The contents of the work at hand represent, however, (most of) the transactions of what explicitly was planned and veridically became the First North American Semiotics Colloquium ever held in the United States. This Colloquium took place on July 28–30, 1975, at the University of South Florida, Tampa, within the wider framework of that Summer's nine-week Linguistic Institute held under the auspices of the Linguistic Society of America. Three "pioneers," Shands, Stankiewicz, and I, who took part in the earlier conference, were in Tampa too, and each is, in fact, a contributor to this new book.

The meeting was assembled for two different but closely interrelated reasons: the primary objective was to provide a formal opportunity for the founding of an organization of U.S. semioticians; an incidental but no less important purpose was to make a scholarly forum available for the ventilation of a wide range of current issues in semiotic theory and practice. The congregation was unusual—indeed, unprecedented—in that it included, over and above a large number of language scientists (among them both the 1975 and the 1976 Presidents of the LSA, the second also a recent President of the Charles S. Peirce Society) teaching or studying at the Linguistic Institute, many invited as well as volunteer North and South American and West European participants with expertise in diverse branches of semiotics, complemented by an exceptionally rich representation from Eastern Europe (Czechoslovakia, Hungary, Poland, Romania, Yugoslavia), and the USSR (the latter in the person of Thomas V. Gamkralidze, of the Georgian Academy of Sciences, in Tbilisi). The Secretary General of the International Association for Semiotic Studies, Umberto Eco, came from Italy, and Roland Posner, now the President of the Deutsche Gesellschaft für Semiotik, from Germany. The Secretary of the Polish Semiotic Society, Jerzy Pelc, was there from Warsaw, as was the Secretary of the Hungarian Semiotic Society, Özséb Horányi, from Budapest, among such other prominent Continental semioticians as Solomon Marcus, from Bucharest, and Ivo Osolsobě, from Brno. Grants supporting the participation of many of our foreign visitors—both world-famous scholars and some of their burgeoning disciples—were generously provided by the American Council of Learned Societies, the Department of State's Board on Foreign Scholarships and Bureau of Cultural and Educational Affairs, the Ford Foundation, and the International Research and Exchanges Board. To all of these private and federal agencies who helped, often acting on short notice, to enable the travel and sustenance of these colleagues, I extend, once again—this time publicly—my warmest appreciation for their timely aid.

Peirce had modestly characterized himself to be only "a pioneer, or rather a backwoodsman, in the work of clearing and opening up" what he called "semiotic." Charles Morris, whose interest in the theory of signs began in the early 1920s, remarked half a century later that he still felt "essentially the same about [his] own work." But it is from the seed sown by autochthonous giants such as Peirce and Morris, the foundational doctrine of semiotics as severally delineated by them, that we all now reap. (When Walt Whitman wrote, "Enclosed and safe within its central heart,/Nestles the seed perfection," was he aware, I wonder, of the etymological resonances of *sēma* and *sēmen,* as Dante must have been in "ogni erba si conosce per lo seme"?)

In conformity with Peirce's belief that the entire universe is perfused with signs, if it is not composed exclusively of signs, the theme that animated the Colloquium and that, accordingly, informs the contents of this book is that of global unity underlying variety, and a spirit of ecumenicalism that, more and more, characterizes contemporary semiotics. However, the specific ways in which signs function in various human sciences are also clearly brought out in this book, which may fairly be taken as a companion volume to a further collection, *Sight, Sound, and Sense,* to follow shortly under the same publisher's imprint. For technical reasons, a few papers delivered *viva voce* could, regrettably, not be included in this volume, notably one on semiotics and the visual arts and another (which its author is expanding into a book) on semiotics and the theater.

It remains for me to report that the conference closed with a business session the principal long-range result of which was the creation, in 1976, of the Semiotic Society of America, incorporated, February last, in the State of New York. With an exceptionally successful first Annual Meeting, at the Georgia Institute of Technology, now behind us, with future meetings scheduled to be held at such centers of excellence as Colorado (1977), Brown (1978), Indiana (1979), and with hundreds of active members joining our circles daily from here and abroad, this collection should also be regarded as a celebration of this consolidating achievement, a milestone in the development of semiotics in North America and wherever, in perpetually widening circles throughout the world, the thought of Peirce is finding stronger and more sympathetic echoes.

Thomas A. Sebeok

Bloomington
February 1, 1977

Criteria for Semiosis

Rulon S. Wells

My fundamental message is a message of caution. We must beware of claiming too much for semiotics. And whatever claims we make, we must be prepared to support.

The danger of claiming too much takes various forms; two or three are most frequent.

First, there is the temptation to assimilate. If we are interested in signs ('signs' in whatever sense we have already established for ourselves), and are interested in other things, we feel the temptation to construe these other things as signs. (There is the opposite temptation too: the temptation to heighten differences; may it be that I am succumbing to *that* temptation?) Many of the current attempts to view art semiotically can be explained, though they cannot be justified, by this temptation.

Somewhat more sophisticated is the attempt to generalize.[1] Often this attempt is inspired by the notion that generalizing is one of the things one does in science. Charles Peirce's semiotics is heavily influenced by this notion and to a considerable extent vitiated by it. There is such a thing as pseudogeneralization, which is empty or sterile generalization, and much of Peirce's work that he regarded as generalization is really only pseudogeneralization.

In between, there is a process that I may call decoding.[2] It consists in treating what appear to be ordinary, straightforward statements as coded messages. 'Code' is used in many senses, but what I have in mind here is the sense in which, say, 'tanker' is a code word for stock prices, 'freighter' is a code word for bond prices, 'north' is a code word for rise, and 'south' is a code word for fall. Given this code, the message 'tanker north' can be read either as clear or as coded; taken as clear, it says that a tanker is to the north, and taken as coded, it says that stock prices rise. Now there are cases where a statement using the word 'language' can be read as if a coded reference to gestures, or to kinship systems, or whatever. When I speak of 'reading as if coded', I am using 'code' metaphorically, for one who does this doesn't suppose that the statement was put into code for the sake of secrecy. Rather, he tries the experiment of taking the word 'language' *as if* it were a code word for this or for that, and sometimes the experiment yields interesting results. The result will be interesting only if enough other words be taken as coded in the same code so that entire, extended discourses can be read as if coded.

Codes will have their limits; not every statement containing the word 'north' can be read as if coded in the above-specified code; for instance, 'Nothing is north of the North Pole' cannot be read this way, nor can 'North is at right angles with East'. A proposed set of code readings will be the more interesting, the larger the set of discourses that can be read either as clear or as coded in this set of code-readings.

When someone proposes, explicitly or implicitly, to give the word 'language' a code-meaning, the ordinary way of describing what he is doing is to say that he is using the word metaphorically. For instance, talk of body language or of the language of flowers, commonly styled metaphorical, may equally well be viewed as a certain kind of coding. A certain kind, not just any kind; the coding system has to be such that, when all the words in a discourse that can be read as coded are so read, the discourse retains the same truth-value that it has when read as clear. This constraint amounts to requiring an isomorphism between clear and coded readings.

The technique exhibited in a rudimentary way in such double readings was brought to explicitness by nineteenth-century mathematicians. I refer to Ernest Nagel's fine history of the episode.[3] It led to fruitful results in algebra, geometry, and symbolic logic, and was a step (1) in making mathematics more abstract, (2) in disengaging the intellectual from the intuitive component of mathematical knowledge, (3) in leading up to David Hilbert's formalism, and (4) in leading up to Hilbert's use of 'interpretation' or modeling to prove consistency. These developments gave geometry a deductive rigor far beyond what it had in Euclid, and they refuted Kant's thesis that intuition plays an indispensable role in mathematics.

But we should recognize that the technique is different from the technique of generalization. That the same formal system can be interpreted in two (or more) ways does not show that these interpretations have a concept in common; just the opposite. This is because the coding, which makes a double reading possible, has to be systematic. The principle of duality in projective geometry allows us, *salva veritate,* to take 'point' as a code word for line, provided that we simultaneously take 'line' as a code word for point. And what point and line have in common is only that they are related to each other by certain symmetries. Point differs from line in the same way as line differs from point. Point and line are like each other in that, in a certain respect, each is different from the other in that same respect.

The example is significant as proving that likeness (resemblance) cannot always be reduced to sharing a property. That kind of likeness which is displayed by the clear meaning and the coded meaning of a code word is not generic likeness; and therefore the possibility of setting up a code in which 'language', 'vocabulary', 'syntax', 'phrase', etc., have coded meanings alongside of their clear meanings does not suffice to establish that there is a semiotic genus of which speech is one species and the phenomena signified by the coded meanings are another species. The formalistic approach is revealing, but it does not reveal generic properties.

There is a particular version of formalism that is proving attractive to semioticians. Every sign has two 'faces' (Saussure): its form and its content. Here I must digress briefly on a point of terminology. In general it is convenient to follow Hjelmslev in drawing *two* distinctions within the sign; in his terminology the two faces are called expression (not form) and content, and then each of these two is subject to a second distinction between its form and its substance. The only *in*convenience of this terminology is that the term formalism becomes inappropriate, and 'expressionalism'' wouldn't do because it is preempted. So I will accept the inconvenience and retain the now inappropriate term 'formalism' to signify concern with the expression-face in abstraction from the content-face.

As one of our important concerns in this Colloquium will be zoosemiotics, I want to call attention to the possibility that when we ascribe signs to brute animals, we are speaking formalistically. I do not lay this down as a thesis; my role here is to ask questions. *May it not be that* the so-called animal signs resemble human signs in their expression-face and yet lack a content-face, in other words, have no meaning?

The hypothesis that wherever there are phenomena that appear to be the expression-faces of signs, there will also be found phenomena that appear to be the content-faces of signs, is a respectable hypothesis; but if it is to be a scientific hypothesis, it must be susceptible of verification, i.e., of confirmation or refutation; and, if it is confirmed by the consequences that it predicts, then it must pass the further test of being compared for simplicity with alternative hypotheses.

What if no alternative hypotheses can be thought of? In the case that concerns us, when the expression-structure is elaborate, it is tempting to say that the only alternative to the hypothesis of an accompanying content-structure is the hypothesis that what appears to be an expression-structure is due to chance, and that the more elaborate the structure, the more improbable is the explanation by chance. Since we are speaking of living organisms, the alternatives can be stated more pointedly in terms of function. Most organic structures have functions, and the more elaborate a structure is, the more likely it is to have some discoverable function.

But in addition to the fact that cases are known of elaborate biological structures that have no justifying function as far as we can see, it is appropriate at this juncture to bring in an entirely new consideration, namely, diachrony. The injection of the diachronic viewpoint affects semiotics in two main ways. First, there is the inertia often displayed in evolution, whereby something—the dorsal plates of dinosaurs, the sabre-teeth of tigers or of boars, the horns of various reptiles and mammals—continues, blindly following along a certain line, to get bigger and bigger, to the point where it ceases to be an asset and even becomes a liability; the phenomenon, in short, that moved Theodor Einer to posit alongside of natural selection a cause which he called 'orthogenesis'. Besides this extreme inertia which is, viewed animistically, blind and intransigent, there is also a lag which would only be called sluggish, but it need not here be distinguished as a separate case; any inertia whether long- or short-lasting spoils a synchronic functional analysis à la Malinowski. The second main way in which the injection of the diachronic viewpoint affects semiotics (and everything else) is that things may *change* function. An organism may perform (accomplish, fulfill) function A by means of structure S, then S may come to serve also, incidentally, function B, then the need for function A may wane, or the need for function B may wax, and function B may come to be the main function served by structure S. Speaking with specific reference to human purposes, Wilhelm Wundt called this phenomenon the heterogony of ends; Hans Vaihinger called it the preponderance of means over end; Gordon Allport, Robert Merton, and others have discussed it.[4] In the first half-century or so of response to Darwin, this phenomenon was put forward as an alternative to finalistic (teleological) explanations; at the present time it deserves consideration as an alternative to semiotical explanations. The hypothesis that plants and brute animals act purposefully was challenged as anthropomorphic; a responsible defense of the hypothesis that they act semiotically will address itself to the same challenge. A teleological explanation of biological phenomena would conceive Nature as a purposive agent, guiding the course of organic evolution; an alternative explanation along the lines I have sketched would see each change as caused *a tergo*.

We may consider a series of species together and find that, *when* considered together, it is as if they made up different and successive stages of one individual. When the old 'teleologische Naturbetrachtung' did this, the counterexplanation was put forward that each stage must be considered separately in its own terms, which means in terms of *its* needs and *its* means. The insects considered in one of Professor Sebeok's papers[5] furnish an example. The third species in the series seems, considered as a later stage of the first and the second, to be fooling his wife; he presents her, it seems, with a package that is all wrapping and no gift, but she discovers this only too late, after he has made his getaway. Now the sceptic would be at once suspicious of the fact that this episode occurs at each copulation. Invariably the wife is fooled. What has happened to the philosopher's insight that deception and lie can only occur against a background of truth? Deception depends on ambiguity; and only he who can tell the truth can deceive (Plato). And the sceptic will shrewdly observe that the semiotic plausibility of the example depends on construing Insect number 3 as a later stage, a more sophisticated and worldly stage, as it were, of numbers 1 and 2. Number 2 was exploratory; he stumbled on a ruse that rescued him, and (for whatever reason) then moved into stage 3, in which, as a steady routine, and without giving the matter any thought, he employed this ploy.

I have cautioned against three dangers: the dangers of assimilating, of generalizing, and of coding. The main question to which I am addressing myself is this: What is the proper business of semioticians; or rather, how do we recognize our business? How do we recognize a sign? Here I have to say that Peirce and Morris gave the inquiry a wrong turn. Besides trying to generalize the concept of sign, they tried to define it. Peirce tells Lady Welby that "I despair of making my own broader conception understood."[6] What reason to think he *has* a conception? More specifically, what reason to think that there is a conception of something common to the icon, the index, and the symbol? It is conspicuous that in his studies of semiotics, Peirce uses as his chief heuristic guide not any inductive study and not any feeling for the distinctively semiotic, but rather the combinatorial possibilities offered him by his three categories.

But it is another aspect of Peirce's philosophy that I concentrate on here. Peirce's philosophy has many aspects and many themes; and it is not a mere heap of ideas from which one can deftly pick out some while leaving the others quite behind. His concept of sign involves interpretant; his concept of interpretant involves mind; his concept of mind is generalized (to include 'quasi-mind') beyond recognition along panpsychist lines dictated by his synechistic idealism. His pragmatism and his anti-Cartesianism must be mentioned in the same breath.

Where a strict Cartesian would limit mind to consciousness, a Peircean would construe it far more widely. Instead of admitting it only where he has to, he would admit it everywhere that he can't be prevented from admitting it. (Descartes seeks to restrict; Peirce, to extend. Descartes seeks, as it were, discontinuities; Peirce, continuities.) Their respective views of transspecific communication nicely exhibit their differences. Peirce socializes with his horse and his canary. Descartes grants to brute animals feelings but not thoughts.[7] No wonder, then, that Peirce refuses to separate thought in the strict sense—logos, ratio—from feeling and from will. His synechism directs him to say that in brutes, the rational element is not lacking altogether but is merely present in imperceptibly low degree.

Without attempting an exhaustive or a conclusive proof that semiosis cannot be defined, I will mention three representative attempts.

First, surrogate. A Sign is a surrogate, or substitute, for that which it signifies. At best this gives the genus of a definition, but not the specific difference, since even if all signs are surrogates, not all surrogates are signs. So next we must seek the specific difference. But it is manifestly idle to define a sign as a significant or semiotical surrogate.

Worse than idle, though, it is also not true. Some signs function in some ways as surrogates, but in no case are we warranted in saying that to be a sign is to be a surrogate. I will show what I mean by making reference to Morris's example (*Signs, Language, and Behavior,* p. 6) of a road sign. How does the message 'The road ahead is blocked by a landslide' function as a sign to the automobile driver? Morris answers that "in some sense . . . the words control . . . behavior . . . in a way similar to (though not identical with) the control which would be exercised by the . . . obstacle. . . . The . . . words are in some sense 'substitutes'. . . ." I find myself obliged to point out that not only does Morris fail to show, but no one before or since him has succeeded in showing, what that sense is.

One sees that Morris hopes to define sign; that he hopes to do it in terms of the concept 'substitute'; and that he hopes to work out a criterion for substitution along these lines, 'x is a substitute for y if x is similar to y in a certain way'. Now why is it that no one has been able to achieve that aim by specifying (in behavioral terms) what the 'certain way' is? The answer is simple. The requisite certain way in which x is similar to y is that it is taken to be substitutable for y. But 'taking' is a mental, not a behavioral notion. Far from defining sign in terms of substitute, we are now thinking of defining substitute in terms of taking; we might as well bypass substitution altogether, and, if we still aspire to define the sign, define signifying in terms of taking. This would be a genuine genus-and-species definition, in that taking-as-a-sign is a species of taking, and '*x* is a sign of *y* to *z*' can be paraphrased as '*z* takes *x* as a sign of *y*'. As my last word upon quitting the subject, I mention that the inspiration for my definition comes from Peirce. Peirce considers the connection between similarity and the judgment of similarity, and controverts the usual view. The usual view is that our minds judge *A* and *B* to be similar because they *are* similar; Peirce holds that, in the last analysis, if *A* and *B* are similar it is because our minds judge them so.[8]

My first objection to the surrogate-conception has been that its assumption about similarity is untenable because it assumes a hysteron proteron. My second objection is that the sense or the way in which a sign is a surrogate is far removed from the ordinary sense or way. Consider Morris's road sign. If I come to a landslide, I back up, turn around, and take some detour to my destination. If, a mile before I would have come to the landslide, I come to a sign, 'Landslide one mile ahead', *and I believe the sign,* I stop traveling on that road, and take some detour to my destination. The landslide makes me stop and take a detour; the believed sign makes me stop and take a detour; here is the similarity between the believed sign and that which it is a sign of. But why should we call this substitution, or surrogation? The sign is not in the same place as the landslide; if it were, it would be superfluous, and if it were put where the landslide was, and the landslide were taken away, then the sign would become false.

Let us not confound signs with replicas. A glass imitation of a diamond is like a diamond in glitter and transparency, though not in the detailed quality of its glitter and not in other physical and chemical properties. An opera singer's understudy passably resembles her in voice, if not in appearance; a movie actor's double resembles him in appearance, if not in the range of his acting abilities. But none of these replicas is a sign; none of them signifies that which it replicates.

As a second representative attempt to define, reduce, or analyze the concept of sign, I choose Dewey's proposal to reduce signifying to inferring. Not that the proposal is original with Dewey; it is the Epicurean concept of sign, set forth by Philodemus in his treatise on signs and copiously reported in Sextus Empiricus. My point of criticism, made with all possible brevity, is that the proposal of Epicurus and Dewey forces on signs a unity that they do not have.

My third choice is thirdness. Thirdness is for Peirce the category of law and of mediation. And it might seem that mediation is what the surrogate-conception was trying to achieve. After all, one of the oldest definitions of the sign is that it 'stands for' its object. But there would be an important difference between Morris and Peirce, even though both talk of substituting and both talk of mediating. It is that whereas the surrogation-theory, as in Morris, points up the identity between sign and object, the thirdness- or mediation-theory points up the distinctness. *In between* the interpreter and the object stands the sign.

Of course, thirdness is many things for Peirce. Perhaps I should invert the statement and say that for Peirce many things are thirds. His favorite example of thirdness is law, but his theory of categories is largely given over to working out the complications, the proliferations, the ramifications of the deceptive utter simplicity of his initial display of one, two, three. As regards the theory of signs, I make only passing mention of his sixty-six varieties of signs and his conception (modeled after mathematics) of degenerate cases, in order to concentrate on the application of the categories to one another (the thirdness of secondness, etc.). After all the complications entailed by this are noted and reckoned with, there will remain the simple fact that the realm of thought is distinct from the realm of actuality. The expression in his terms of that simple fact will be that actuality (as a whole) is a second to thought (as a whole). Now the fact that semiosis is unanalyzable—that it may be treatable as a variety of thirdness, but that we are unable to specify in a non-redundant way *what* variety of thirdness it is—will manifest itself in Peirce's system this way, that there will be some formula containing the word 'thirdness', such that the proposition consisting of 'semiosis is identical with' followed by that formula will be added to Peirce's system (not deducible within it), and will have the status of a synthetic a priori proposition, not of an analytic proposition. Peirce is able to disguise from himself the need for synthetic a priori propositions connecting his thought-world with actuality by assigning such propositions the status of hypotheses needing further investigation, with the hope that sufficient investigation will present them no longer as synthetic a priori, but as analytic. For the purposes of the present colloquium, it is enough to say that so far the attempt to define semiosis as a species of thirdness has not succeeded and shows no prospect of succeeding.

One last point about attempts to define the sign: there may be circles of interdefinability. Cases are known where there is a set of concepts such that any member of that set may be defined in terms of one or more other members of the set, but no member can be defined otherwise. (Example: In logic, 'or' can be defined in terms of 'not' and 'and'; also, 'and' can be defined in terms of 'not' and 'or'.) It is a familiar doctrine in analytic philosophy that ethical notions form such a set; and R. M. Chisholm[9] has argued that behavioral definitions of purpose and the like appeal to a notion of intentionality, in which case intending, purposing, seeking, trying, etc., form an inter-definability-set. Peirce expressly (4.530) rejects the definition of a sign as a substitute, but in the definition (in a letter to Lady Welby, already quoted) he himself offers, he defines it in terms of determination. But determination, if it is to yield a result that is neither too wide nor too narrow, must be understood to mean something like intention. And Peirce himself was aware of the interdefinability of 'sign' and 'mind'. Here, then, is an interdefinability-set: intention, sign, mind.

It might be thought that all definition is circular in this way, but it is not so. For example, when Russell defined the concept of number it was urged against him by Joseph[10] that his definition of number was circular because he defined the number one as a class and a class is *one* class, so that he was defining one in terms of one. Russell successfully refuted this objection, and therefore I am not making a point that can be made of all definition when I say that the concept of sign can only be defined circularly as a member of some interdefinability-set. And interdefinability is tantamount to indefinability, since we think of definability as being an asymmetrical relation.

More modest than attempts to define signs are attempts to classify them. Ernst Cassirer, for example, in *An Essay on Man,* classifies signs into signals and symbols. Cassirer says that symbols have a new dimension; this dimension is, however loath he is to admit it, the dimension of intentionality explored by Brentano, Meinong, and Husserl, and applied to present-day philosophy by Chisholm, as remarked above. I mention, but do not develop, the objection that Cassirer neither justifies nor illuminates his metaphor of dimension; instead, I propose to accept Cassirer's distinction and to give it a turn that he never thinks of giving it.

To explain myself I must sketch a philosophy of classification. When there is a genus with two species, it may be that species *A* is characterized by two positive properties, the generic property that it shares with *B* and its specific difference that differentiates it from *B;* and correspondingly for *B.* This according to Aristotle's biological writings is the structure of a good classification. But what if the structure is that *A* has just one positive property, the generic property, and *B* has two positive properties, the generic property and also a *differentia specifica?* We can, if we like, redescribe this by saying that each of the two species, *A* and *B,* has two properties, one generic and one specific, provided that we go on to say that they differ in that the specific property of *A* is a negative, or privative, property, and the specific property of *B* is a positive property. This is the way in which Aristotle treats plant, brute animal, and man. (In other words, Aristotle's treatment of the three kingdoms does not conform to his own strictures on classification.) Plant is living; brute animal is plant plus something (mobile and sensitive); man is brute animal plus something (rational).

Now by Cassirer's account the relation between signal and symbol is that symbols are signals plus something. They fit the second pattern, rather than the first, which is to say that sign, if it deserves to be called a genus at all, is a genus of the second sort, not of the first. The new turn that I propose to give to Cassirer's account is to align it with Saussure's. Let us consider identifying Cassirer's signal with Saussure's signifiant, and his symbol with Saussure's signe. Then the property which, added to a signal, gives a symbol would be the property of having a signifié. The dimension which, according to my suggestion, symbols add to signals is the dimension of content, or meaning.

It is not my claim that this is what Cassirer really had in mind; neither is it my claim that we ought as I suggest to identify Cassirer's new 'dimension' with Saussure's second 'face'. My self-chosen role in this paper being the role of questioner and not of answerer, I content myself with having made the suggestion. I do, of course, make this much of a claim, that the questions I pose are serious questions, worthy of investigation, not idle or wild questions.

If we do match up Cassirer's contrast with Saussure's, then certain adjustments in Saussure's conceptual framework and in his terminology are called for. To speak of a signifiant that doesn't signify, a signifié that isn't signified, an expression (Hjelmslev) that doesn't express, a content that isn't the content of anything—every one of these locutions seems to be a *contradictio in adjecto*. The reason is the same for all: all are relative terms; to be related is built into them. But we can perform on built-in properties an operation of subtraction, such as Hume does when he writes: "Every effect necessarily presupposes a cause; effect being a relative term, of which cause is the correlative. But this does not prove that every being must be preceded by a cause; no more than it follows, because every husband must have a wife, that therefore every man must be married."[11] There being no terms in ordinary language for the derelativized results of these four semiotic terms, as there is 'man' for 'husband' derelativized, we might use some prefix and speak of quasi-expressions or semi-expressions or the like.

But it may seem that in Saussure the real difficulty remains untouched, and demands something more than 'adjustment'. According to him (Part II, Ch. 4), signifiant and signifié presuppose each other so intimately that each would be shapeless without the other. But Saussure himself resolves the difficulty. "Linguistics then works in the borderland where the elements of sound and thought combine; their combination produces a form, not a substance." (This passage is the textual basis for Hjelmslev's distinguishing, as noted above, between the contrast of form and substance and the contrast of expression and content.) It is not the expression-substance and the content-substance that presuppose each other, but their forms; when an expression-substance is used to signify a content, then expression-form and content-form emerge. Form and substance are not correlative, i.e., do not presuppose each other; the same substance may (functioning in different systems) have different forms, or it may function in no system and so have no form; and the same form may be the form of different substances.

Having introduced the Saussure-Hjelmslev distinction between form and substance, we may now say that it furnishes us the terms that we hitherto lacked. Instead of a quasi-expression or a semi-expression, the same purpose will be served if we speak of an expression-substance, and similarly of a content-substance.

The import for semiotics is momentous. Semiotics is primarily the study of signs, and (as a built-in property) a sign has a signifiant and a signifié, an expression and a content. But there may be expression-substance without expression, and the semiotician may include them in his study, even though they are not among his primary objects, because they are relevant to his primary objects. The semiotician will want to know which facts of semiosis are necessary, which contingent; and a part of this question is the question, which expression-substances could be expressions and which ones could not be. The evolutionary version of this question would be, which systems of expression-substances that are not expressions might evolve into systems of expression-substances that are expressions, and, in particular, from what did genuine human expressions evolve? And the study of what Cassirer calls signals might be relevant to semiotics even if signals are not signs. I will return to the subject of evolution at the end of this paper.

I have considered two ways of delimiting signs. The first way, definition, went to its doomed failure. The second way, classification, encountered a major question: might it not turn out that an alleged classification of signs into species A and B could be regarded as a distinction between signs proper, A, and certain non-signs, B, that were potentially the substance for signs? The possibility was illustrated by Cassirer's distinction between symbols and signals. Now, in the last part of my paper, I will consider a third way of delimiting signs, the way that I regard as most promising. Whether or not we agree that symbols (in Cassirer's sense) are the only signs, they are certainly signs par excellence. Let us then examine the properties of symbols, other than the built-in property of being intentional, and see whether, on the basis of these, we can find any warrant for calling other things signs, though not signs par excellence. The method is proposed by Plato in the Phaedo (100a), where Socrates says, "This was the method which I adopted: I first assumed some principle which I judged to be the strongest, and then I affirmed as true whatever seemed to agree with this . . . ; and that which disagreed I regarded as untrue." But I modify this method in a Peircean way; I replace the dichotomy, agree or disagree, by a series: wholly agree, largely agree, some-what agree, no more agree than disagree, etc. The resulting modified method is called by Aristotle the method of more and less.

A being that has intentions also has volitions, has freedom, is capable of arbitrary decisions, has open-ended or infinite power, understands mere pos-sibility, and is capable of signifying negation. At least a *human* being has these several powers. But must every being that has one of them have all?

In general, when we specify more than property as a criterion, or as a necessary condition, for some concept, we should anticipate the possibility that there are things having *n* of these properties but not the remaining *m-n* properties. A. Ingraham, as reported by Ogden and Richards, entertainingly described the possibility using the example 'wall'. C. D. Broad and Hilary Putnam have developed the idea further, the former using the metaphor of 'degrees of freedom' and the latter coining the label 'cluster-concepts'.[12] The import of these insights for my touchstone is that we must not expect a single touch of the touchstone to answer the question whether this or that is a sign, nor must we expect that the answer will be either yes or no. A phenomenon examined by the touchstone may turn out to have some but not all of the properties that speech-signs, the signs par excellence, have; there will be degrees of closeness to the paradigm case.

The first two properties of a signifier, intending and willing, are both expressed in ordinary language by 'mean'. When communication using language-signs occurs, the speaker wills to emit something that will be taken as a sign by the hearer. In other and plainer words, the speaker means some-thing that is taken as meaningful by the hearer. According to the scholastic language reintroduced by Brentano into modern philosophy, when the hearer takes something, *x,* as a sign of something, *y,* he intends *y,* and *y* is called the intentional object of *x.* This technical sense of 'intend' is easily distinguished from the more familiar sense in which for example someone intends to keep a promise and in which 'intention' means the same as 'intent' and 'intentional' means the same as 'deliberate, on purpose'. The familiar and the technically philosophical sense of the verb 'intend' and derivatives are easily distin-guished, but in semiosis par excellence there is a certain necessary connection between them: the speaker intends in the familiar sense, and the hearer intends in the philosophical sense: the speaker intends$_f$ that the hearer shall intend$_p$ such and such.

When the communication is nonlinguistic, there are analogues to speaker and hearer: in plastic art, artist and spectator (observer, esthete); in music, musician (split into composer and performer) and audience.

It is common parlance to speak of signs that are not intended in the familiar sense; a cloudy sky as a sign of rain is an easy example. Human beings may exhibit signs of this sort: a red face is a sign of being hot (though ambiguously, because it is also a sign of being angry, of being embarrassed, and of being strangled), a bluish-white face is a sign of being cold. These will not be signs par excellence, because there is no signifier; there is not, for example, Mother Nature.

Taking the touchstone seriously will lead to surprising and seemingly objectionable results; such as, that not all speech is signification par excellence. Things that are said 'spontaneously', that are 'blurted out', might not count as willed. But why should this perplex us? There is nothing odd about saying that *only* speech, but not *all* speech, is semiosis par excellence. But no doubt every utterance is an utterance that *could* have been uttered intentionally (deliberately, on purpose), and this is what people have in mind when they say that speech is essentially intentional.

The next-mentioned property after intention (deliberateness) and intentionality is freedom. For my part, it is not my intention, nor my pretension, to solve the questions of freedom, but only to peg one set of questions to another. When the bees dance their nectar-dance, do they give their signs freely? I suppose the general opinion would be negative; a common way of putting it, influenced by computers, would be to say that they are 'programmed' to do what they do; we find no occasion to say that one bee might refuse to participate in the dance if (like Achilles) he was angry at the other bees, or was engaged in a campaign to show that he was his own master. Of course as we get to know the bees better we may start to find occasions to say these things, in which case the nectar-dance would cease to seem an example of unfreedom.

Freedom has indefinitely many manifestations; one of them is the capacity for arbitrary decisions. Leibniz[13] was fond of saying that 'liberty of indifference' was a fiction and that where there is a perfect balancing of motive forces, a being will be moved by neither, and in particular where there is a perfect balancing of reasons, a reasonable being will do neither. There is one case he didn't sufficiently consider. He did amply consider such cases as that of the traveler at the crossroads who weighs the reasons for going left against the reasons for going right and, finding them equal, goes neither to the left nor to the right, i.e., comes to a standstill. But he didn't sufficiently consider the case where the traveler weighs the reasons for keeping going against the reasons for coming to a standstill and finds them equal; he considered that case, to be sure, but not sufficiently, because he contented himself with saying that it couldn't happen. The case where the alternatives are to move and to come to a standstill, i.e., to move and not to move, is of interest because it is protected, as it were, i.e., it is assured of existence, by the Law of Excluded Middle, which means that it is the case where it is logically impossible to say, "Neither alternative will be followed." Leibniz did not propose to repeal the Law of Excluded Middle, but he did propose to withdraw challenges to it from the arena of choice; in such cases one could not say, "Neither alternative will be followed," but one could say, and he did propose to say, "Neither alternative will be *chosen*." His philosophical opponent, Samuel Clarke, defended the possibility of choice under these conditions—arbitrary choice, and without going into the deeper philosophical issues of the controversy I may say that at the very least Clarke's contention fits prima facie appearances better than does Leibniz's. When high-speed vehicles came into use and it became advisable to establish a convention, either that vehicles keep to the right side of the road or else that they keep to the left side, it was immediately apparent that the choice would be arbitrary. And in empirical fact it frequently proves to be the case that, when some group of human beings is confronted with an arbitrary choice between *A* and *B*, one subgroup arbitrarily chooses *A* and the other subgroup arbitrarily chooses *B*. In the case of automobiles, it is inconvenient that some nations made the left-side choice and some the right, but whichever choice was made, it was an arbitrary choice, in defiance of Leibniz's Principle of Sufficient Reason, and having no reason in human right-handedness or in anything else. Units of measurement exhibit, most of them, the same arbitrariness; the English yard may be based on the human body, and the metric-system meter may be based on the aliquot division of the circumference of the earth, but though these applications suggest the choice of unit it could fairly be said of them that they were not (*pace* Leibniz) reasons in any respectable sense, but rather were admittedly extrinsic and strictly irrelevant appeals where genuine good reasons were lacking.

All this bears on 'l'arbitraire du signe'. Human beings are not, as a rule, happy to make arbitrary choices; in fact, it is their last recourse. Now of course Saussure didn't mean that at the first parliament human beings considered what name to give to the tree and some said arbor, some said arbre, some said Baum, some said tree; it was the other aspect of arbitrariness that he was focusing on. It was exactly because the choice on the part of some speakers to say arbor was arbitrary that their successors continued to say arbor for no better reason than that their forebears had; and so when because of externally caused sound-change *their* successors replaced arbor by arbre, there was nothing to stop them.

The willingness to exercise arbitrary power admits of degrees. The word 'arbitrary' suggests 'despotic', 'tyrannical', 'dictatorial', and so there is the further suggestion that nice people would not exercise arbitrary power. But a fuller discussion of the arbitrary would divest the word of these suggestions and would treat as a mark of intelligence the recognition that an enormous number of decisions, major and minor, are arbitrary. That is, the more intelligent one is, the more will one, in facing or in considering situations that call for arbitrary decisions, recognize them as of this type.

That someone recognizes the need for arbitrary decision does not entail that he acts on his recognition. It is for this reason that we posit another factor in the psyche besides intelligence, namely personality. I should accordingly reformulate my characterization of freedom as including 'the capacity for arbitrary decisions'. Since this capacity includes a factor of personality as well as a factor of intelligence, and since only intelligence is relevant as a criterion for semiosis, I reformulate my proposition of two pages above as follows: Freedom has indefinitely many manifestations; one of them is the capacity to understand which decisions are arbitrary.

The open-ended or infinite power of the human mind has been claimed but never adequately analyzed. The infinity claimed is a so-called potential infinite. It involves the unknown future and the concept of non-actual possibilities, in the following way. A description of a past event need not involve non-actual possibilities. Thus, a description of all the objects that a certain human being has signified, up to a specified date, will be a finite list and yet will do justice to the facts. The same cannot be said of the task of being prepared to describe the future, not-yet-signified significations, whether of a person still living or of one not yet even born. Whether this is because the future is inherently indeterminate or because, though determinate, it is not known to us, is a perennial metaphysical question which does not concern the would-be describer. In either case, the list of one who would describe future human significations, and who wants to be sure that his list will not prove incomplete, must be a list of possibilities, including non-actualized possibilities, and each possibility must be either included in the list or precluded from it, and even if there are infinitely many possibilities that the lister is in a position to preclude, still—such is the claim—infinitely many possibilities will remain.

To assess this claim would be too detailed for the present paper, but it is evident that there is some great difference between the list a describer must have at hand if he is to be prepared to describe everything signified by a human being and the list he must have if he is to be prepared to describe everything that could be signified by a bee. It is true that if we were content with high probability, rather than certainty, our list would not prove incomplete; a list much more like the list adequate for a bee would be adequate for a human being; in any case a finite list, rather than an infinite one. And it is quite possible that there is some finite list that would in fact never prove incomplete. But what we are trying to avoid is not just a list that *would* prove incomplete but a list that *might* prove incomplete.

My discussion of infinite power has also, unavoidably, discussed mere possibility. In finishing my comment, then, on my list of powers that in semiosis par excellence accompany the semiotic power, it remains only to speak of negation.

The power to express negation marks the highest achievement of semiosis; without it, even human semiosis lacks the power to express abstract thought. Philosophers had made this point from time to time, but it was most forcibly brought to the world's attention by Freud (*Traumdeutung,* especially Section VI-C, and "Die Verneinung" of 1925, translated in Volume 19 of the Standard Edition). The dream-language lacks any word for 'not', with enormous consequences. One consequence is ambiguity as regards wishing and fearing; to fear x is to wish for non-x, and since (whatever x may be) x and non-x are depicted in the same way in dreams, they are distinguished only by the feeling-tone, i.e., by the difference in the affect—wish or fear, respectively—accompanying the dream. The connection between negation and possibility is prescribed by the Law of Excluded Middle, $p \lor \sim p$, together with the Law of Non-Contradiction, $\sim(p\& \sim p)$. The connection is that possibilities come in pairs, such that at least one (so as not to violate Excluded Middle) and at most one (so as not to violate Non-Contradiction) of each pair is actual. I particularly call attention to the point that only human language has a general sign for negation, though various special cases can be expressed nonlinguistically (e.g., prohibition can be expressed by a conventional gesture such as an upraised hand).

It is sometimes maintained, e.g. (among moderns), by Descartes and by Cassirer, that the difference between brute and human is a difference of kind, not of degree. The position I have taken in the present paper may seem to make the same commitment. The next point I want to make, and the final point of my paper, is that a difference in kind between A and B does not preclude evolution from A to B. To see this, all we have to do is to understand the logic of 'change'.

It is common parlance to speak of one thing changing into another, and it is a common philosophical move to contend that change is really replacement, or succession. When the boy changes into the man, the boy as such ceases to be and in his stead a man comes into being. This philosophical viewpoint may be captious when applied to individuals, i.e., to things having what philosophers call *continued* identity, but when applied to abstract beings it makes perfect sense. Three cannot change into four; as Plato put it in the Phaedo (102–5), when evenness advances, three retreats. Nor can two change into three; but yet a family of two can change into a family of three. Numbers cannot change; two cannot change into three. But numbers *can* change; the number of people in a family can change from two to three. The number two (which is a number) cannot change, but the number of people in a family (which is also a number) can change. The example proves that the word 'number' is ambiguous as between two different kinds of things. It is part of the 'logic' (in the sense of Wittgenstein, Waismann, and Wisdom) of phrases signifying numbers of the second sort that they have continued identity, as individuals do, and are subject in part to the same conditions.

Now for an example that concerns organic evolution. The human being is in process of evolution in various ways. One of the ways is that he is losing teeth. This is the evolutionary meaning of our wisdom teeth. Evolution being gradual, a species that had thirty-two teeth does not all of a sudden turn into, i.e., become replaced by, a species that has twenty-eight teeth. There are various distinct ways in which this gradual loss of four teeth could occur; one of these ways, the way we are actually following, is that the four rearmost teeth are neither fully normal, healthy teeth nor merely vestigial teeth, but are defective teeth which erupt much later than the others and for which there is not sufficient room.

The example is, then, that though thirty-two cannot change into twenty-eight, yet thirty-two teeth can change into twenty-eight teeth, and moreover can do it gradually.

The general pattern of gradual transition will be this. At one stage, s_1, we will find instances that clearly answer to the description A; at some later stage, s_4, we will find instances that clearly answer to the description B, logically incompatible with A; in between, we will find a stage s_2 where there are instances which, though not clear instances of A, yet fit description A better than B; and in between s_2 and s_4 a stage s_3 where there are instances which, though not clear instances of B, yet fit description B better than they fit A. And so on, without any preassignable limit to the number of intermediate stages that can be discriminated. As regards our evolution toward a species with twenty-eight teeth, I take it that we are now in something like stage s_2; it is apter to describe us as having thirty-two than as having twenty-eight teeth, and yet the description has to be qualified.

The logic of the word 'change' is the logic virtually used not only by those who speak of evolution but by those, e.g., historians, who speak of transition from one period of history to another. For example, Cassirer, as noted by Randall,[14] held that the Middle Ages were a distinct, i.e., a conceptually discrete, period from the Renaissance, while granting (as he could not help doing) that the transition from the one to the other was chronologically continuous. And, coming back to organic evolution, this same logic is applicable in particular to the evolution from non-human to human, and from the absence to the presence of semiosis.

I made a point of mentioning Cassirer, because I had mentioned him

earlier in connection with signals and symbols. In the *Essay on Man* he is so
emphatic in claiming that symbols are a different order (a different dimension,
a different kind) from signals that transition from one to the other seems out
of the question. But the knowledgeable reader will see that exactly the same
logic makes a transition from the Middle Ages to the Renaissance out of the
question. And in one sense this is true. The Middle Ages, defined by their
nature and not by their date, can never change into the Renaissance or anything else. The Middle Ages do not change; when the Renaissance approaches, the Middle Ages simply withdraw. This is true, in the typological
sense, and the only thing to add is that besides the typological there is the
chronological sense of change. Ambiguity is part of the logic of the word
'change'; change is impossible or is possible according as that which changes
is characterized typologically (formally) or chronologically (materially), the
latter being the characterization which warrants our speaking of continued
identity throughout change.

Cassirer gave his life to the study of change; but I have searched his
writings in vain for evidence that he ever grasped this distinction and brought
it into focus as a theme. I must say the same of Humboldt. Indeed, Humboldt
is at pains to display his confusion. He says, "So natürlich die Annahme
allmähliger Ausbildung der Sprache ist, so konnte die Erfindung nur mit
einem Schlage geschehen."[15] The reason is that "der Mensch ist nur Mensch
durch Sprache; um aber die Sprache zu erfinden, müsste er schon Mensch
sein." Now the phrase "mit einem Schlage" sounds chronological, as if it
referred to time, but just there is where the confusion lies. The phrase 'at one
stroke' is infected by the same ambiguity to which 'change' is subject; and the
formal fact that humanity is lacking 'until' the power of speech is present and
vice versa is independent of and has no bearing on the material question
whether every living organism that is human is clearly human, or on the
material question whether in every succession of generations from clearly
non-human ancestors to clearly human descendants there is a last ancestor that
is clearly non-human and the very next generation—the child (immediate
descendant) of this last, clearly non-human generation—is clearly human.
Humboldt's doctrine is plausible if taken formally, groundless if taken materially.

The ambiguity, and the distinction which resolves it, are to be taken into
account in all discussions of evolution, whether of man, or of human speech,
or of anything else. I discussed the general pattern of change from A to B. In
the special case where A = non-B (meaning here by 'non-B' not just any
member of the complement of B, but some member that is similar to B), e.g.,
the case where some non-human brute changes into man, it will always be

plausible to say, speaking formally, that non-*B* changes at one stroke into *B*. But this formal truth exercises no constraint on matter, which can evade the formal sharpness by presenting instances that are in between (on the border-line, indeterminate).

Linguists have instituted a concept that copes with this fact. It is the concept of performance, as contrasted with competence. The concept has been put to many uses, and these have not been clearly distinguished from one another, nor has it been proved that they necessarily go together. But one use, perhaps the original use, has been to reconcile the ascription of a certain infinite power—speech—to man with the fact that only a finite portion of this power is actually exercised. It would be quite in keeping with this established use to deal with organisms of which we were doubtful whether to say that they had speech by saying that they definitely have speech competence, rudimentary though their performance may be.

Throughout this paper my leading idea has been to judge the less clear cases by the clearer cases, taking speech as the supremely clear case of semiosis. It has not been my intention to reject any alleged case, but only to urge that the allegation needs to be supported. I can put my point in terms of a contrast introduced by geometers, highlighted by Kant, and signalized by Cassirer.[16] The very concept of a datum (a given) comes from Greek geometers; and they oppose the *data* of a problem to the *quaesita* as beginning and end, respectively. The contrast is expressed more neatly with German words than with Greek, Latin, or English ones. My point, then, has been that the unity of semiotics is not something given to us but something to be sought: it is not *gegeben,* but *aufgegeben* as an *Aufgabe.*

NOTES

1. In Wells (1963)§§ 4ff. I discuss pseudo-generality.

2. Kahn (1967) deals with codes. Of particular interest here are codes that are not, except by the coder and his intended recipient, recognized as codes; such codes are discussed by Kahn under the rubric "steganography." See especially pp. 516, 542, 794.

3. Nagel (1939).

4. Vaihinger (1924) pp. xxx, xxxix; Merton (1957) p. 199; Stevenson (1944) 194–8.

5. Sebeok (1977).

6. Peirce (1953) p. 29 (letter of December 23, 1908), quoted in Ogden and Richards (1938) p. 288; not in Peirce (1931) Volume 3.

7. Peirce (1931) §§1.314, 7.379 fn. 17; Descartes, passages in Malcolm (1973), especially pp. 6–7.

8. Peirce (1931) §§4.157 (p. 135); 7.498 (pp. 300–1).

9. Chisholm (1957), Chapter 11.

10. As reported by John Wisdom, Mind 47 (1938) 468 (reprinted in Wisdom (1953) p. 69; see also Joseph (1916) pp. 552–3 fn. 2.

11. Hume (1888) p. 82 (§1.3.3).

12. Ogden and Richards (1938) p. 46; Broad (1933) pp. 117, 125; Putnam (1962) p. 378.

13. Leibniz's exchange (1715–16) of letters with Samuel Clarke is "the most frequently cited of all eighteenth-century philosophical controversies" (Leibniz [1956] p. vii). The text is in every major edition and in most selected editions of Leibniz's philosophical writings; the 1956 edition I have chosen to cite has valuable notes and appendices.

14. Randall (1949) p. 719.

15. Humboldt (1843) p. 252 = (1905) p. 15 (§13); quoted by Müller (1862) pp. 345–6, Steinthal (1966) p. 106.

16. Kant (1781) pp. 287–8/343–4; 304/361; 483–4/512; 497–8/526; 508/536; 647/675; 669/697 (page numbers refer to First Edition/Second Edition). Cassirer (1918) p. 274; (1946) p. 287.

REFERENCES

Broad, C. D. 1920. "The relation between induction and probability, II," Mind 29.11–45.

———— 1933. *An Examination of McTaggart's Philosophy,* Volume I. Cambridge: Cambridge University Press.

Cassirer, Ernst. 1918. *Kants Leben und Lehre.* Berlin: Bruno Cassirer.

———— 1944. *An Essay on Man.* New Haven: Yale University Press.

———— 1946. *The Myth of the State.* New Haven: Yale University Press.

Humboldt, Wilhelm von. 1843. *Gesammelte Werke,* Volume 3. Berlin: Reimer.

———— 1905. *Gesammelte Schriften,* Volume 4, edited by Albert Leitzmann. Berlin: Königlich Preussische Akademie der Wissenschaften.

Hume, David. 1888. *A Treatise of Human Nature,* edited by L. A. Selby-Bigge. Oxford: Clarendon Press.

Joseph, H. W. B. 1916. *An Introduction to Logic,* Second Edition. Oxford: Clarendon Press.

Kahn, David. 1967. *The Codebreakers.* New York: Macmillan.

Kant, Immanuel. 1781. *Kritik der reinen Vernunft.* Riga: Hartknoch.

Leibniz, G. W. 1956. *The Leibniz-Clarke Correspondence,* edited by H. G. Alexander. Manchester: Manchester University Press.

Malcolm, Norman. 1963. "Thoughtless brutes," *American Philosophical Association. Proceedings and Addresses* 46.5–20.

Merton, Robert K. 1957. *Social Theory and Social Structure,* Second Edition. Glencoe, Ill.: Free Press.

Morris, Charles. 1946. *Signs, Language, and Behavior.* New York: Prentice-Hall.

Müller, F. Max. 1862. *Lectures on the Science of Language,* Second Edition. New York: Scribner.

Nagel, Ernest. 1939. "The formation of modern conceptions of formal logic in the development of geometry," *Osiris* 7.142–244.

Ogden, C. K., and I. A. Richards. 1938. *The Meaning of Meaning,* Fifth Edition. London: Kegan Paul.

Peirce, C. S. 1931. *Collected Papers* (eight volumes, 1931–58). Cambridge, Mass.: Harvard University Press. [Citation is by volume and numbered section, not by volume and page.]

———— 1953. *Letters to Lady Welby,* edited by Irwin C. Lieb. New Haven: Whitlock's.

Putnam, Hilary. 1962. "The analytic and the synthetic," *Minnesota Studies in the Philosophy of Science* 3.358–97.

Randall, J. H., Jr. 1949. "Cassirer's theory of history as illustrated in his treatment of Renaissance thought," *The Philosophy of Ernst Cassirer,* edited by Paul Arthur Schilpp, pp. 689–728. Evanston: The Library of Living Philosophers.

Sebeok, T. A. 1977. "Semiosis in Nature and Culture," *Proceedings of the International Symposium on Semiotics and Theories of Symbolic Behavior in Eastern Europe and the West*. Lisse: Peter de Ridder Press.

Steinthal, Heymann von. 1966. "Wilhelm von Humboldt," *Portraits of Linguists,* edited by Thomas A. Sebeok, 1.102–20. Bloomington: Indiana University Press.

Stevenson, C. L. 1944. *Ethics and Language*. New Haven: Yale University Press.

Vaihinger, Hans. 1924. *Philosophy of As-If*. London: Kegan Paul.

Wells, R. S. 1963. "Is Frege's concept of function valid?" *Journal of Philosophy* 60.719–30.

Wisdom, John. 1953. *Philosophy and Psycho-Analysis*. Oxford: Blackwells.

Peirce's Theory of Signs

J. Jay Zeman

The lifetime of Charles Sanders Peirce spanned a period of tremendous change and development in human knowledge, in the sciences in general. He was a young man of twenty in the year that *Origin of Species* was published; he approached the end of his life just before Albert Einstein presented us with General Relativity. His lifetime saw the emergence of psychology as a discipline separate from philosophy, a birth attended by philosopher-psychologists such as his good friend William James. The work of Peirce, like that of the other American Pragmatists, reflects the ferment of the times. His thought bears the imprint of science, not the science of that Nineteenth Century which, as Loren Eiseley has remarked, "regarded the 'laws' of nature as imbued with a kind of structural finality, an integral determinism, which it was the scientists' duty to describe,"[1] but rather, of science as open, as intrinsically revisable, as radically empirical. Working from the model of science in this latter sense, Peirce held that philosophy, and indeed logic itself, must ultimately return to experience for validation (2.227).[2]

As a man of science in the open sense and as a logician, Peirce concentrated heavily on what science had to teach philosophy; he emphasized the intellectual aspect of human experience; he examined habit and law; he devoted much energy to the study of logic itself, logic in the narrower sense of deductive symbolic logic as well as in the broader sense of the general theory of signs, or semiotic.

Peirce's semiotic is not a detached, independent element of his philosophy, but interpenetrates and is interpenetrated by his thought as a whole. Peirce held that all thought—indeed, I would say, all experience—is by signs; his theory of signs is, then, a theory of experience, a theory of consciousness. The examination of so central an aspect of Peirce's thought requires a preliminary view of the structure of that thought. Peirce held that logic—along with ethics and esthetics—is a normative science (5.36), and

> before we can attack any normative science, any science which proposes to separate the sheep from the goats, it is plain that there must be a preliminary inquiry which shall justify the attempt to establish such dualism (5.37).

What he proposes is a

> science of phenomenology [which] must be taken as the basis upon which normative science is to be erected and [which] accordingly must claim our first attention (5.39).

The heart of the Peircean phenomenology is Peirce's system of categories; the categories are basic to the understanding not only of Peirce's concept of normative science, but of his theory of signs and indeed of his thought as a whole.

> The *list of categories* ... is a table of conceptions drawn from the logical analysis of thought and regarded as applicable to being. This description applies not merely to the list published by me ... but also to the categories of Aristotle and to those of Kant (1.300).

Aristotle listed ten categories and Kant twelve; Peirce employs three. Their names are, simply enough, *first, second,* and *third,* or *firstness, secondness,* and *thirdness.*

By far the most difficult of the categories to discuss is firstness. Firstness is, among other things, the category of *feeling,* by which Peirce means

> an instance of that kind of consciousness which involves no analysis, comparison or any process whatsoever, nor consists in whole or in part of any act by which one stretch of consciousness is distinguished from another, which has its own positive quality which consists in nothing else, and which is of itself all that it is, however it may have been brought about; so that if this feeling is present during a lapse of time, it is wholly and equally present at every moment of that time. ... A feeling, then, is not an event, a happening, a coming to pass, ... a feeling is a *state,* which is in its entirety in every moment of time as long as it endures (1.306).

Firstness, the category of feeling in this sense, is preeminently the category of the *prereflexive.* The difficult thing about talking about firsts is that when we recognize that something is grasped as a first, its firstness as firstness effectively evanesces. I cannot give you a first, I can merely point to where you might find one and subsequently recognize that you *had* found it. Significantly, the places where firsts may most easily be located and recognized have strong esthetic connections. Sitting back and enjoying a piece of music (without reflecting on the enjoyment) is close to experiencing a first.

Firstness is immediacy, firstness is the prereflexive. When reflection does occur, however, we enter the realm of secondness. Secondness is the category of the *actual existent,* and as such is the easiest of the Peircean categories to discuss. It is the category of the other recognized as other; it is the knock on the door which interrupts the musical reverie; it is the unexpected rear-end collision; it is the sudden confrontation with a person you'd rather not confront. Something is a second insofar as it is, and in particular, insofar as it is an object to a subject. Seconds are unique existences, unique in space and time. For example, specific observations as recorded in a laboratory, whether physics or psychology, are seconds. While firstness is essentially atemporal, secondness provides the discrete, distinguishable points which we order by the time sequence.

The brute thereness, the unquestionable existence of seconds might lead us to think of secondness as the category of the "really real." Peirce would consider this to be an inadequate analysis. Reality, he held, is more than a matter of discrete events occurring at given points in space-time. Reality is also a matter of the *relations between* events, and here is where his category of thirdness enters. Thirdness is the category of law, of habit, of continuity, of relatedness. Tycho Brahe's recorded observations of the positions of the planet Mars at given times are seconds. Kepler's laws, worked out to unify that body of data, are thirds. If we look back to that musical performance we earlier gave as a place to hunt for firsts, we may comment that the performance in its unreflected immediacy is firstness; in the actual space-time thereness of its individual notes it is secondness; and in the identifiable structurings relating its notes, rhythms, harmonies, it is thirdness. We shall now move away from remarks specifically about Peirce's categories; we shall see many examples of their application in what follows, which has to do with Peirce's theory of signs.

"A sign," Peirce tells us,

> ... is something which stands to somebody for something in some respect or capacity. It addresses somebody, that is, creates in the mind of that person an equivalent sign, or perhaps a more developed sign. That sign which it creates I call the *interpretant* of the first sign. The sign stands for something, its *object* (2.228).

Peirce here is discussing the sign as it participates in semiosis, the sign relation. There are a number of ways of subdividing the matter of Peirce's semiotic; one of them is based on the fact that we may identify three *relata* in the semiosical relation as understood by Peirce: these are the sign itself, and the above-mentioned object and interpretant. The interpretant itself is a sign (2.228) which Peirce calls the "proper significate effect" of the original sign (5.475). As Charles Morris has pointed out, "Semiotic . . . is not concerned with the study of a particular kind of object, but with ordinary objects in so far (and only in so far) as they participate in semiosis."[3] I would suggest that the participation of an object in semiosis as a sign implies a dual nature for that object. On the one hand, the sign—and this includes interpretants—is an object "in the world"; it is empirically describable in terms of its effects in a variety of ways as is any object in the world—it exists, so to speak, in a "public forum." Insofar as it is in this forum, it is accessible to you in the same way that it is accessible to me. But as a sign, it also stands in a "private forum." It is accessible to me in a way which by its very nature is cut off from you—it is an "element of my consciousness" (of course, I infer that it is accessible to you too in this unique way—unique in this case to *you*). The interpretant as a sign shares this dual nature. It is an event in my body in principle observable by a variety of means, means that vary from the poker player's experienced eye to such devices as the polygraph and electroence-phalograph. But in the private forum, it *is* my consciousness. Morris speaks of the *interpreter* as a fourth component of semiosis,[4] and Peirce speaks of the interpretant as being produced "in a mind." I would like to suggest that the interpretant is not "in" a mind or an interpreter the way that peanut butter is in a jar, but rather that interpretants, or proper significate effects of signs, *constitute* the interpreter or mind; the interpreter, then, is a historically exist-ing continuum of interpretants, and the interpretant, correlatively, is a cross section or snapshot of the interpreter—the cross section may, but need not be, at an instant of time. Incidentally, this view of the interpreter as a continuum of interpretants (which are signs) throws some light, I think, on Peirce's at first curious-appearing view that *man is a sign* (5.310ff.). There is an interesting connection here from a perhaps unexpected direction. The concept of the interpreter as historical continuum of interpretants is closely akin to the concept of ego developed by Sartre in *The Transcendence of the Ego.*[5] The Sartrean ego emerges in the process of reflection on consciousness. In such reflection present consciousness becomes consciousness of (previous) consciousness, which (previous) consciousness is then *reflected* conscious-ness; the ego emerges as an object which is the unity of "consciousnesses of . . ." the multitude of "things"—material and abstract—states, qualities, and activities of which we can be conscious. The "consciousness of . . ." which can be reflected upon I see as a Sartrean analog of the interpretant; the ego which emerges in the process of reflection would then be the interpreter.

At this point we may note something of a difficulty in Peirce's discussion of the sign. 2.228, quoted above, continues:

> [A sign] stands for [its] object, not in all respects, but in reference to a sort of idea, which I have sometimes called the *ground* of the [sign].

The "sometimes" in this assertion would seem to have reference chiefly to Peirce's "On a New List of Categories" (1.551). Unfortunately, the "New List" was published in 1867, some thirty years before the passage in 2.228 was written. One suspects that we may be seeing here what Murray Murphey calls "a typically Peircean procedure: having set forth a doctrine with appropriate terminology, Peirce revises and refines the content of the doctrine while retaining the form and terminology unchanged. Thus, extensive revisions of position pass unnoticed under a shell of changeless terminology, to the utter confusion of the reader."[6] Peirce's thought underwent considerable development in those thirty years, and there is a legitimate question as to whether the 'ground' of 1897 is the same as that of 1867. A fair assumption is that Peirce himself saw a continuity between the two, because of his using the same term and his explicit reference to earlier uses of it.

Although Peirce devotes a fair amount of attention to the ground in the "New List," he discusses it hardly at all in his later years, although he uses it in the perplexing fashion of 2.228; it is perhaps best to seek understanding of his later use of 'ground' by examining its employment in this passage. First of all, we note that ground, when added to object and interpretant, makes a triad; this is typically Peircean, and involves a classification by his categories, with ground, object, and interpretant as first, second, and third respectively. Peirce states:

> In consequence of every [sign] being thus connected with three things, the ground, the object, and the interpretant, the science of semiotic has three branches. The first is called by Duns Scotus *grammatica speculativa*. We may term it *pure grammar*. It has for its task to ascertain what must be true of the [signs] used by every scientific intelligence in order that they may embody any *meaning* (2.229).

So the ground of a sign is intimately associated with pure grammar, which is the study of interrelationships between signs themselves; it would appear that the ground of the sign, then, has a close connection with the sign itself. And we note that elsewhere (and elsewhen—1885) Peirce asserts that "a sign is in a conjoint relation to the thing denoted and to the mind" (3.360). In this passage Peirce explicitly makes the sign the first *relatum* in semiosis. In the analysis of Morris, the *relata* in the semiosical relation are "sign vehicle," "*denotatum*," and "interpretant." On the basis of this analysis of semiosis, Morris distinguishes respectively three "dimensions" of semiotic—the syntactic, the semantic, and the pragmatic—the syntactic dimension corresponds to Peirce's *pure grammar*.

It is worthwhile taking a look at Peirce's assertion that pure grammar "has for its task to ascertain what must be true of the [signs] used by every scientific intelligence in order that they may embody any *meaning*" (2.229). It may seem peculiar for Peirce to speak of meaning in this context, since Peircean "meaning" has at its very center the concept of *possible effect*—the meaning of something in a definite sense is, for Peirce, its possible effects; note Peirce's "pragmatic maxim":

> Consider what effects that might conceivably have practical bearing we conceive the object of our conception to have. Then our conception of these effects is the whole of our conception of the object (5.402).

Indeed, we find Murray Murphey discussing a passage very similar to 2.229, but from the much earlier New List:

> Peirce describes speculative grammar as treating "of the formal conditions of symbols having meaning, that is of the reference of symbols in general to their grounds or imputed characters . . ." (1.559), thereby indicating how far he was from the idea of pragmatism in 1867 [which is the theory of meaning summarized in the "pragmatic maxim" (5.402) quoted above].[7]

The Peirce of the New List, of 1867, may have been far from the idea of pragmatism, but in 2.229, written about 1897 when he was well into pragmatism, he speaks of speculative (pure) grammar and meaning in almost the same terms as thirty years previously. How does the asserted relationship between pure grammar and meaning mesh with the pragmatic concept of meaning as possible effects? About 1903, Peirce answers this:

> A word has meaning for us in so far as we are able to make use of it in communicating our knowledge to others and in getting at the knowledge that others seek to communicate to us. That is the lowest grade of meaning (8.176).

A sign does not communicate *in vacuo,* but in a context, in relationship to other signs; a paradigm of such relationship is the grammatical structure of language. That there be such a grammatical structure is a necessary condition for the signs of language to be able to communicate, and so, by the above passage, to have meaning (in the sense of the lowest grade of meaning). It would be in this sense of meaning that pure grammar "has as its task to ascertain what must be true of . . . [signs] . . . in order that they may embody meaning" (2.229). The passage from 8.176 goes on to indicate that there is more to meaning than this "lowest grade":

> The meaning of a word is more fully the sum total of all the conditional predictions which the person who uses it *intends* to make himself responsible for or intends to deny.

The full meaning of meaning does indeed involve possible consequences. But insofar as relatedness to other signs is a necessary condition of a sign's communicating, speculative (or pure) grammar is the study of what must be true of signs "in order that they may embody any *meaning*" (2.229).

Speculative, or pure, grammar (of which we shall see more anon) is the first branch of Peirce's semiotic, corresponding to the "ground" of the sign—or to what Morris called the "sign vehicle."

> The second [branch] is logic proper. It is the science of what is necessarily true of the [signs] of any scientific intelligence in order that they hold of any *object*, that is, may be true. Or say, logic proper is the formal science of the truth of representations (2.229).

Peirce clearly sees logic proper here from the semantic point of view; note that Morris's "dimension of semiotic" corresponding to the *denotatum* or object of the sign is the semantic dimension.

Considerable study has been devoted to what Peirce calls "logic proper," which is a subject, or group of subjects, warranting special attention in itself. Much of the material in this area is involved and specialized, and so we shall not discuss this topic in technical detail in this paper; however, a few general remarks about his accomplishments here are in order, since he clearly considered "logic proper" to be an integral part of his theory of signs.

For Peirce, logic proper is "the formal science of the truth of representations." Another way to characterize it would be to follow Dewey, and call logic in this sense "The Theory of Inquiry." Peirce divides logic from this point of view into deductive, inductive, and abductive, or retroductive logic (hypothesis formation). The division is by the Peircean categories (though it is not completely, in this case, clear how the division works). Peirce tells us that

> Retroduction and Induction face opposite ways.... The order of the march of suggestion in retroduction is from experience to hypothesis. A great many people who may be admirably trained in divinity, or in the humanities, or in law and equity, but who are certainly not well trained in scientific reasoning, imagine that Induction should follow the same course.... On the contrary, the only sound procedure for induction, whose business consists in testing a hypothesis already recommended by the retroductive procedure, is to take up the predictions of experience which it conditionally makes, and then try the experiment and see whether it turns out as it was virtually predicted in the hypothesis that it would (2.755).

Note that the concept of induction to which Peirce objects here is the same as that embodied in that essentially worthless distinction between inductive and deductive logic that continues to be perpetrated upon countless undergraduates in introductory logic, speech, and writing courses: "Inductive logic argues from particulars to generals, while deductive logic argues from generals to particulars."

An extended discussion of "logic proper," including inductive and abductive logic, would necessarily take us far afield from what is generally considered semiotic. We note that Peirce's best-known philosophical writings, the essays on the "Fixation of Belief" (5.358ff.) and "How to Make Our Ideas Clear" (5.388ff.) are studies of logic as the general theory of inquiry. This fact is illustrative of the central position of semiotic in Peirce's thought. As we have remarked, Peirce's semiotic is not an isolated, separate part of that thought, but is integral to his philosophy as a whole. In preparing a paper of so limited a scope as the present one must be, however, we must choose carefully the paths to be followed in detail. We shall not pursue inductive and abductive logic further, then, and shall take a brief look at Peirce's deductive logic, which he set out in great detail and with great skill.

First of all, Peirce saw formal deductive logic as an analytic tool; the purpose of a system of symbolic logic is "simply and solely the investigation of the theory of logic, and not at all the construction of a calculus to aid the drawing of inferences" (4.373). A calculus for Peirce is a computing aid of some kind, designed to shorten, say, the drawing of inferences; a logic, on the other hand, is supposed to break inferences down into their most basic steps and so to exhibit the deductive process involved. In a number of places, Peirce gives us what may be considered postulate sets for symbolic logic; examples are the "icons of the algebra of logic" of his 1885 "Contribution to the philosophy of notation" (3.359ff.), and the "Rules of illative transformation" of his "Existential graphs" (4.372–584). The 1885 "icons" include a complete axiomatization of the classical propositional calculus[8] as well as a considerable chunk of material on quantification and the logic of relatives. The later (1897 and after) transformation rules for Peirce's existential graphs are postulates for a successful and ingenious logic in a non-standard notation. The rules of transformation for the graphs include a complete formulation not only of the classical propositional calculus, but of the full quantification theory with identity[9] as well. In addition, this later work of Peirce is loaded with suggestions that Peirce himself was unable to exploit fully, but which anticipated by decades contemporary developments in symbolic logic; notable here is a beginning development of what is effectively a "possible worlds" semantics for modal logic (4.512ff.).[10]

Although Peirce presents sets of axioms (the 1885 "icons") or rules of inference for his logics, a little examination shows that his basic orientation toward deductive logic is a *semantical* one, as we might be led to expect from his association of "logic proper" with the *object* of a sign. The icons of the algebra of logic are justified by him on what we recognize as truth-functional, and so semantic, grounds (see 3.384, for example) and the most basic sign of the systems of existential graphs, the "sheet of assertion" on which logical transformations are carried out, is "considered as representing the universe of discourse" (4.396); such representation is a semantical matter. But contemporary logic makes a distinction that Peirce did not make. It is necessary to study logic not only from a radically semantical point of view, in which propositions are thought of as being true or false, but also from a *syntactic* or *proof-theoretical* point of view, in which the deducibility of propositions from each other is studied without reference to interpretations in universes of any sort, and so without reference to truth and falsity.

Peirce failed to distinguish between logic as proof-theoretical and logic as semantical, but he can hardly be faulted for that; Gottlob Frege, who with Peirce must be considered a co-founder of contemporary logic, also failed to make the distinction[11] and even Whitehead and Russell are fuzzy about it. Indeed, a clear recognition of the necessity for distinguishing between logical syntax and semantics does not arise until later, with the developments in logic and the foundations of math which culminated in Gödel's celebrated completeness and incompleteness results of 1930 and 1931 respectively.

We have mentioned Peirce's first and second branches of semiotic. The first, pure grammar, is associated with the "ground" of the sign, or with the sign itself. The second, "logic proper," is associated with the object of the sign, for Peirce. The third branch arises because of the role of the interpretant in semiosis, and is called by Peirce

> *pure rhetoric.* Its task is to ascertain the laws by which in every scientific intelligence one sign gives birth to another, and especially one thought brings forth another (2.229).

Peirce also calls this branch of semiotic "speculative rhetoric" and sometimes "methodeutic"; this science

> would treat of the formal condition of the force of symbols, or their power of appealing to a mind, that is, of their reference in general to interpretants (8.342).

Peirce calls speculative rhetoric "the highest and most living branch of logic" (2.332). (Note that here he is using the word "logic" to refer to semiotic as a whole, rather than to deductive logic; this is a usage explicitly adopted by him in 2.227.) From Peirce's remarks on speculative rhetoric, it is clear that he considered it an important science; it also seems clear that he devoted considerable thought to it. Unfortunately, he presents no systematic study of it. About 1902, he remarks that "The practical want of a good treatment of this subject is acute" (2.105). And further, although the number of works upon Methodeutic since Bacon's *Novum Organum* has been large, none has been greatly illuminative. . . . THE book on the subject remains to be written, and what I am chiefly concerned to do is to make the writing of it more possible. I do not claim that the part of the present volume [never completed] which deals with Speculative Rhetoric will approach that ideal (2.109–10).

Speculative rhetoric was to be, for Peirce, "a method for discovering methods" (2.108) in human inquiry in general (2.110); the longing for such a science is deeply rooted in Peirce, and goes back to his earlier days—see, for example, 3.364, which is from the "Philosophy of notation" paper of 1885. The project, however, remains uncompleted. This "highest and most living branch of logic" is a matter of scattered treatments and vague content in Peirce's writing. It does, however, occupy a key place in the architectonic of Peirce's philosophy. An interesting, if somewhat difficult, task would be to reconstruct, based on the structure of Peirce's philosophy, what a Peircean speculative rhetoric might look like.

Of the three branches of Peirce's semiotic, then, the third, speculative rhetoric, is radically incomplete, and the second, "logic proper," when studied in detail, carries us into areas of Peirce's philosophy and symbolic logic not commonly thought of as belonging to the theory of signs. Much, perhaps most, of the material we commonly associate with Peirce's semiotic falls under the first branch of the theory of signs, speculative grammar. I now propose to discuss some of the major topics treated by Peirce under this heading.

A major thrust of Peirce's speculative grammar is a detailed and complex classification of signs. In a definite sense, even the most basic part of speculative grammar, the description of the semiosical relation itself, is a classification of signs. The interpretant is a sign (2.228), and the object is, at least often, a sign. So the description of semiosis gives us a triple viewpoint from which to observe signs in action: signs functioning as signs properly so called, signs as objects of semiosis, and signs as effects of semiosis (interpretants). Peirce elaborates the theory of sign, object, and interpretant in a variety of ways. In his "Survey of pragmaticism," written about 1906, he discussed different kinds of interpretant; the classification is again by the categories. His opening remark here, by the way, illustrates the epistemological importance that he attached to this kind of classification:

> Now the problem of what the "meaning" of an intellectual concept is can only be solved by the study of the interpretants, or proper significate effects, of signs. These we find to be of three general classes with some important subdivisions. The first proper significate effect of a sign is a feeling produced by it. There is almost always a feeling which we come to interpret as evidence that we

comprehend the proper effect of the sign, although the foundation of truth in this is frequently very slight. This "emotional interpretant," as I call it, may amount to much more than that feeling of recognition; and in some cases, it is the only proper significate effect that the sign produces. Thus, the performance of a piece of concerted music is a sign. It conveys, and is intended to convey, the composer's musical ideas; but these usually consist merely in a series of feelings (5.475).

The emotional interpretant is a very good example of a first. It is experience "at its most immediate." As such it is unreflected upon, and is *recognized* only in a "later moment." John Dewey gives, in a discussion of immediate experience, an excellent description of the kind of thing involved in the emotional interpretant:

> Immediacy of existence is ineffable. But there is nothing mystical about such ineffability; it expresses the fact that of direct existence it is futile to say anything to one's self and impossible to say anything to another. Discourse can but intimate conditions which if followed out may lead one to *have* an existence. Things in their immediacy are unknown and unknowable, not because they are remote or behind some impenetrable wall of sensation of ideas, but because knowledge has no concern with them. For knowledge is a memorandum of conditions of their appearance, concerned, that is, with sequences, coexistences, relations. Immediate things may be *pointed to* by words, but not described or defined.[12]

Note that Peirce draws his example of an emotional interpretant from esthetic experience, where we are very likely to be in significant immediate contact with the objects involved. An anecdote told of Schubert (whether apocryphal or not) illustrates the key role of the immediate, and so of the emotional interpretant, in esthetic experience. The composer had played one of his pieces on the piano, and afterwards was asked by a lady who had been listening, "Oh, Maestro, what does it *mean?*" Whereupon he sat back down at the pianoforte and played the composition again. Any answer to her question other than the providing of the immediate experience of the music would have missed the point, for the point was found precisely in the ineffable immediacy of the experience—in the Peircean emotional interpretant which was its effect.

Esthetic experience may be the *locus* where the emotional interpretant is most easily recognized, but this interpretant is by no means restricted to experience in the arts. Rather, it is an element of experience in general; in fact, "If a sign produces any further proper significate effect [beyond the emotional interpretant], it will do so through the mediation of the emotional interpretant" (5.475).

When a sign produces an effect beyond (and with the mediation of) the emotional interpretant, Peirce tells us,

such further effect will always involve an effort. I call it [the effect, the effort]
the energetic interpretant. The effort may be a muscular one, as it is in the case
of the command to ground arms; but it is much more usually an exertion upon
the Inner World, a mental effort (5.475).

Where the emotional interpretant is clearly a first, the energetic interpretant is
a second. A key here is the word "effort." Secondness is the category of the
other, of "struggle," of effort—the *action* of an effort implies the *reaction* of
an other. In classroom work on this subject, I will commonly interrupt the
lecture at this point with an injunction to one of the note-taking students to
"Look here!" or some such. The student invariably does, often with some
surprise. I point out that the overt action, the effort, involved in looking here
is itself an interpretant, the energetic interpretant connected with the sign
"Look here!" Peirce points out that the energetic interpretant need not be as
overt as that; a mere shifting of attention, for example, would count as an
energetic interpretant (I would suggest, however, that any energetic interpretant is in principle observable, although instrumentation [EEG, etc.] may be
required to observe it).

The energetic interpretant, however, "never can be the meaning of an
intellectual concept, since it is a single act, [while] such a concept is of a
general nature" (5.475). When we speak of interpretants in terms of *meanings* we enter the realm of what Peirce called the "logical interpretant." A
quick characterization of the logical interpretant would be to say it is a "general concept." Peirce speaks of "first logical interpretants" (5.480) of the
phenomena that suggest them as being the initial conjectures arising in problematic situations. He sees a second stage in the logical interpretant as arising
when

> these first logical interpretants stimulate us to various voluntary performances in
> the inner world. We imagine ourselves in various situations and animated by
> various motives; and we proceed to trace out the alternative lines of conduct
> which the conjectures would leave open to us. We are, moreover, led by the
> same inward activity, to remark different ways in which our conjectures could
> be slightly modified. The logical interpretant must, therefore, be in a relatively
> future tense (5.481).

We see the logical interpretant itself being classified by the categories, as
having a first, a second, and—we might expect—a third stage. Indeed, after
the activity referred to in this last passage has so taken

> the form of experimentation in the inner world . . . the interpreter will have
> formed the habit of acting in a given way whenever he may desire a given kind
> of result. The real and living logical conclusion *is* that habit; the verbal formula-
> tion merely expresses it. . . . The deliberately formed, self-analyzing habit—
> self-analyzing because formed by the aid of analysis of the exercises that

nourished it—is the living definition, the veritable and final logical interpretant (5.491).

In speaking of "logic proper," the second branch of Peirce's semiotic, we saw that an excursion of any depth into the topic would involve us in an intimate way with Peirce's philosophy; the same would doubtless be true of speculative rhetoric (that "highest and most living branch of logic"), had Peirce developed it in any detail. In our examination of the theory of the logical interpretant, we see that the same is true of speculative grammar. "The deliberately formed, self-analyzing habit . . . is . . . the veritable and final logical interpretant"; in such ways does Peirce tie this branch of semiotic in with the center of his philosophy. The concept of habit for Peirce may fairly be identified with thirdness; note that for Peirce "habit" is not restricted to our ordinary use of the word. The habits by which I deal with my environment are just one species of what Peirce calls generically "habit." Any regularity, any disposition—including, for example, the laws of physics—counts as habit, as *thirdness* for Peirce. And thirdness, habit, is preeminently the category of reality (cf. 5.93ff.). So once again do we see Peirce's semiotic as integral to his thought as a whole.

As we move into the further study of Peirce's speculative grammar, we are struck by the great wealth of material available; indeed, some wags might suggest that we would be better off a little poorer. About 1903, he tells us that

> signs are divisible by three trichotomies; first, according as the sign in itself is a mere quality, is an actual existent, or is a general law; secondly, according as the relation of the sign to its object consists in the sign's having some character in itself, or in some existential relation to that object, or in its relation to an interpretant; thirdly, according as its Interpretant represents it as a sign of possibility or as a sign of fact or as a sign of reason (2.243).

So at this point, Peirce sees the *relata* in the semiosical relation—sign, object, and interpretant—as defining three trichotomic divisions of signs; the first he calls the division into *Qualisigns, Sinsigns,* and *Legisigns* (2.244); the second, into *Icons, Indexes,* and *Symbols* (2.247); and the third into *Rhemes, Dicisigns,* and *Arguments* (2.250). These three trichotomies he sees as giving rise to ten classes of signs (2.254ff.). Several years later, in his correspondence with Lady Welby, he expands the list of *trichotomies* to ten (8.344 ff.), which gives rise, it would seem, to no fewer than *sixty-six classes* of signs.[13]

I do not propose to enter here into a discussion of this later classification of signs. Peirce himself did not complete work on the classification, and a fair amount of what he does say is conjecture. Speculative work in this area may be found in the papers of Weiss and Burks and of Sanders referred to in note 13. To give a taste of Peirce's classification of signs appropriate to the present paper, it seems sufficient to examine briefly the earlier classification of signs by the three trichotomies of 2.243ff. We shall, in this discussion, leave to the last the trichotomy which Peirce says is the one he most frequently uses (8.368), that of Icon, Index, and Symbol.

The first of the trichotomies is based on the sign "as it is in itself," and from this point of view,

> a sign is either of the nature of an appearance, when I call it a *qualisign* or secondly, it is an individual object or event, when I call it a *sinsign* (the syllable *sin* being the first syllable of *sem*el, *sim*ul, *sin*gular, etc.); or thirdly, it is of the nature of a general type, when I call it a *legisign*. As we use the term 'word' in most cases, saying that 'the' is one 'word' and 'an' is a second 'word', a 'word' is a legisign. But when we say of a page in a book that it has 250 'words' upon it, of which twenty are 'the's', the 'word' is a sinsign. A sinsign so embodying a legisign, I term a 'replica' of the legisign. The difference between a legisign and a qualisign, neither of which is an individual thing, is that a legisign has a definite identity, though usually admitting a great variety of appearances. Thus, &, *and,* and the sound [of the printed 'and'] are all one word. The qualisign, on the other hand, has no identity. It is the mere quality of an appearance and is not exactly the same throughout a second. Instead of identity, it has *great similarity,* and cannot differ much without being called another qualisign (8.334).

As we might expect, the branch of this trichotomy most difficult to understand is that associated with firstness, the qualisign. Peirce offers some help elsewhere with the kind of thing he here calls qualisigns, indicating that they are

> objects which are signs so far as they are merely possible, but felt to be positively possible; as, for example, the seventh ray that passes through the three intersections of opposite sides of Pascal's hexagram (8.347).

As we indicated, we shall turn now to what Peirce has to say about the third trichotomy of signs, which is "In regard to its relation to a signified interpretant"; here,

> a sign is either a Rheme, a Dicent, or an Argument. This corresponds to the old division, Term, Proposition, and Argument, modified so as to be applicable to signs generally. A *Term* is simply a class-name or proper-name. . . . A Rheme is any sign that is not true nor false . . . (8.337).

We note that in what is probably Peirce's most extended discussion of rhemes, in his work on the existential graphs (see 4.438ff.), he uses 'rheme' virtually synonymously with the way contemporary logicians use the term 'predicate.' The predicate 'x is red', for example, is a sign which cannot be spoken of as being true or false (until a quantifier or other such index is added to tell which or how many x's we are talking about). Peirce goes on about propositions:

> A *proposition* as I use that term, is a dicent symbol. A dicent is not an assertion, but is a sign capable of being asserted. But an assertion is a dicent. According to

my present view . . . the act of assertion is not a pure act of signification. It is an exhibition of the fact that one subjects oneself to the penalties visited on a liar if the proposition asserted is not true. An act of judgment is the self-recognition of a belief; and a belief consists in the deliberate acceptance of a proposition as a basis for conduct (8.337).

Peirce goes on to comment that he thinks "this position is open to doubt." Perhaps, but the tentative assertion of it shows again how closely connected to his philosophy as a whole his semiotic is. The conjectures about propositions, judgment, belief, and conduct in this passage are very much those of Peirce the pragmatic philosopher. He goes on about the *argument:*

Holding, then, that a Dicent does not assert, I naturally hold that an Argument need not actually be submitted or urged. I therefore define an argument as a sign which is represented in its signified interpretant not as a Sign of that interpretant (the conclusion) [for that would be to urge or submit it][14] but *as if* it were a Sign of the Interpretant. . . . I define a dicent as a sign represented in its signified interpretant *as if it were* in a Real Relation to its Object. (Or as being so, if it is asserted.) A rheme is defined as a sign which is represented in its signified interpretant as *if it were* a character or mark (or as being so) (8.337).

He goes on to expand on this by holding that a sign may "appeal to its interpretant" in one of three ways, depending on whether it is rheme, dicent, or argument:

1st, an argument only may be *submitted* to its interpretant, as something the reasonableness of which will be acknowledged.

2nd, an argument or dicent may be *urged* upon the interpretant by an act of insistence.

3rd, an argument or dicent may be, and a rheme can only be, presented to the interpretant for contemplation (8.338).

In connection with Peirce's talking about signs "being presented to the interpretant," note that this is virtually the same as being presented to the *interpreter* in a given "moment" of consciousness.

We now turn to that trichotomy of signs which Peirce felt he used most often, which indeed he saw as the most fundamental division of signs (2.275), and which is probably the best known to students of the theory of signs; this is the division of signs into *icons, indexes,* and *symbols.* Peirce tells us that

an analysis of the essence of a sign . . . leads to a proof that every sign is determined by its object, either first, by partaking in the characters of the object, when I call the sign an *Icon;* secondly, by being really and in its individual existence connected with the individual object, when I call the sign an *Index;* thirdly, by more or less approximate certainty that it will be interpreted as denoting the object, in consequence of a habit (which term I use as including a natural disposition), when I call the sign a *Symbol* (4.531).

So this division of signs comes about because signs have objects, and is based on the way that the sign represents its object.

The key feature of an icon is that it bears a resemblance of some sort to its object, "whether any such Object actually exists or not" (2.247). The resemblance may be the extreme likeness of a photograph (2.281), or it may be more subtle; under any circumstances, "Each Icon partakes of some more or less overt character of its Object" (4.531). This partaking can be of a complex sort:

> Particularly deserving of notice are icons in which the likeness is aided by conventional rules. Thus, an algebraic formula is an icon, rendered such by the rules of commutation, association, and distribution of the symbols. It may seem at first glance that it is an arbitrary classification to call an algebraic expression an icon; that it might as well, or better, be regarded as a compound conventional sign. But it is not so. For a great distinguishing property of the icon is that by the direct observation of it other truths concerning its object can be discovered than those which suffice to determine its construction (2.279).

The icon in a very definite sense partakes of the life of its object. Once it is set down, inferences about it become inferences about the object, insofar as it is iconic. A mathematical figure of speech would be to say that the icon is a *mapping* of its object, or a morphism of it. The mapping function may be very like an identity function, as is the case with photographs viewed as icons; on the other hand, it may be complex and conventional. We have employed a mathematical analogy in speaking of icons; the reverse of this coin is that icons are of key importance in mathematics:

> The reasoning of mathematicians will be found to turn chiefly upon the use of likenesses, which are the very hinges of the gates of their science. The utility of likenesses to mathematicians consists in their suggesting in a very precise way, new aspects of supposed states of things (2.281).

An icon represents by resembling. An index, on the other hand, need bear no resemblance to its object. The key thing about an index is that it has a direct existential connection with its object. The uses of ordinary English are reliable in our discourse about indexes; the index finger is used to point to something, for example. The pointing-to is a direct existential connection with the pointed-to, and so is an index in the Peircean sense. When *tumor, dolor, rubor* and *calor* are present, inflammation is *indicated* to the physician; swelling, pain, redness and heat are indexes of inflammation. You will find the party tomorrow night by looking for the house with the white picket fence—that fence, by its connection to the house, is an index of the house and so of the party. "Indices . . . furnish positive assurance of the reality and the nearness of their objects. But with the assurance there goes no insight into the nature of those Objects" (4.531). The fence tells you where the party is, but it does not tell you whether the party will be dull, wild, etc.

It is important, by the way, to note that signs by no means need be purely icons or indexes (or symbols, either). The sign in front of a shop is indexical by its connection with the shop. But it also may be iconic, by, say, bearing a picture of a book to indicate that the shop is a bookstore.

We have looked at icons and indexes; now,

> A Symbol is a [sign] whose Representative character consists precisely in its being a rule that will determine its Interpretant. All words, sentences, books, and other conventional signs are Symbols (2.292).

The employment of icons and indexes is a necessary condition of communication but the conceptualization that is so essential a part of human interaction with the environment rests directly on symbols:

> Symbols grow. They come into being by development out of other signs, particularly from icons, or from mixed signs partaking of the nature of icons and symbols. We think only in signs. These mental signs are of mixed nature; the symbol-parts of them are called concepts (2.300).

We have attempted in this paper to give a taste of Peirce's theory of signs. Obviously, as the taste is not the complete meal, so short a paper as this must omit much of the detail of so large a topic as Peirce's semiotic. Actually, this paper may be looked upon, in its incompleteness, as a kind of iconic representation of the semiotic of Peirce. For, as is the case with much of Peirce's later work, his classification of signs and the semiotic as a whole is by no means complete; it is as if the later Peirce had an overabundance of potentially fruitful insights, which would require another lifetime to exploit fully. However, it was Peirce who remarked that

> the opinion which is fated to be ultimately agreed to by all who investigate is the truth, and the object represented by this opinion is the real (5.407).

The full exploitation of what any one man begins is, for Peirce, a matter for the community of investigators to complete, and that completion may be indefinitely far away (5.408). Given Peirce's view of scientific inquiry as a community effort, with the community extended in time as well as in space, it would be unreasonable to expect him to come to closure in all that he began. Certainly his semiotic is a phase of his work which he did not complete. But he began it, and pointed out a variety of possible paths to follow, paths promising both to the Peirce scholar and to the semiotician with only a passing interest in Peirce. It is to be hoped that we will ably make use of the guideposts he left us.

NOTES

1. Loren Eiseley, "The Intellectual Antecedents of the *Descent of Man,*" in *Sexual Selection and the Descent of Man,* ed. Bernard Campbell, Chicago: Aldine, 1972.

2. *The Collected Papers of C. S. Peirce,* vols. 1–6, ed. Charles Hartshorne and Paul Weiss, 1931–5; vols. 7–8, ed. A. W. Burks, 1958, Cambridge: Harvard. Quotations from the *Collected Papers* are referenced in the standard manner of Peirce scholarship, parenthesized within the text. The first numeral in the reference is the volume number, and the number to the right of the point is the paragraph. Thus 2.227 refers to paragraph 227 of volume 2.

3. Charles Morris, *Foundations of the Theory of Signs,* IEUS, vol. 1, no. 2, Chicago: University of Chicago Press, 1938, p. 4.

4. Ibid., p. 3.

5. Jean Paul Sartre, *The Transcendence of the Ego,* tr. by Forrest Williams and Robert Kirkpatrick, New York: Noonday, 1957.

6. Murray Murphey, *The Development of Peirce's Philosophy,* Cambridge: Harvard, 1961, pp. 88–9.

7. Ibid., pp. 91–2.

8. Arthur Prior, "Peirce's Axioms for the Propositional Calculus," *Journal of Symbolic Logic* 23 (1958), 135–6.

9. Jay Zeman, "The Graphical Logic of C. S. Peirce," Doctoral Dissertation, University of Chicago, 1964.

10. For possible world semantics, see, for example, J. Jay Zeman, *Modal Logic,* Oxford, 1973; on Peirce in this connection, see Zeman, "Peirce's Logical Graphs," *Semiotica* 12 (1974), 239–56.

11. Gottlob Frege, "Begriffschift," *From Frege to Gödel,* ed. Jean van Heijenoort, Harvard, 1967, p. 13.

12. John Dewey, *Experience and Nature,* Dover 1958 (originally 1925), pp. 85–6.

13. For detailed discussions of these divisions, see Gary Sanders, "Peirce's sixty-six signs?" *Transactions of the C. S. Peirce Society* 6 (1970), pp. 3–16, and Paul Weiss and A. W. Burks, "Peirce's sixty-six signs," *The Journal of Philosophy* 42 (1945), pp. 383–8.

14. The brackets are Peirce's.

Logical Basis of Semiotics

Henry Hiż

When we want to say something, often we say it in words. We convey information, an opinion, an opposition, a question, a command; we tell a story, give an impression, reprimand, or confess in words, in sentences, in linguistic utterances. How the meaning is carried in words is the business of semantics, a part of linguistics.

Often meanings are not conveyed in words. By our dress we tell something about ourselves or about the occasion. The hostess—in some circles—shows respect to the guests by wearing a formal gown. An Appeals Court in New York barred a Roman Catholic priest from wearing clerical garb while serving as a lawyer in a criminal trial. The court held that the clerical collar was "a continuing visible communication to the jury" and this would prevent a fair trial.[1] A Bachrach photograph shows a distinguished businessman, wearing his immaculate shirt and necktie, with the standard expression on his face radiating success, comfort, confidence, and reliability. These businessmen have a different look about them than the kings in the eighteenth-century (or, for that matter, most centuries) pictures in the style of "king-realism." The standard expression on the face of a monarch is perhaps pompous but does not show any curiosity. This was to show that a discussion with him was not possible. (In that respect, David's picture of Napoleon is different; it portrays an intense and alert man, standing near his working-desk, with a stain of ink on his white trousers. Napoleon, a self-made monarch, liked this picture and did not allow the stain on the trousers to be painted over.)

Semiotics deals with meaning conveyed by any medium, not only by speech. Semiotics is therefore a generalization of semantics.[2] I will use the term *semiotic property* to refer to those properties which create meaning. Semantic properties are those semiotic properties that belong to speech. Speech has not only semantic properties. A sentence may be long; it may contain seventy words, twenty of which are monosyllabic. These are not semantic properties though they may in some unusual circumstances contribute to semantic properties, i.e., to the meaning of the sentence. Many objects, paintings, buildings, music compositions, customs, have meaning. But not all properties of these objects have semiotic roles. A painting has length and width; it weighs a few pounds and is worth some sum of money. Those properties of the painting are not semiotically significant. A painting may have aesthetic values, but neither are these semiotic properties. One of the main difficulties in establishing semiotics as a field of systematic studies is to distinguish those properties of objects which play a role in meaning from extrasemiotic properties. In particular, semiotics may abstract from the aesthetic values of objects. Linguistics developed rapidly when it abstracted from considering which texts are beautiful, or in good style. In the long run, the fact that linguistics does not study sentences as artistically valuable has proven useful even for stylistics, which today uses some results and techniques of general linguistics. Progress in a science requires delimitation of topics. Social history of art records what different classes liked in different periods—and does not say whether they were right or whether they had good taste or poor taste. Iconography deals with the subject matter of works of art and not with their social role or with their artistic values.[3] Iconography is a special case of semiotics, as semantics is. Semiotics can learn from semantics and from iconography, although most of the particular methods of semantics or of iconography are too closely adjusted to the objects they study, namely languages and arts, to be directly applicable to semiotics, which is to be the study of meaning wherever it occurs. Another science which is a particular case of semiotics is model theory, which is that part of logic which deals with the relations between formal languages and their possible interpretations. Again, it is clear that semiotics cannot follow in details what model theory is doing, because model theory in its essential steps uses the structure of a formalized language and puts a limitation on models which it will consider. Only certain very general investigations of model theory may be helpful to semiotics and will be used below.

To delimit properly the semantic role of linguistic utterances, and similarly the semiotic role of our other communicative behavior, one may note that our utterances not only communicate their content but show something more about us. Our way of speaking betrays us as coming from a dialectal region, a social class, or a profession, or as pretending to know something about the subject matter, as coherent or disorganized, stylish or stupid, arrogant or polite. Our listeners are forming their opinion about us on the basis of what we say and how we speak, even if we do not speak about ourselves but about birdwatching, Giacometti, or category theory. The listeners conclude from the fact of our utterance not only what it says but also that we, the speaker, say it. But this is not the same thing. A sentence does not say that it is said. Nothing about the sentence or about the speaker follows from the sentence. From a sentence follows only what follows from its content.

If I say that Epicure performed euthanasia on himself, you are directly informed that Epicure performed euthanasia on himself. You may conclude from this that he took his life voluntarily. Indirectly, from my saying it, and not from the sentence I have uttered, you know something about me. First of all, you know that I know that Epicure performed euthanasia on himself. Furthermore, with varying degree of substantiation, you gather that I have read a book about ancient philosophers, that I am interested in ancient philosophy, or in Epicurean philosophy, or in the problem of euthanasia. You may wonder why I chose to call it *euthanasia performed on himself* rather than *suicide*. You may suppose that I have read about the event in Diogenes Laertios where it is described in detail. But this is not what was said. The difference is between what you were told and what you noticed. You were told something about the mode of Epicure's death. And from that you rightly conclude that he decided to end his life. From what you noticed you infer my acquaintance with Diogenes Laertios. From the Euclidean axioms follow many statements about figures, lines, sets of points, but nothing about Greek culture. From the fact that Euclid wrote the axioms of geometry follows a lot about Greek culture of his time. We notice the presence of an advanced abstract intuition and use of axiomatic systems.

The concept of noticing is not semantic or even semiotic, though sometimes the term *sign* is used in connection with it. We notice that wood gets soft and take it as a sign of termites; we notice that a friend is coughing and conclude that he has bronchitis. But we were not told by anybody about softening of wood, termites, coughing, or bronchitis. Our ways of noticing things and generally of acquiring knowledge do not belong to semiotics. The only acquisition of knowledge with which semiotics deals is that of being told. A piece of wood does not tell us that there are termites in it. Nature does not tell us anything, though writers often use this metaphor. We are told this or that by elements of various systems of communication.

I am not trying here to define systems of communications; I am only drawing a distinction between noticing and being told. The latter is always in a "language," in a "system," in English or Italian, in conventions governing dress, in a tonal system of Western music (before Webern and Schoenberg). It is plausible that all our perception is done in some "categories of mind" and even that these categories are related to a language in which reports of our perception are stated, but those are different questions than the simple one which I am not addressing. We see ink as black if our vision is proper. But we understand the sentence *The ink is black* if our command of English is proper. We are told that ink is black if we hear the sentence *Ink is black* and understand English or if we hear the sentence *Inchiostro è nero* and we understand Italian. Similarly, we are told something by a painting when besides perceiving the colors we group the color patches into proper sets, if we are trained in interpreting them, if we are familiar with the style in which the painting was made. Otherwise we may either see it asemiotically, as just an interplay of color patches, or we may misunderstand it. An asemiotic interpretation occurs, for example, in listening to music if one perceives the rhythm in three with the first stressed and distinguishes it from the rhythm in three with the third stressed but does not know that the first is music to dance a waltz by and the other is a mazurka. A lot of the so-called aesthetic experiences may be asemiotic: experiencing the rhythm of the distribution of pilasters in the façade of a Renaissance palace, for instance.[4] Even when one has already given a semiotic interpretation to an object one may in addition give an asemiotic interpretation and by this assign to the object a more penetrating structure. For instance, the façade of the Notre Dame de Paris can be viewed, and is often viewed, as composed of two equal squares overlapping each other by half. Whether this structure has a semiotic counterpart—whether it expresses something—is a matter of dispute among art historians.[5] We observe the proportions of the façade, but we are not told anything by them.

There are borderline cases between being told and noticing. A recording tells us that the telephone number that we have dialed is disconnected. Here the original speaker did not address us directly. When the recording was made, the person was addressing anybody who might be calling a disconnected number. A busy signal tells us that the other party is using the line; the long ringing signal tells us that the line is not busy. The speaker in all those cases may be taken to be the telephone system which in our culture is a partner in communication. We tell it, by dialing, that we want such and such a party and it follows our request or tells us that it cannot satisfy it and why. But when in our receiver there is no signal whatsoever we are not told anything by the telephone system. We did not reach it. And we notice that we did not reach it and gather that our telephone is out of order. This example also shows that the intention of communication can be fairly remote in an act of communication.

An explanation of the meaning of a sentence or of the meaning of a picture, a building, or a sonata is a difficult task. From all previous discussions (and there have been many, from Plato on) it is clearly naive to think that a part of a picture represents something and that the meaning of the picture is the sum of the meanings of the parts. Moreover, it does not seem very useful to consider that a picture has symbols which stand for, or represent, or denote some entities. And that holds not only for abstract, nonobjective art, but also for realistic pictures. A representational, denotational semiotics says that a part of David's picture *Marat Assassinated*[6] represents the body of Marat, another part a knife, another a towel, another a drop of blood. One will not go very far with a representational semiotics. No part of a picture, no symbol, stands for death, or for the body of Marat being in the bathtub. As a matter of fact, the bathtub itself is not shown at all; it is all covered by towels, sheets, and blankets. We also may infer that there is a source of light somewhere behind Marat's head. But the lamp, candle, or window does not appear in the picture. We infer it from the distribution of shadows and from the technique of painting the wall darker closer to the supposed source of light and progressively lighter toward the other side. It is as if the scene is larger than its part shown in the frame. There are many·facts conveyed by the picture. More precisely, there are many English sentences which we infer from the picture. Those sentences are jointly the meaning of the picture. Thus I will not say that the picture represents Marat, the towels, the knife, etc., but that from the picture one infers that Marat's body lies in a bathtub, that his blood is coagulating, that there is a lamp, candle, or window to the left of Marat's head, etc.

The meaning of a sentence in a natural language is also, roughly speaking, the set of its consequences. Less roughly, to the meaning of a sentence belongs any sentence that is a consequence of the first sentence taken not alone but with other sentences which we know, or assumed before. For we do not draw consequences from an isolated sentence but from it taken with a lot of other, mostly banal, sentences which often remain tacit. Still more precisely, the meaning of a sentence is the difference between what one can infer with the new sentence and what one can infer without it.

Let A be a set of assumptions,[7] $Cn(X)$ the set of consequences of X, $X \cup Y$ the set of X augmented by the set Y, $X - Y$ the set X with all the members of Y deleted, $\{\alpha\}$ the set having α as its only element; $\alpha \in X$ is read α *is a member of* X.[8]

1. Meaning $(\alpha, A) = Cn(A \cup \{\alpha\}) - Cn(A)$

In this way, the meaning of a sentence may change, if the set A of accepted sentences changes. For some studies the set A of accepted sentences is taken to be constant (for instance, the common knowledge of a linguistic group). In others, it may change as the conversation progresses.[9] In the extreme case A

may be empty and then we have the meaning of the sentence α in isolation. Of course, this is only one of many senses of *meaning* as applied to utterances. It is the information meaning and not, for instance, a psychological meaning, which may be useful if one studies the surprise value or the commercial value of an utterance. The information meaning is useful in linguistic semantics, and one may try to utilize a similar idea for a more general semiotics where one takes as α not a sentence but a behavior, a costume, a picture, a musical composition, a building, etc. To study this extention of logical semantics to general semiotics, let us look more closely at the concept of consequence by means of which meaning is defined. Logicians accept the following principles for it.[10]

2. If $\alpha \in$ Cn(A), then $\alpha \in S$ and $A \subset S$[11]

If α is a consequence of A, then α is a sentence and A is a set of sentences. Sentences are, of course, in a language and the concept of consequence is relative to that language.

3. $A \subset$ Cn(A)

A set of sentences is included in the set of its consequences; in other words, each sentence from among sentences A is a consequence of sentences A. In particular, each sentence is a consequence of the set consisting of that sentence alone.

4. Cn(Cn(A)) = Cn(A)

This is the closure principle. The consequences of consequences of a set are just the consequences of it.

5. If $\alpha \in$ Cn(A), then there is a finite set B, such that $B \subset A$ and $\alpha \in$ Cn(B).

This is called the compactness principle. If a sentence is a consequence of a set of sentences, then it is also a consequence of a finite part of the set. Whatever follows from infinitely many sentences follows already from a finite selection of those sentences.

There are usually other principles of consequence given which show how this concept combines with specific constructions present in the considered language. For the language of logic, one states that a contradictory set has every sentence as a consequence of it.

6. If $\alpha \in$ Cn(A), then Cn($A \cup \{not\ \alpha\}$) = S

In principles 2–4, the concept of consequence is used very generally. There may be several more specific concepts of consequence. Often, one uses a specification of a consequence which is provability. α is provable from A if

there is a finite sequence of applications of some rules of inference which lead
from A to α. Another specification of the concept of consequence is the
semantic consequence which is the preservation of truth; α is a semantic
consequence of A if α is true whenever all sentences of A are true; that means,
no matter how sentences of A are understood, no matter how they are interpreted, if they are true in that interpretation, then the sentence α is true in that
interpretation as well.[12] The various specific concepts of consequence are not
at all equivalent but they all have the properties stated in principles 2–4.

To come now to semiotics, we want to make consequences not from
sentences but from a picture and a set of sentences. From what we know or
assume (however provisionally, fictitiously, or for fun) and from a picture we
infer consequences. The consequences are English sentences. Let us therefore
include in our study some objects in addition to sentences. Those objects may
be called *meaningful objects* (abbreviated as *Mo*). Sentences are among meaningful objects and therefore semantics of a natural or of a formal language is a
particular case of semiotics. Just as sentences are in some language or
another, so meaningful objects are in one or another convention. It does not
make much sense to speak of a sentence in abstraction of a particular language
and it should not make any more sense to speak about the meaning or the
content of a picture outside a convention. What has meaning in Christian
iconography, say a halo, may not have meaning in Moslem or in Buddhist
iconography. Or it may have a different meaning. An eagle on an American
coin is not a symbol of St. John's Gospel but of the U.S. government. What
counts as a picture of a flower is relative to a style, a period, a culture.[13] In all
statements here when S appears it is to be taken as S *in the language L* and
when *Mo* occurs it is to be read as *Mo in the Convention C*.[14] One may
generalize the concept of consequence to the concept of semiotic consequence
(symbolically *Iocn*) and one may state some principles for it.

7. If $\alpha \in \text{Iocn}(A)$, then $\alpha \in S$ and if $\beta \in A$, then $\beta \in Mo$ or $\beta \in S$.

If α is a semiotic consequence of the set A, then α is a sentence in a language
and every member of A is either a sentence in that language or a meaningful
object in a convention. A particular case of conventions in which meaningful
objects are formed are languages with sentences. Thus semiotic consequences
are sentences inferable from a meaningful object (a ritual, a drawing) and
from sentences assumed.[15] Semiotic consequences contain the semantic consequences of those assumed sentences:

8. If $\alpha \in \text{Iocn}(A)$ and $B = $ the set of all the sentences in A, then
   $\text{Iocn}(B) = \text{Cn}(B)$

The closure principle is similar to 4:

9. Iocn (Iocn(A)) = Iocn(A)

The problem of compactness with respect to the semiotic consequence is a subtle one. Applying the idea of 5, if α is a semiotic consequence of a meaningful object and of a set of assumptions, then a finite number of those assumptions should suffice to infer it:

10. If $\alpha \in$ Iocn($A \cup B$), $B \subset S$, and for no β, $\beta \in A$ and $\beta \in S$, then there are finite sets C and D such that $C \subset A$ and $D \subset B$ and $\alpha \in$ Iocn($C \cup D$).

The truth of principle 10 may be questioned. And so is the truth of 5. There are higher order formal languages for which 5 is false. Therefore, before one assents to an application of 10 one has to examine the convention in which the studied objects are coined and the grammatical features of the sentences that are assumed. The matter is complicated and future research on semiotics should bring results concerning the applicability and limitations of 10 which will contribute to our understanding of the differences between the formal structures of various conventions. Incidentally, another kind of compactness may be of interest. Namely, instead of, or in addition to, the compactness of the set of assumptions, we may speak about the compactness of the picture itself. There are meaningful objects in a convention which have as their part (in the case of a picture, a physical part) another meaningful object in that convention. If you divide David's painting in half vertically, the left half is still a painting in the classical convention together with the usual assumptions and gives as a semantic consequence *A man was killed with a knife*. A part of a picture may be discontiguous; it may consist of a fragment here and a fragment there. Triptychs and comic strips are discontiguous meaningful objects. Normally, a picture can be taken to be a two-dimensional continuum of points. Can a finite selection of points of the picture be considered a picture? And is it true that whatever is conveyed semiotically by a continuum of points can also be conveyed by a finite selection of them? An affirmative answer may be called the hypothesis of pointillism:

11. If $\alpha \in$ Iocn($\{\beta\} \cup A$) and β is a meaningful object in a convention, then there is a finite part γ of β such that γ is a meaningful object in that convention and $\alpha \in$ Iocn($\{\gamma\} \cup A$).

The pointillist hypothesis is a statement which may be viewed as a claim in psychology or physiology of perception, or in epistemology. But neither a point (in the geometric sense) nor a finite set of points is perceivable in isolation. I do not claim that a geometric point is not perceivable at all; certainly we perceive the intersection of two lines, that is, we see the point of intersection. But it requires the context of the two lines. The pointillist hypothesis is false if a point is understood as a circle with radius zero. However, if a point is understood as a minimal meaningful object, a meaningful object of which no proper part is a meaningful object, then the hypothesis may well be true. Then it is not a physiological hypothesis. Speaking about minimal meaningful objects is like speaking about words or morphemes. They are repeatable entities. It does not matter whether you take a word or a picture or a musical composition to be a physical event with definite time and space coordinates or whether you think about them more abstractly. Among some objects there is a relation of repetition and this is what makes the objects meaningful. Nothing unrepeatable is meaningful. But further analysis of repetion may lead to the conclusion that in a natural language only sentences and texts are repeatable primarily, and words, morphemes—or perhaps phonemes—are so only derivatively. Repetition of a sentence is a particular case of the relation of consequence. The hypothesis of compactness says that a consequence of a picture is a consequence of a finite selection of meaningful objects which are parts of the picture.[16] Before one can really say whether the hypothesis is true, much more study must be done about the foundations of semiotics. Here, an important idea is that not all properties of a picture are semiotic properties. It may very well be that, as Goodman wants, a picture is unrepeatable—with all its qualities.[17] But semiotically it is repeatable; there may be another picture with the same consequences.[18] Aesthetic properties and technical mastery of a painting or of a building do not go into consequences which are English sentences.[19]

The semiotic meaning of a meaningful object depends on the set of assumed sentences or other meaningful objects and consists of the increase of the field of consequences of the set augmented by that meaningful object.

12. Semiotic meaning $(\alpha, A) = \text{Iocn}(\{\alpha\} \cup A) - \text{Iocn}\{A\}$

The semiotic meaning of an object depends both on what kind of meaningful object α is, that is, to what convention it belongs, and on the content of the set A of assumed sentences and possibly of other meaningful objects. In what language we have to read an inscription or hear an utterance is not stated in the inscription or in the utterance. We understand the utterance as being in a particular language. Similarly, we guess what convention or style a painting is in and we "read" it accordingly. The reading of a text with understanding and the understanding of a painting consist in drawing the consequences from it plus an appropriate set of assumptions. In an ordinary discourse the assumptions are taken from common knowledge. In art they are found in the real or fantastic realm. A picture of Bacchus awakes in the spectator a number of stories from Greek mythology and they are used in our drawing of inferences from the picture. The semiotics with which people look at a picture varies depending on what they know and what other pictures they have seen and remember. Our ability to shift the system of assumptions, the story in which we place a sentence or a picture, is an important feature of our thinking. For a sentence in a conversation, what was said before is accepted as true and relevant, and is used for making consequences and therefore affecting the meaning of the sentence. And the environment of a picture may affect its meaning. If in conversation a sentence is used twice, then the meaning of its second occurrence is quite different from its meaning the first time. Because the meaning, according to 1, is only what the sentence said that is new, no part of the meaning of the first occurrence of the sentence is in the meaning of the second occurrence. Maybe it will be considered meaningless without, at least, some variation in intonation. If tolerable at all, the meaning of the second contains, perhaps, statements about the meaning of the first, that it is important, that it really is so, or that it was said. Now, suppose you see two identical pictures (say, two copies of the same photograph) hanging side by side. Though we can force ourselves to contemplate one of them separately, in the arrangement they are affecting or annihilating each other. We will make only comments about their similarity. This technique may be used to add to the meaning of the picture. Andy Warhol put in a picture 20 pictures of Marilyn Monroe, and we conclude that her appearance was for mass consumption.[20]

A sentence, or a text, or a picture often makes an allusion to another meaningful object; a religious painting to the Gospel, Brahms' violin concerto in D to a čardash. We can define allusion using the terminology just developed.

13. β alludes to γ relative to A if and only if, for some α,
$\alpha \in \text{Iocn}(\{\beta\} \cup \{\gamma\} \cup A)$ and not $(\alpha \in \text{Iocn}(\{\beta\} \cup A)$ and not $(\alpha \in \text{Iocn}(\{\gamma\} \cup A))$.

Two objects in different texts allude to each other when there is a consequence of the two objects which is not a consequence of each of them separately. For instance the sentence *To buy or not to buy* has as an allusion the consequence: *Do not worry about being, think about buying.* In this and similar cases we form a text of which the first sentence is the old one and the second sentence is the new allusion. So that $\alpha \in \textit{Iocn}(\{\beta\} \cup \{\gamma\}A)$ in 13 could be replaced by $\alpha \in \text{Iocn}(\{\beta\gamma\} \cup A)$. But this specification is inappropriate when β and γ are in different conventions, different media like painting and the Gospel, and we cannot form a text by juxtaposing them. Note that according to 13, when β alludes to γ, then γ alludes to β as well. There may be an advantage in keeping the relation of alluding symmetric. A Renaissance Entombment alludes to the

Gospel and the Gospel to the Renaissance Entombment. The meaning of the text of the Gospel may stay the same but the set of its allusions changes with time. We associate with the text of the Gospel Renaissance paintings.

The definition of allusion (13) presents some interesting difficulties. If β and γ are axioms in an independent axiomatization, then often there are consequences of the two axioms which are not consequences of each of them separately. We say in such a case that the axiomatic system does not accept a split. But then from 13 it seems to follow that the two axioms are allusions to each other—which is counterintuitive. To rule out such cases, it may suffice to require that β and γ be in different texts. A proof, or a system, is a typical text. To the fact that a proof is a text testifies the ease of inserting into a proof such phrases as *hence, and, on the other hand*. Two axioms of an unsplittable axiom system are fragments of the same text. But if β and γ are to be of different texts, the definition fits well. However, this calls for a definition of a text. Or for stating some principles governing texts as such. The task of characterizing the concept of text is particularly difficult, as we do not know enough facts about texts. The grammar of texts, or discourse analysis, is not a very advanced science.

To return for a moment to David's picture; on the table by the bathtub is carved "À Marat, David." However, we do not conclude that just after Marat was killed and before his body was removed from the bathtub David carved an inscription on the table. It is not a unusual signature; we take it as an essential part of the picture, we draw conclusions from that part. Still, it is on a different order, as if in a different language or manner of speaking. The realism of a painting does not require that there be only one convention used in it. Here there are two. The carving is not for real in one convention and the scene of Marat's death is not for real in the other. Note also that the shapes of the letters make the carving look like a Roman inscription. This is an allusion to the fact that during the French Revolution Roman civic virtues were revered. And the inscription is a personal tribute of David to Marat.[21] The history of painting has taught us to operate with more than one system in a picture and to see their interplay. In *Nativity* by Caravaggio there is Mary and the Baby and Joseph and an ox—and, in addition, St. Francis and St. Lawrence. There is also a flying angel. We are not told that St. Francis was present at the Nativity as we are told the ox was. We know that we must conclude from this picture that St. Francis was there in another—perhaps spiritual—sense. A similar mixture of conventions occurs in all the many pictures in which, beside a scene of Nativity or of Crucifixion, a benefactor of a church is kneeling. We know he was not there. We learn the combined convention of the two orders though each order by itself may be in the same convention, as it is in Caravaggio. This kind of combination of conventions may be distinguished from a joined representation of two orders of supposed reality. For instance, as in very many paintings, in *Pietà* by Perugino the body of Christ does not have much weight. It is lying on two Marys' laps but their dresses have no folds. What is conveyed is that the celestial order is different from the terrestrial one. There are numerous Crucifixions where the body of Christ does not really hang on the cross but floats in the air. Here we do not have two conventions; we have two worlds spoken about by one convention. A consequence of Perugino's *Pietà* is that there are two kinds of reality and that Christ's body is not totally subject to physical laws.

The logical or semantical concept of consequence requires some principles which will combine it with some important words in the language—in particular, with the logical connectives. Statement 6 binds the concept of consequence with negation. How about negation in general semiotics? Among the consequences of a picture or a building, there are negative sentences. A consequence of Perugino's *Pietà* is, *The body of Christ is not a purely physical object.* It is not easy to study directly the connection between consequence and various parts of a painting or various ways the painting is put together from its component parts. An imposition of linguistic structures on a painting or on a building, or even on a poem, is a dangerous enterprise. But from a painting may follow a negative sentence, or a conjunction, and therefore indirectly there is a link between a painting and logical connectives. Similarly, a Renaissance palace tells us that the landlord is not afraid of military attack. A Roman palace makes a negative allusion to a castle. There are on it no corbels supporting a machicolation. But many Florentine palaces actually do have relictish corbels and minute machicolations, making a positive allusion to military architecture. If a meaningful object is making a negative allusion to another meaningful object, they may be considered to be in some sort of negation relation. But one has to be careful with negation—both in English grammar and in general semiotics. There are paintings which together with a usual set of assumptions are contradictory: the set of consequences is the set of all sentences. An interrogative can be a consequence of a picture as well. In Caravaggio's *Calling of St. Matthew,* Christ and St. Peter approach a pool of gamblers. The gamblers are not surprised to see the Biblical figures. One of them asks: *Do you call my gambling partner?* Negation, conjunction, interrogation are therefore among consequences of pictures.

There is an old controversy whether art or art criticism is more difficult. About poetry Montaigne wrote that *il est plus aisé de la faire que de la conoistre.* Later, in the eighteenth century Philippe Destouches, a theatre writer, was of the opposite opinion: *La critique est aisée, l'art est difficile.*[22] To me it seems that the theory of art, especially its semiotics, is in a rather primitive stage, but I cannot say that about art. Art exists in all cultures, theory of art in some cultures only. Reflection about art and customs is like reflection about language; people speak in all cultures but write grammars only in a few. Therefore, I am siding with Montaigne.

NOTES

1. *The New York Times,* April 8, 1975.
2. In taking semiotics as a generalization of semantics I follow Roman Jakobson.
3. Fundamental ideas of iconography are explained, e.g., in Erwin Panofsky's book *Meaning in Visual Arts,* Anchor Books, New York, 1955 (especially pp. 26–54) and in Meyer Schapiro's *Words and Pictures,* Mouton, The Hague, 1973.
4. The distinction between semiotic and asemiotic (there called *semantic* and *asemantic*) interpretation was discussed in Stanisław Ossowski's influential book *U Podstaw Estetyki* (At the Foundations of Aesthetics), Warsaw, 1933 and later editions.
5. Many medieval buildings have simple geometric proportions of squares, equilateral triangles, etc. Some historians connect it with the Pythagorean and Platonic claim that the ideal structures of the cosmos have simple geometric proportions, a view held by theologians of Chartres in the XII century. Others think that the simplicity and the frequency of occurrence of proportions are due to the fact that medieval builders did not have good measuring instruments. See Władysław Tatarkiewicz, *History of Aesthetics,* Mouton, The Hague, 1970.
6. Brussels, Musée Royal des Beaux Arts.
7. *A* are not only assumptions in the sense of sentences which are just assumed but not known; among *A* there may be both known sentences and sentences accepted hypothetically.
8. For the acceptance of statements like 1, 2, etc., one does not have to believe in the existence of sets as kinds of things different from buildings, tables, pictures, people, or sentences. To say that Jane is a member of the set of women is the same as to say simply that Jane is a woman. To use the phraseology α *is a member of the set A* is just a *façon de parler* which is stylistically useful. But it must be carefully distinguished from speaking about sets in another, collective, sense. Hence, if Jane is a lawyer we can figuratively say she is a member of the set of lawyers but also, now literally, that she is a member of the Bar. For the Bar is an entity, an organization actually composed of Jane and other members. Similarly, a picture is a collective set of its points, patches, strokes of paint; and a building is a collection of its parts, of bricks, stones, tiles which went into its construction. In the first, distributive, sense, the term *set* is spurious. In the second, collective, sense it is not. Formula 1 may be read less crisply but philosophically less misleadingly as follows:

The meaning of a sentence α with respect to sentences A is the joint consequences of A and α which are not consequences of the sentences A alone.

A result of such a reading is that *meaning* itself is a form of speech only; in fact, some sentences are meanings of a sentence when assumptions are made. But as I am not very certain about the existence not only of sets but of other entities as well, including pictures, sentences, and Jane, I can equally well use the phraseology of set theory as the phraseology of concretism sketched above, provided that I do not confuse the collective with the distributive sense of *set*. The distinction comes from Leśniewski;

my skepticism about the existence of any particular thing is expressed in "Aletheic Semantic Theory," *The Philosophical Forum,* 1 (1969) and in "On the Assertions of Existence," *Logic and Ontology,* Milton K. Munitz, editor, New York University Press (1973).

9. This is the point of departure of some recent studies of presuppositions by Richard Smaby.

10. These principles were first stated by Tarski (see his *Logic, Semantics, Metamathematics,* Oxford, 1956, pp. 31, 32, 63, 64).

11. 'S' here stands for *sentence* and '⊂' is the sign for inclusion, so that 'A ⊂ S' can be read *all A are sentences.*

12. This concept was also introduced in the logical literature by Tarski (ibid., pp. 409–420).

13. This point has been made by many writers. Nelson Goodman in *Languages of Art* (Bobbs-Merrill, 1968) reminds us of this fact in radical terms (in particular, pp. 37–39).

14. The word *convention* is perhaps misleading. I do not intend to suggest that some people actually make conventions concerning meaning. Such conscious acts are exceptions. Neither is language established by conventions in the sense of agreements. Instead of the term *convention,* writers use *system* or *symbolic system.*

15. It is not clear whether one can draw conclusions from meaningful objects which are not sentences without using some sentences as assumptions. If one cannot, then it will be correct to add to 7 an extra clause: in A there is a α such that $\alpha \in S$. If with assumptions a picture gives a sentence as its consequence, it does not mean that somebody actually recites this sentence.

16. This is not principle 10. Rather, it is a statement in a theory of meaningful objects which refers to subdivisions of a meaningful object into meaningful objects. 10 is concerned with a set, in the distributive sense, of meaningful objects. The compactness hypothesis which I now refer to deals with a set, in the collective sense, of meaningful objects and takes the set itself as a meaningful object.

17. See the book cited in note 13.

18. The accuracy of repetition may still be a matter of degree. If somebody makes a copy of David's picture without the mastery of David, we may not be able to draw the same conclusions from the facial expression of the cadaver about what kind of man he was or how he faced his death. But an accurate copy of *Marat Assassinated* may carry all the same semiotic information without preserving all the aesthetic properties. To say *This picture is beautiful* is not to make an inference from the picture. It is a metastatement.

19. That a sentence is repeatable is assured by 3. But to state a similar principle for meaningful objects is more difficult and may require introduction of the concept of repetition as a new primitive concept.

20. I owe this example to Sol Worth.

21. Mieczysław Wallis, "Napisy w obrazach" (Inscriptions in pictures. In Polish), *Studia Semiotyczne,* II, 1971.

22. See the book cited in note 5.

Poetics and Verbal Art

Edward Stankiewicz

About a hundred years ago, Gerard Manley Hopkins defined the study of poetry or poetics (by which he meant, as we do, the study of verbal art in all its forms and modes) as a "baby science," which he proposed to study in a precise and scientific way or, as he put it, with a "microscope and dissecting knife" (106). Although the study of verbal art is at least as old as the study of the other sciences of man, the recent proliferation of works on poetics testifies to its perennial versatility and vitality.[1]

What seems to be the distinctive feature of twentieth century poetics is that it has set up its tent under the double banner of structuralism and linguistics. As Piaget has observed, the term "structuralism" has come to hold for our century the same kind of fascination that words like "organism," "system," "determinism," or "causality" held for other periods (Bastide: 93). In the simplest terms, structuralism implies the quest for the intrinsic behind the extrinsic, the obligatory behind the contingent, and the invariant behind the variant. However, the various schools of structuralist poetics, like linguistics itself, have assigned to these qualities the most diverse interpretations, depending on differences in philosophical outlook, local traditions and fashions, and the pressure of neighboring disciplines.

The Russian Formalists, the keenest students of literary theory some fifty years ago, identified the search for the invariant in literature with the separation of the intrinsic features of literature (what they called its "literariness") from its sociological, ideological, emotional, or referential functions and causes. Thereby they hoped to convert the study of literature into an autonomous and nomothetic science.

The Formalist program may be seen (and was seen by them) as a part of a more general movement that was taking place at the same time in a number of disciplines, but especially in art history and linguistics, the two fields that were most closely related to the study of verbal art. In art history the new lines of investigation were drawn by Wölfflin, who proposed to replace the study of subject matter and of the great monuments of the past with that of pure visual forms treated as a system of opposed, historically alternating values. In linguistics it was above all Ferdinand de Saussure who insisted on the autonomy of linguistics as a science "en elle-même et pour elle-même," and who established this autonomy by drawing a sharp distinction between *langue* and *parole,* i.e., by treating language as a formal system of relations apart from its material realizations. Language, wrote Saussure, is "form, not substance."

These developments coincided at the turn of the century with the emergence of a new, experimental poetry, remarkable in its scope and variety. By renouncing its subservience to extra-literary causes, the new poetry set as its aim the construction of "pure," inner-directed and tightly organized forms that would, in the words of Edgar Allan Poe, have the precision of "a mathematical formula" and that would resort to language for its invention and inspiration. "Grammar, dry grammar," wrote Baudelaire, "becomes the magic of evocation," while Mallarmé advised his friend Degas that "it is not with ideas that one makes a poem, but with words" (Valéry, 1958: 63). Combined with this effort was a distrust of language as a vehicle of meaning (misinterpreted by a long linguistic tradition as the equivalent of referential meaning) and an attempt to assimilate poetry to non-representational art. "Pure poetry," according to Valéry, "need not carry any communicable meaning but should resemble dance and magic formulas." He envied the musician the purity of his art and exhorted the poet "to draw a pure, ideal voice from practical and soiled language, a maid of all work" (1958: 81).

The modern poets-turned-theoreticians thus became the true founders of modern theoretical poetics which sought to define the general characteristics of verbal art by overcoming the one-sided historicism of the nineteenth-century approach to literature which had dominated the scene since Herder's declaration that "no theory of the beautiful is possible without history" (Wellek: 2).

The views of several generations of poets (Poe, Baudelaire, Mallarmé, Belyj, Pound, Valéry), however, gave a particular direction to the further development of poetics. To begin with, they were intended to lend theoretical dignity to the kind of art they themselves were producing but were ill-fitted to forms of art based on different principles (e.g., realistic prose); second, they placed a high premium on innovation at the expense of tradition; third, they exaggerated the formal properties of poetry, tending to disregard its semantic aspects. The place of meaning in this scheme was unambiguously described by Archibald MacLeish: "A poem should be equal to: not true/A poem should not mean, but be," while the titles of such works as *Philosophy of Composition* (E. A. Poe), *How is the Overcoat of Gogol' Made?* (B. Ejxenbaum), *The Morphology of the Folk-Tale* (V. Propp), *How to Make Verses* (V. Majakovskij) testify to the heavy emphasis placed on the technical aspects of verbal art. "A new form," wrote Šklovskij, "does not arise to express a new content, but in order to replace an old form." The study of poetic form above and apart from meaning could not but lead the Formalists to a study of the formal "devices" or techniques that allegedly were sufficient to cope with the esthetics of literary works.

The development of literature was further interpreted by the Formalists as a self-regulating process, involving a constant change of forms, and the principle accounting for this phenomenon was seen in the "law" of "de-familiarization" or "de-automatization," i.e., in the awakening of perception that is stultified by familiarity with old forms. Thus the question of the function of poetry or of its meaning was not dismissed; its burden was merely shifted to the external form and psychology of perception. And just as the mere arrangement of color and line was believed by some contemporary painters to provide a "bridge between the visible and the invisible," in the same way poetry was presumably capable, through the magic of form and by severing its ties with external reality, to convey a deeper, "trans-sense" reality.

The pre-World War II period witnessed in addition various efforts to define poetry in opposition to "ordinary" language. Thus it has been defined (by Carnap, I. A. Richards, R. Ingarden) as the language of "pseudo-statements" (in opposition to referential language that deals with true/false statements), as the language of emotion (Croce, S. Langer), or as the language of "connotations and attitudes" (Ogden and Richards). Along more linguistic lines, it has often, though vaguely enough, been described as a "deviation" from language, as a more expressive form of language, or as a language that draws attention to the sign-vehicle itself. The last view was especially popular with the Formalists, but it was also embraced by their followers of the Prague Circle. Poetic language, according to one of the leading theoreticians of that Circle, is "une langue fonctionnelle ayant pour but la désautomatisation des moyens d'expressions, une langue où tout élément linguistique, même celui qu'habituellement on remarque le moins, peut prendre la valeur d'une procédé nettement téléologique'' (Mukařovský, 1931: 288). It will be noted that the Formalist concept of de-familiarization is retained in this definition but is given a decisive linguistic slant. And what may be said in general about the Prague Circle is that they, more than any other contemporary school, established a close connection between linguistics and poetics, treating them as complementary aspects of the same study. To the credit of the Prague structuralists it must be added that they rejected the atomistic study of poetic ''devices'' and recognized the will-o'-the-wisp of a poetics that does not come to grips with the question of meaning. Thus we read in one of the *Theses* of the Prague Linguistic Circle that ''poetry reveals to us language not as a ready-made static system, but as creative energy,'' while another of the *Theses* points out that ''what remains least elaborated from a methodological point of view is poetic semantics of the words, phrases and compositional units of a certain length. The diverse functions of tropes and figures have so far remained unexplored'' (1929: 20).

At the Fourth International Congress of Linguists (*Actes:* 1938), Mukařovský defined ''poetic language'' as a meta-language, i.e., as a verbal activity that refers to itself. This proposal had the advantage of incorporating the recent contribution of Bühler, who in his ''Sprach-Organon'' recognized the referential, expressive, and appellative functions as the three basic functions of language, Since, like poetic language, the last two functions suspend the question of the truth-value of the message, the opposition poetic-non-poetic language could no longer be considered coterminous with the opposition of non-referential and referential function. But Mukařovský's proposal raised in turn the question of the difference between poetry and meta-language in the proper, logical sense of that term, i.e., of a ''language'' in which the message refers to the code, or to special, artificial codes. A solution to this problem was offered by Jakobson in his paper ''Linguistics and Poetics,'' which expanded Bühler's model by adding to it three more linguistic functions, and where the difference between the poetic and the meta-linguistic functions is defined as follows: in meta-language ''the sequence is used to build an equation,'' while in poetic language the ''equation is used to build a sequence'' (1960: 358). It should be apparent that this definition places the emphasis on the formal, syntagmatic structure of the message, remaining in line with Jakobson's earlier (and since reiterated) formulation of poetry as a language in which the ''fixation is on the message itself'' (1971: 662). While the other dimensions of language—the referential, phatic, expressive, and meta-linguistic—are specified positively in terms of their semantic functions, poetic language is defined negatively in opposition to these functions (with which it may, nevertheless, intersect), and positively as a verbal sequence built on the parallelism (''equivalence'') of its linguistic elements.

The tradition of Formalism and of a structuralist poetics has in the last decade received the strongest support from the French School of poetics, which has given a new twist to this tradition by combining the tenets of Formalism and of structural linguistics with the objectives of an ideological and extra-literary (Marxist or psychoanalytic) character. The leading representatives of this school do not tire of emphasizing the intransitive, "metalinguistic" character of poetic discourse, the priority of an abstract code over the concrete poetic message, and the derivative nature of poetic forms from their linguistic substratum. Literature, according to R. Barthes, is "une activité tautologique, comme celle de ces machines cybernetiques construites pour elles-mêmes" (1964: 148). The literary code, by analogy with the Saussurean approach to language, is treated as a closed system and as the only legitimate object of study, whereas the general properties of the poetic text as a particular type of message are ignored. The individual text is declared to be inaccessible and lacking in interpersonal meaning since, it is argued, each reader may bring to it any interpretation he wishes. "La poétique," writes Todorov, "est en quelque sorte un langage—non le seul—dont dispose la littérature pour se parler. Chacune d'elles est un langage qui traite de l'autre; et en même temps chacune ne traite que d'elle-même" (1968: 164). Literary analysis swings like a pendulum between the poetic text and the code, inasmuch as the text is used to arrive at the distinctive properties of the code while the code is expected to explain the text or to refer to itself. The literary code is defined abstractly as a "set of possibilities," but is interpreted concretely as an inventory of devices that are in part drawn from traditional rhetoric and in part from the categories of language. The two types of devices are not kept apart but tend to merge into each other, as when Todorov (in his *Grammaire du Décaméron*) equates sexual passion with the optative and the tasks of the hero in fairy tales with the conditional or subjunctive. The members of the French School, like classical Rhetoricians, show a strong predilection for classificatory schemes and taxonomies. Thus Barthes has established an ingenious distinction between the "readable" (*lisible*) and the "writeable" (*scriptible*), a distinction that cleaves the entire history of literature and any modern text in two. No bridge unites the "readable" and the "writeable," since the first refers to the paraphraseable content of a given work and the second to its esthetic superstructure that remains "absolutely intransitive." The literary text is likened by him to an onion: no matter how much you peel it, you get the same layers of skin without ever reaching a kernel.

In his latest work (*Le plaisir du texte*), Barthes treats literature as a hedonistic activity in which the "neutral" word teases suggestively with meanings it never intended to deliver ("c'est le seintillement même qui séduit," and "vous voulez qu'il arrive quelque chose et il n'arrive rien"

(1973: 23), and where the problem of meaning is precluded in advance. It would not be unfair to conclude that the school of French structuralists, which started out by declaring its allegiance to linguistics and to structuralism, has not contributed to the development of either. Having taken over from Saussure the antinomy between *langue* and *parole* and his indifference to the latter, it has ignored the study of the distinctive features of the poetic message (message being mistakenly identified with the realizations of *parole*), and instead of studying the types and interrelations of historically given poetic codes, it posits a reified poetic code which it interprets atomistically as a catalog of formal devices.

Before proceeding to the noncritical part of this paper, it is worth having a glance at classical poetics, which grappled with the issues of poetry that are still pertinent and reached, like many a modern theory, semantically incomplete results.

The founder of theoretical poetics, Aristotle, was probably the first to maintain that the value of art lies in the work itself (*Ethic Nic.* II, 1105a) and that the propositions of poetry are neither true nor false (*De interpret.*, 17a2). He had also an acute awareness of the other functions of language, for he opposed poetry and the modal statements of language, together with forms of persuasion and command (which he assigned to Poetics and Rhetoric respectively), to the referential function of language (*lógos apofantikòs*, which he treats under Logic). These Aristotelian distinctions provided the model for a functional approach to language that was overlooked by Saussure but that was amply developed by the Stoics and the British philosophers of language (Locke, Hobbes, and Berkeley), to be taken up again in our own times by Bühler and philosophers of language. Aristotle also advanced some specific proposals about the function of poetry in his analysis of Tragedy. Although he was sensitive to the critical role of poetic form, he insisted that the poet should be "the maker of plots, rather than of verses." "Tragedy," he proceeded, "is an imitation of action," though not of real action, which is the concern of history, but of action that belongs to the realm of the probable. "Poetry," he concluded, "is a higher thing than history"; it is "more philosophical" and "tends to express the universal," while history deals merely with the particular (*Poetics*, 1451a36). Unfortunately, we are not told what "more philosophical" is supposed to mean.

And, as though to acknowledge the shortcomings of his semantic theory, Aristotle added to it some further elements—to wit, that the function of Tragedy is to "inspire fear and pity," that the roots of poetry lie in "the instinct for harmony and rhythm," or, finally, that the poetic impulse is beyond rational explanation, for it "implies either a happy gift of nature or a strain of madness." It is the above definitions of poetry—that of mimesis, catharsis, or supernatural inspiration—that were destined to have a successful career in Western criticism.

The ideas of mimesis and of the poet as a seer are echoed in the works of Shakespeare. "The purpose of playing," we read in *Hamlet* (III, 2), "whose end, both at first and now, was and is, to hold, as 'twere, the mirror up to nature, to show virtue her own feature, scorn her own image, and the very age and body of the time his form and pressure," while Theseus in *A Midsummer-Night's Dream* (V, 1) gives us what amounts to a Romantic formula of the poet as visionary and as a man moved by powerful emotions: "The lunatic, the lover and the poet are of imagination all compact. . . . The poet's eye, in fine frenzy rolling . . . does glance from heaven to earth, from earth to heaven."

The solid kernel to be found in the above definitions is that poetry does not sever its relations with the other functions of language, but that it is multi-functional. The sharp separation of the artistic from the other functions is, on the whole, a modern invention. It is contradicted by the existence of long traditions of realistic and didactic art and by our experience with minor or larger forms of literature that convey—to one extent or another—referential, expressive, appellative, and socializing (phatic) functions (e.g., the novel, dirge, ritual formula, advertisement, lyric poem, hymn). The view of an art for its own sake was certainly far from those traditions of literature that encouraged simultaneous poetic and non-poetic interpretations of a work (e.g., the medieval tradition of four types of literary exegesis), that urged a search for the truth behind the poetic garb (Dante's *"mirate la dottrina che s'asconde sotto il velame degli versi strani"* [*Inf.* IX, 62/63]), or recommended instruction and delight (*prodesse et delectare*) as the goal of all poetry. The capacity of art to express a variety of functions is also known from the history of painting if we but think of the works of Leonardo and Dürer which, in their observation and rendering of phenomena, have served as invaluable sources of factual information.

The esthetic function of a work, furthermore, cannot be decided in internal terms alone: the identification of the artistic function may vary with changes in style and the attitude of the reader. Works of art executed primarily for non-esthetic purposes (ritual masks, goblets, wedding songs, or laments) may be approached from a purely esthetic angle if the non-esthetic intentions are forgotten or purposely ignored. On the other hand, works that were conceived and interpreted as art may in the course of time lose their esthetic impact and function as pure historic facts. Nor are the artistic and non-artistic effects in a complementary relationship: Balzac's novels can tell us more about French bourgeois society than contemporary chronicles, while Plato's *Dialogues* may be considered artistically superior to the plays of Voltaire.

If poetic works appear to us nevertheless as works of artifice or "fiction," compelling us to suspend the question of their referential or social functions, it is not because their words are emptied of their inherent meaning and the sentences lose their propositional function, but because the overall organization of poetic texts compels us to view them primarily from an esthetic angle. Poetry may tell profound truths or bold lies (or, as is so often the case, blur the distinction between the two), but these questions remain ultimately peripheral to the central poetic enterprise. The poetic text creates its own universe and points of reference, a "microcosmos" (or, as the followers of Aristotle would say, a "heterocosmos") in which all the elements and parts of the message are employed for the purpose of mutual support and for confrontation. Poetic discourse is thus more complex and richer than "ordinary" language, for it does not preclude the other functions of language but incorporates them, and transcends them.

The specific character of the poetic message would also argue against the treatment of poetry as a "function of language" on a par with the other linguistic functions, or as a special "poetic language," unless of course we treat these terms metaphorically. The reason for recognizing different linguistic functions must certainly lie in the fact that these functions are expressed by elements inherent in the linguistic code. Thus the referential function depends for its implementation on the use of a predicate (see below), while the appellative, expressive, and phatic functions are rendered by special linguistic forms and constructions.[2] But since the "poetic function" does not depend on special elements of the linguistic code (for some qualifications, see below), it must be treated entirely as a matter of the organization of the message, and not as a separate functional language.

Another characteristic of verbal art that sets it apart from everyday language is its capacity to combine with other systems of signs, or more specifically, with non-verbal arts. This capacity also exists in ordinary discourse which may combine with visual signs (e.g., body gestures); but the non-verbal signs and arts penetrate poetry in a more profound way, yielding a scale of hybrid forms. The manner and range of this penetration depend on the character of literature (i.e., oral or written) and on its genre.

Lyrical poetry (as the term suggests) has been associated everywhere with music and with dance, whereas dramatic art is inseparable from pantomime and the visual arts (e.g., the sets and costumes of the stage). The non-verbal component is particularly strong in oral literature that involves performance in which pantomime, music, and the very style of delivery (e.g., tempo) modify and may even dominate the verbal material. And since every written text can be read aloud, it too can be subject to modifications in the process of delivery.

Written poetry is, in turn, intimately connected with the graphic arts, as is the case with emblems, cartoons, or any illustrated texts. The very typographic arrangements of a poem on the page signal the poetic form and become a part of the composition. This interaction between the visual and verbal forms of expression has been on the increase in modern verse, where the experiments of Mallarmé, Apollinaire, and Majakovskij, the graphic patterns of free verse, and concrete poetry have tended to blur the distinction between the visual and verbal arts.

In considering the crucial problem of the relation between the linguistic code and the poetic message, it is necessary to point out that (1) the linguistic elements of the latter may be, but need not be, different from those of non-poetic speech, and (2) that they are endowed in poetry with functions that they do not carry in non-poetic speech.

An examination of the first problem does confront us with the fact that literature indeed employs features that are at variance from those used in "ordinary" discourse, though poetry does not in this sense differ from those special languages (professional slang, children's language) that likewise abound in such features. The use of deviant forms or unusual linguistic constructions in poetry has been connected with particular literary traditions and schools, and with special purposes and literary genres. Thus the use of the *e muet* is a feature peculiar to French verse, Greek poetry assigned different dialects to different poetic genres, Homer and the Serbo-Croatian epic song are composed in special, inter-dialectal koines, while the poetic guilds of Ireland and Iceland employed special, esoteric languages. The use of neologisms, archaisms, and unusual word order is pervasive in all forms of poetry.

The study of such phenomena must turn, however, from a purely mechanistic enumeration of features to considerations of their function in works of art. The use or prohibition of such features may serve iconically to mark a specific genre or poetic form as well as to modulate its internal structure; e.g., the characterization of the narrator or protagonist by dialectal or archaic forms, the reversal of word order for the purpose of foregrounding thematically crucial words or sentences.

The second problem of the special functions of linguistic elements in literature comes to the fore primarily in the study of integral poetic texts, and not in that of sporadic poetic devices or of the "applied" poetry of "ordinary" language. This "applied poetry" is by no means uninteresting, since "ordinary" language is not homogeneous but consists of a gamut of styles that move from outer-directed, referential, or socializing functions towards texts that are in their entirety set on the poetic function. At the most "prosaic" end of that gamut is scientific language, which stipulates as narrowly as possible the meaning of its terms and which coins special terms in order to obtain a maximal fit between the message and its reference, while closer to the poetic pole are those messages in which practical expediency is relaxed (e.g., leisurely conversations, sermons, or love letters). It is the latter type of message that makes the greatest use of "applied poetry" in the form of stereotyped formulas and "small genres" (e.g., literary quotations, puns, jokes, proverbs) or of semi-poetic expressions and styles. The borderline between such messages and "pure" poetry is never sharp; in some periods or social groups a premium on the "matter of fact" prevails even in leisurely discourse, as it did, for example, in the seventeenth-century Royal Society, which sought to banish metaphor "out of all civil society" (Abrams: 285), while in others the most practical utterances become infused with poetic expressions as, for example, the court decisions in Africa, which conclude with proverbs, or the philosophical works of Descartes, which have been found to be richer in metaphor than the contemporary plays of French playwrights.

The central object of poetics, however, is the poetic text as a message which hinges as a whole on the poetic function and which emerges from the interaction between individual creativity and the poetic codes of a given period, place, or social milieu. The poetic text is also the area of encounter between the linguistic code and the superimposed formal and semantic codes of poetry. The relation between these two kinds of code is not unilateral, but one of interdependence: the linguistic code defines (but does not determine) the possibilities of the poetic codes, while the latter modify and enrich the meanings of the underlying verbal material.

One of the prominent features of the literary text is that it severs its ties with the *hic et nunc* of the ordinary speech act at the same time as it asserts its independence from external aims. The problem of the speech act has largely been ignored in modern linguistics, which has focussed its attention on the properties of the code. In reality, the code and the message present two complementary aspects of language. The basic types of sentence—the question, statement, and command—and the categories of mood and the shifters (the "indexical symbols") are elements of the code that are oriented toward the message and that serve to establish a relation between the participants of the speech-act and the narrated event. Only the existence of such a relation, or what Peirce called the "conjunction of Secondness and Thirdness" (Dewey: 91) enables language to perform its referential and social functions and to build a bridge between the speakers and the world.

In poetry, on the other hand, the role of the speech-event and the relation between its participants are basically transformed. The speech-act loses its situation-bound, extra-textual status and overlaps with the narrated event in the message. The addressor of the message, the author, enters the message as a literary "device" and assumes the role (as Baxtin would say) of one of the voices in the polyphony of the text, even though in the end all the voices are his own. Nor is the reader/listener an addressee in the ordinary sense: he is a ubiquitous, non-specified interpreter, a kind of eavesdropper who must decode the message without any clues from the sender or external context. The only information that is available to him is that supplied by the text itself, and by his literary competence, i.e., by the knowledge of the literary code(s) and of other literary texts against which he projects and interprets the meaning of the message.

Poetry is thus, as Valéry said, "strange discourse, as though made by someone other than the speaker and addressed to someone other than the reader. In short, it is a language within a language" (1958: 63). The removal of the text from external context modifies the semantic values of those grammatical categories which in ordinary discourse define the relation of the participants to each other and to the narrated event. Thus questions and commands acquire the function of poetic "devices" (e.g., of reported speech or of internal dialogs), while the indexical categories of time and person are relativized with respect to each other and in accordance with the internal logic of a work. Thus the opposition between past and present tense may serve to distinguish the voice of the narrator from the foregounded speech of the characters, it may sharpen the contrast between central and peripheral actions, or it may be iconically associated with different genres (e.g., the prevalent past tense of the epic vs. the present tense of lyrical poetry and of plays). Similar shifts of meaning also affect the use of person, inasmuch as the first person designates a fictitious addressor and the second person a fictitious addressee. The modern attempts by novelists to adopt the "dramatic mode" and to suppress the role of the omniscient author have merely shown in how many different guises the author may enter into the work—as the principal narrator, as a narrator who shares the stage with other narrators, or as a pseudo-narrator who speaks through his characters in direct or reported speech. The peculiar relation which obtains between the narrator and the narrated event shapes not only the character of the modern novel, but participates in the articulation of literature into the major genres which assign a different place to the narrator-author. In epic poetry (including fiction) the author shares the stage and interferes with the speech of his characters; in lyrical poetry he generally overlaps with and speaks for his character(s); while in drama it is the characters that speak and act for the author. For even when the playwright tries to step out from the play to turn to the audience directly (as, for example, in the plays of Brecht), his address is always interpreted as an integral part and continuation of the play. By the same token, the spectators are expected to respect the border of the stage and not to transgress it in order to punish the villain. The boundary between the internal and external context of a work is not totally fixed, and allows for fluctuations in the process of reading. And just as the work cannot completely suspend its reference to the external world, in the same way it cannot entirely cancel its relation to an external context.

The emphasis on the external context of a work is most compelling in texts which combine, like a collage, artistic and non-artistic components (e.g., the realistic novel with its frequent digressions of a referential nature) or which employ special, "extra-textual" devices (e.g., the epilogue and prologue) to create a distance between the author and the work and explicitly to place the latter in a historical and social setting.

The internal structure of the text, which reinterprets the meanings of the grammatical categories that in "ordinary" language pertain to the speech-act, also transforms the value of the formal elements of language. This effect is not achieved directly by endowing these elements with some evocative, synesthetic or magic powers (as claimed by the Romantics and mystics of all time), but by using them as the building blocks of the text's composition. It is the composition or formal organization of a work which enriches the value of the underlying linguistic material, bringing into play the elements of all linguistic levels and endowing them with peculiar semantic weight. This interaction between meaning and form converts poetry into a code of a special kind, or, as Novalis would have it, "into a language to the second power" (93). The nature of this code is most palpable in verse, since verse represents the poetic composition in its optimal and most condensed form. Here the selection and arrangement of sound, the length of a sentence, the choice of word order, the distribution of word and sentence boundaries, and even the mere repetition of lines and words all participate in the construction of the whole, while they serve to shape the meanings of its parts.

The interpenetration of meaning and form is even more conspicuous in the pivotal element of verse, in rhyme, where parallelism of sound at the end of lines is inextricably connected with parallelism of sense.

The modern concern with form at the expense of meaning has distracted modern poetics from the study of the function of form, and more broadly from the study of the very function of poetry. The insistence on the "symmetry between sound and meaning" and the inclination to treat poetry as a semantically purposeless activity that can be likened to music or to dance have tended to skirt the central issue of its function: the meaning of the poetic message as structured form. For even verse, the most systematic of poetic forms, is not merely a structure of unfolding parallelisms of sound and meaning, but a process in which the parallelisms of form *serve* to create parallelisms of meaning. This process transcends the limits of verse and presupposes for its implementation a special organization of the poetic text that applies both to its formal and its semantic dimensions.

The basic formal properties of the poetic text are its tendency towards closure and the articulation of the text into discrete, equivalent parts. These two properties, we may note, were also singled out by Aristotle. "Tragedy," he wrote, "[is] closed action of a definite size [which is] differentiated in all its parts" (*Poetics,* 1449b24). The first of these features guarantees the self-focused, discontinuous character of the text, while the second defines its internal structure.

The tendency towards closure marks both the limits of the discrete parts and of the work as a whole, but it is most conspicuous at the outer boundaries of the work, i.e., at its beginning and end. The compositional devices that delimit the beginning and especially the end of a work constitute a frame which defines the work like the curtain or stage in the theater, or the frame of a painting, and which separates it from other forms of verbal discourse. This frame is occasionally of a non-verbal character (e.g., refrains consisting of nonsense words or of musical themes); but, being generally verbal, it differs thematically and/or formally from the rest of the text. Examples of such frames are the prologues and epilogues of plays and novels, the preambles of oral epic poetry, the final couplet in a Shakespearean sonnet, the epigrammatic endings in lyrical poetry, the use of the proverb at the end of Serbo-Croatian epic songs.

The second feature that articulates the text into a series of parts is counterbalanced by a tendency to unify them into larger wholes. The individual parts, such as the couplets and stanzas of verse, the scenes and acts in a play, the chapters in a novel are relatively independent and equivalent, since each successive part repeats with some variation the basic formal properties of its antecedents in the temporal unfolding of the text. Semantically, the parts seem to be even more independent, allowing for sudden shifts of theme, as does the famous sonnet by Ronsard, *Sur la mort de Marie,* in which the quatrains describe the fading of a rose (*Comme on voit sur la branche au mois de mai la rose...*), while the tercets switch to the death of the beloved (*Ainsi en ta première et jeune nouveauté*). While in ordinary discourse, and especially in scientific prose, we tend to speak about one thing at a time, the poet deals with a variety of things all at once, or, as Shakespeare says in the passage quoted above, he throws his glances "from heaven to earth and from earth to heaven."

An opposite, but in essence concomitant, feature of the division of the text into a series of parts is the tendency to integrate these parts into progressively more complex wholes, up to the unity of the total text. This integration is achieved by combining the principle of succession with the principle of simultaneity which forces us to grasp the successive elements of time as if they were equivalent elements in space. The combination of the two principles complicates the syntagmatic structure of the poetic message, opposing it to the ordinary message which is based on a single principle of linearity and which, as Saussure has pointed out (following here the views of the seventeenth- and eighteenth-century philosophers of language [Aarsleff: 103/4]), is one of the principal features of language and a corollary of the temporal character of speech.

The syntagmatic complexity of the poetic message was firmly grasped by Diderot at a time when Lessing (in *Laocoon*) tried to justify the superiority of poetry over painting by emphasizing its ability to present action in a linear succession: "C'est [l'esprit du poëte] qui fait que les choses sont dites et representées tout à la fois... et que le discours n'est plus seulement un enchaînement de termes énergiques, qui exposent la pensée avec force et noblesse, mais que c'est encore un tissue d'hieroglyphes entassés les uns sur les autres qui la peignent" (374).[3] The principle of simultaneity in succession also applies to other arts, and its role in music was described along similar lines by Mozart, who claimed to compose his works "in the mind" and to perceive the parts "all at once... like a fine picture or a beautiful statue" (VII).[4]

The principle of simultaneity does not contradict the principle of succession but, on the contrary, enhances it and brings it more sharply to the fore. While the linear progression is endowed in ordinary language with an iconic function (e.g., the irreversibility of the verbs in the phrase *veni, vidi, vici,* which reflects the actual order of events), in poetry it is exploited in more complex ways, involving not only the perception of duration but the structure of the plot, the vicissitudes of the heroes, and the formal structure itself. The successive order is persistently felt, even when the author rearranges the sequence of events, or when the central plot is stalled by minor plots or counterplots. The principle of succession dominates in the theater, as it did in the classical epic, and lies at the basis of such literary forms as the *catena* or the palindrome, in which the reversibility of the sequence merely corroborates the importance of the order of succession. It is also implicit in the compositional structure, which concentrates all its energy around the terminal point (the *pointe*), or in which the last part carries, like the tercets of a sonnet, the weight of the preceding, less significant parts.

The principle of simultaneity compels us, on the other hand, to comprehend the elements of the sequence in their simultaneous presence, imparting to the progressive movement of the text a retroactive impulse. This forward and backward movement is most clearly felt in verse, where each line leads inevitably to a succeeding line, while the latter in turn looks back to its antecedent, with which it forms a higher, inseparable union. The same pattern asserts itself in plays and in artistic prose, where each individual segment or motive may anticipate the occurrence of a similar segment or illuminate the structure of the whole. Thus the train in one of the early sections of *Anna Karenina* (Ch. 18) is the very train under which she finds death at the end of the work. The opening line of Mickiewicz's *Crimean Sonnets,* "Wpłynąłem na suchego przestwór oceanu" ("I sailed out into the expanse of the dry ocean")—indeed, the entire first sonnet—anticipates the dynamic movement of the entire cycle of sonnets (which describe alternatively a voyage by sea and by land) and mirrors the semantic opposition which informs the entire composition. The plays within *Hamlet* are a part of the sequential development and are also a metaphor for the whole play.

The combination of the successive and simultaneous dimensions is differently exploited in various genres and traditions that assign a different importance to the one or the other principle. Plays and narrative fiction tend to emphasize the order of succession (through action and the temporal development of plots), whereas short lyrical poems can more fully exploit the simultaneous order of all their parts. There is also a difference between works that are destined for reading and those destined for oral delivery, where the mind cannot easily retain the totality of the successive parts. This limitation of memory is compensated by the use of supplementary, integrating features, like music, or by the listeners' familiarity with the text. What makes all poetry an art of "difficult reading," however, is precisely the fact that the principle of succession is at every step complicated and resisted by the principle of simultaneity, which compels attention to the structure as a whole. The difficult form of modern poetry is but a consequence of the increased emphasis on the role of simultaneity at the expense of the principle of contiguity. The ideal of Valéry to combine "le simultané de la vision avec le successif de la parole" (*Oeuvres* I, 625) was not merely a quest for a new form, but was connected with the search for a new language of "daring" metaphors which could be grasped only within the confines of highly condensed texts.

The central issue of poetry is not, however, the formal structure of the message, but—as has been suggested above—the creation of "poetic meaning" by means of structured form. The form of a poetic message is the indispensable framework within which the disparate semantic components are compressed and confronted for the purpose of revealing the "unity in variety." The poetic text is set on a metaphoric process which involves the discovery of resemblance in difference and of difference in resemblance and which is, as in a nutshell, represented by the metaphor in the narrow sense of the word. For the proper function of the metaphor is the conjunction of opposites with a view to bringing forth their underlying similarity. Contrary to commonly held opinion, the metaphor does not imply any shift in meaning as it does not neutralize or alter the distinctive semantic features of the conjoined terms, but, on the contrary, sharpens their opposition while it draws attention to their common trait. The metaphor contained in the line from Mickiewicz quoted above compels us to see the similarity in the difference between the steppe and the sea and to view them as variants of a more abstract semantic unity. But if the single metaphor works in the small, the poetic text builds its metaphoric process on a larger scale, enriching it with properties that stem from the very unfolding of the message. In his article "Poetics and Linguistics," cited above, Roman Jakobson defined poetry in a marvelously compact and compelling formula as the "projection of the principle of equivalence from the axis of selection into the axis of combination" (358), i.e., as a sequence that is built on the alternation of equivalents that are either "synonymous" (similar) or "antonymous" (dissimilar). But this definition is too restrictive and makes poetry too dependent upon and parallel to language. It is too restrictive in that a poetic text built on the mere succession of similarities or dissimilarities would remain a static structure without a goal or integrating movement, whereas an adequate definition of poetry should capture the dynamic and creative aspects that characterize any work of art. The poetic text further differs from the paradigmatic system of a language (the "axis of selection") in that it does not, like the latter, merely involve either/or alternatives but combines, in the complex dialectics of poetry, the either/or with the both/and possibilities. The semantic equivalents, that is, do not follow each other in sequence like the parallel lines of a poem, but they interpenetrate and illumine each other, producing, in the words of Goethe, "wonderful reflections . . . which moving from mirror to mirror do not pale, but ignite each other" (173).[5] The concept is close to that of the Neoplatonists of Florence who in their hermetic, half-mystical way believed that beauty, in assuming the shifting guises of Proteus, reflects the oneness of Pan, and that Pan cannot reveal himself in any other form than through the ever-changing Proteus. "Nor do contrariety and discord between various elements," wrote Pico della Mirandola in his treatise on Beauty, "suffice to constitute [it], but by due proportion the contrariety must become united and the discord made concordant; and this may be offered as the true definition of Beauty, namely that it is nothing else than an amicable enmity and a concordant discord" (88).[6]

The exploration of similarity in dissimilarity and of dissimilarity in similarity in verbal art, as opposed to other arts, is supported by the structure of language itself, since every meaningful unit is both opposed and similar to other meaningful units. The pattern of differences and similarities encompasses all levels of language so that identity or resemblance on one level (e.g., lexical) entails a difference on another (e.g., morphological or syntactical), producing a constant interplay of similarities and dissimilarities in poetry. The metaphoric process engages the poet in an incessant exploration of the resources of language, but the choices of what is similar and dissimilar are always his own and it is they that make up the "vision" of his poetry. But the poet further transcends the limits of language by creating entire works whose themes, plots, actions, and heroes are constructed on the principle of similarity in difference.

The application of this principle to the structure of narrative is most tangible in folklore and in the literature based on it, since folklore reduces to the simplest schemes the relations that in original works of literature are more complicated and intertwined. These narratives include such universal themes as the return of the hero after years of wandering (as in *Ulysses*), the transformations of man into animal (as in the *Metamorphoses* of Ovid), the worlds of giants and dwarfs (as in *Gulliver's Travels*), the blindness of the sighted and the seeing of the blind (as in *Oedipus Rex*). All these tales contain the elements of wonder and surprise that come with the recognition that the split realities which appear before us are basically the same, and that the conflicting differences conceal a basic unity. The interplay and conjunction of opposites unfolds with the work as a whole, so that resemblances established in one part of a work are transformed into differences in another part, creating shifting perspectives that strive to be resolved in a unified vision or in a synthesis that is never finally resolved. The quality of such transformations was cogently defined by Gerard Manley Hopkins: "[Poetry] makes of each resemblance a reason for surprise in the next difference, and of each difference a reason for surprise in the next resemblance . . . and resemblances and antitheses themselves are made to make up a wider difference" (p. 105).

The metamorphoses that are developed in a text (and which especially mark the great works of fiction) engage the reader's constant attention, for he must formulate at each point of his reading, by means of provisionally formed hypotheses, the proper meaning and direction of the text. The forward and backward movement of the text along the syntagmatic axis, its retardation and acceleration, compression and extension are complicated paradigmatically by the hierarchical structure of its components (by the characters "in the round" and characters "in the flat," by peripheral and central actions, by the utterance of the author and the utterances of the character) which make the text into a multi-dimensional and multi-layered structure within which the reader is expected to find the unifying links. "Our wills and fates do so contrary run/That our devices still are overthrown,/Our thoughts are ours, their ends none of our own," says the Player King in *Hamlet,* and this saying illustrates, indeed, not only the conflicting elements and lines of a text, but also the tension it creates between itself and the reader.

Inasmuch as the poetic message is an intentional, goal-directed and creative act, it always strives to say something new. Its newness is not of a practical or referential nature, but lies in the creation of a meaningful metaphoric structure in which the means (the form) amalgamate with the ends (the content). The poetic message is a goal in itself, and as such it is ''memorable'' and enters the collective consciousness as a concrete cultural fact. The founder of a typology of visual art forms, H. Wölfflin, was acutely aware of this (in contrast to some modern structuralists) when he asserted that ''die Kunst steht überhaupt nicht im Allgemeinen, sondern im einzelnen Werk'' (217).

But although the intention of the artist is always to create *de novo,* he never creates *de nihilo,* and his effort is always informed by the norms or codes of a given art. Knowledge of the formal and semantic codes also guides the reader in his interpretation of a poetic message, and if the message is to have an interpersonal and communicable meaning, the codes that are mustered at both ends of the ''channel'' must basically (though not completely) coincide. The contemporary emphasis on the rights of the reader to interpret the text in any way he wants opens the gates to a free-for-all subjectivism and often marks the refusal of literary criticism to limit itself to the intrinsic properties of art.

The problem of innovation cannot be separated from that of tradition, just as the question of the individual text cannot be separated from that of the collective code. Code and message constantly interact, and the change of code is brought about through innovations in individual messages which redefine the limits of the code. The relation of code and message, however, presents a gamut of possibilities that vary according to literary form, oral or written type of literature, school, and period. The highly codified small literary forms, which belong largely to the oral tradition (proverbs, riddles, fixed metaphors), are least susceptible to personal invention, while oral literature as a whole treats the relation of innovation to tradition in a different way from written literature. Moving essentially on a single synchronic plane (which itself comprises a series of diachonic layers), oral literature combines a maximal adherence to the collective code with a minimal adhérence to any specific text. The individual text emerges only in the process of actual performance in which the non-verbal elements (music and pantomime) play no less a role than the verbal material. The longer texts of oral literature thus acquire an existence similar to that of an abstract code, while the role of the performers of such texts comes close to that of their actual authors. Written literature, on the other hand, observes to a maximal degree the integrity of the individual fixed text and achieves innovation by breaking the rules of the governing code(s). The changeable status of literary codes and the fixed character of the written texts introduces into "learned" literature a historical dimension which complicates the reading of any individual text. For the "memorable" texts of the past exist side by side with the texts of the present, composing with them an open and continuous series. The interpretation of any written text thus presupposes not only a knowledge of the underlying poetic and linguistic codes (knowledge of the latter being a prerequisite of any verbal message) but also a familiarity with other texts to which the given text may explicitly allude. The poetic text is consequently as context-bound and open-ended as any non-poetic message, except that the latter is anchored to an external (situational) context, whereas the former refers primarily (though not exclusively) to other homogeneous texts. It can always be interpreted metonymically, as a part of a larger text (as a poem in a cycle, as a part of a trilogy, or as a representative work of a certain school), or metaphorically, as an echo of another text (as, for example, Pushkin's *Pamjatnik* with respect to Horace's *Exegi monumentum,* or Joyce's *Ulysses* with respect to Homer's *Odyssey*). The conjunction of such texts not only affects the interpretation of each text, but puts them, like any metaphor, in a state of mutual irritation that expands the meanings of both.

The covert or overt use of allusions is a conspicuous feature of modern poetry (as in the works of Joyce, Eliot, Pound, or Mandel'štam), which has condensed the internal structure of the text and expanded its reference to other texts. By doing so it has become a literature of an elite which demands the closest collaboration of the reader with the author. For example, the two-stanza poem by Yeats, *The Scholars,* ends with the unexpected couplet, "Lord, what would they say/Did their Catullus walk that way?" However, knowledge of Catullus's poem *Vivamus, mea Lesbia* reveals immediately the affinity between the two poems in theme and formal organization. Both poems establish the opposition between the young and the old (in Yeats: "old, learned bald heads" vs. "young men, tossing in their beds," and in Catullus: "Vivamus, mea Lesbia, atque amemus" vs. "rumoresque senum severiorum"), between learning and ignorance, hope and despair— oppositions which complement each other within and across the two poems.[7] The lack of extra-textual knowledge which would make the reader miss the point of Yeats's allusion need not vitiate the comprehension and enjoyment of his poem, but both poems gain in fullness and completion when read in conjunction with each other.

An extra-textual, internalized dimension is nevertheless indispensable for the full interpretation of any literary work, though it may vary again according to time and literary tradition, and according to various literary forms. It is this dimension that involves the active participation of the reader and completes the meaning of individual texts.

In the first place, the reader is expected to be able to place the message within a more general type, i.e., within one of the major literary genres. Knowing the distinctive (both positive and negative) features of the basic genres, the reader can restrict the range of his expectations and exclude those interpretations that are alien to the given genre. Without knowledge of the literary types (knowledge internalized in the process of earlier readings), the reader could not decide whether the work in question is a pastiche or parody, to what extent it adheres to the rules of the given genre, or if it tries to establish a new form (as happened when the Romantics elevated the letter to a literary form, or tried to fuse the features of different genres). A knowledge of compositional form, which generally varies according to the basic genres (e.g., lyrical poetry is, on the whole, composed in verse), serves likewise as a guide to the reading of a text. Thus it is well known that diverse metrical patterns are associated with different functions and are capable of evoking the content of poetic works. According to Valéry, the rhythm of the ten-syllable line and its association with Dante's *endecasillabo* suggested to him the theme of *Le Cimitière marin;* in the same way the Russian iambic meters imply (at least during the nineteenth century) a high, rhetorical tone, while the trochaic meters evoke the light, sung motif of folkloristic verse.

A command of the literary code—i.e., literary competence—is essential for the interpretation of entire poetic sub-types, such as the allegory and the fable, whose overt textual meanings must be complemented by reference to the implied, non-verbalized sense. An open-ended, latent dimension also underlies such popular forms as the proverb, whose internal meaning is completed only by matching it with a corresponding external context, or the riddle that always implies more than one solution. The latent meanings may, as in the forms cited, underlie the meanings of entire texts or they may surround the meanings of individual words, elevating them to the status of symbols. The symbolic meaning which is superposed upon the ordinary lexical meaning of words may be a part of the broader cultural tradition (the Christian symbols of the cross and the rose), of a given period or poetic school (the mythological symbolism of the Renaissance), or of individual poets and texts (Blake or Yeats). Furthermore, the ''allegorical'' and ''symbolic'' interpretations of a text may combine, as, for example, in the *Divine Comedy*, which must be read both with an eye to its allegorical meaning (stipulated by the canons of medieval poetics) and with an understanding of its symbols (e.g., the beasts in the *Inferno*). However, no poetry is entirely free of a symbolic layer, since every lexical element can be endowed with supplementary, non-''literal'' meanings. The metaphoric process itself compels us to look for the deeper, multi-layered meanings that are set off by the collision of opposites and radiate beyond the surface of the text. Thus the tragic meaning of *Othello* lies not only in the conflict between the Moor's jealousy and Iago's hatred, or on a deeper level between the parallel sins of pride and envy, but also in the tension between two opposite visions of the world. Similarly, the various divergent lines of *Hamlet* converge to expose the tension between crime and duty, thought and action, freedom and fate, but even more profoundly, the ambiguity of man ("the beauty of the world" and "the quintessence of dust") and of the human condition.

The quest for symbolic meanings has often led in modern poetry (as in the works of the Symbolists) to the proliferation of private symbols that tend to blur the clarity of a text in the same way as the density of allusions hampers its understanding. The two types of trans-textual reference are nevertheless implicit in the poetic process that enlarges the meaning of individual texts and moves them closer to each other. In going beyond the limits of the text, poetry also establishes links with other arts, in the same way in which the plurality of its functions puts it in the broader context of non-artistic systems and activities.

NOTES

1. This paper is a further development of reflections in poetics that I have presented in two recent papers: "Structural poetics and linguistics" (1974: 1) and "The poetic text as a linguistic structure" (1974: 2). For a fuller bibliography and discussion of certain points, see especially 1974: 1.

2. For the need to distinguish the expression of the various functions in the code vs. the message, see Stankiewicz, 1964, 242 ff.

3. There is some reason to believe that Lessing was influenced by and grasped the ideas of Diderot whose *Discours sur la poesie dramatique* he translated in 1760. In the chapter "De la pantomime" Diderot repeated some of the principles he had formulated in his *Lettre* of 1751. According to E. M. Szarota (1959: 163ff.), Lessing planned to write a follow-up to the *Laokoon* in which he intended to defend the superiority of dramatic art over other literary genres precisely on the grounds that it combined more than any other genre the principle of succession with that of simultaneity.

4. The full passage of Mozart's letter reads: "My object enlarges itself, becomes methodised and defined, and the whole, though it be long, stands almost complete and finished in my mind, so that I can survey it, like a fine picture or beautiful statue, at a glance. Nor do I hear in my imagination the parts successively, but I hear them as it were all at once."

5. The quotation is taken from Cassirer (1945) and refers to the effects of colors in crystals. The German text reads: "entoptische Erscheinungen . . . welche gleichfalls von Spiegel zu Spiegel nicht etwas verbleichen, sondern sich erst recht entzünden." On Goethe's concepts of *Polarität* and *Steigerung* and the use he made of them in his esthetic and scientific writings, see Jolles, 1957.

6. On the use and interpretation of the Neoplatonist concepts by Goethe and the Romantics, see Wind, Chs. 5 and 13, and M. H. Abrams, 1972, 183 ff.

7. A closer analysis of the two poems and their full texts are given in Stankiewicz, 1974: 2.

REFERENCES

Aarsleff, Hans. 1974. "The Traditions of Condillac," *Studies in the History of Linguistics: Traditions and Paradigms,* edited by Dell Hymes. Bloomington, Ind.

Abrams, M. H. 1953. *The Mirror and the Lamp: Romantic Theory and the Critical Tradition.* New York.

———. 1971. *Natural Supernaturalism. Tradition and Revolution in Romantic Literature.* New York.

Aristotle. *The Works of Aristotle translated into English.* Vols 9, 11, edited by W. D. Ross. Oxford.

Barthes, Roland. 1953. *Le degré zero de l'écriture.* Paris. Engl. transl. 1968. *Writing Degree Zero. Elements of Semiology.* Boston.

———. 1964. *Essais critiques.* Paris.

———. 1973. *Le plaisir du texte.* Paris.

Bastide, Roger (ed.). 1962. *Sens et usages du terme structure dans les sciences humaines et sociales.* The Hague.

Cassirer, Ernst. 1945. "Thomas Manns Goethe Bild. Studie über Lotte in Weimar," *The Germanic Review* 20.3.

Dewey, John. 1946. "Peirce's Theory of the Linguistic Sign, Thought and Meaning," *The Journal of Philosophy,* 85–95.

Diderot, Denis. 1875. "Lettre sur les sourds et muets," *Oeuvres complètes,* I. Paris. Cited by Mario Praz. 1967. *Mnemosyne. The Parallel between Literature and the Visual Arts.* Bollingen Series, 35, 16. Washington. Footnote 6.

Hopkins, Gerard Manley. 1959. "Poetic diction" and "On the origin of beauty." *The Journals and Papers,* edited by H. House, 84–114. London.

Jakobson, Roman. 1960. "Linguistics and Poetics," *Style in Language,* edited by T. A. Sebeok, 350–77. Boston and New York.

———. 1971. "Linguistics in Relation to Other Sciences," *Selected Writings,* 2. The Hague.

Jolles, M. 1957. *Goethes Kunstanschauung.* Bern.

Mozart, Wolfgang Amadeus. 1968. *Letters,* edited by H. Mersmann. New York.

Mukařovský, Jan. 1931. "La phonologie et la poétique," *Travaux du Cercle linguistique de Prague,* 4, 278–288.

———. 1938. "La denomination poétique et la fonction esthétique de la langue," *Actes du Quatrième Congrès International de Linguistes,* 98–104. Copenhagen.

Novalis. 1945–46. *Gesammelte Werke,* ed. Carl Seeling. Vol. 3.

Osborne, H. 1970. *Aesthetics and art theory: An historical introduction.* New York.

Pico della Mirandola. *On the General Nature of Beauty (Della bellezza in commune).* Cited after Edgar Wind. 1968. *Pagan Mysteries in the Renaissance.* New York.

Stankiewicz, Edward. 1964. "Problems of Emotive Language," *Approaches to Semiotics,* edited by T. A. Sebeok, et al. The Hague.

———. 1974. "The Poetic Text as a Linguistic Structure," *Sciences of Language.* Tokyo.

————. 1974. "Structural Poetics and Linguistics," *Current Trends in Linguistics,* 12. The Hague, 629–59. *Theses of the Prague Circle*—Thèses presentées au Premier Congrés des philologues slaves. 1929. TCLP 1.5–29.

Szarota, Elida Maria. 1959. *Lessings 'Laokoon.' Eine Kampfschrift für eine realistische Kunst und Poesie.* Weimar.

Todorov, Tzvetan. 1968. "Poétique," *Qu'est-ce-que le structuralisme,* edited by O. Ducrot, et al. Paris.

————. 1969. *Grammaire du Décaméron.* The Hague.

Valéry, Paul. 1957–60. *Oeuvres,* ed. Jean Hytier. Bibliothèque de la Pleiade, Paris.

————. 1958. *The Art of Poetry,* transl. by Denise Folliot. New York.

Wellek, Rene. 1974. "Poetics, Interpretation and Criticism," *The Modern Language Review,* 69, 4.

Wölfflin, Heinrich. 1933. "Kunstgeschichtliche Kunstbegriffe. Eine Revision," *Logos* 22.

Unexpected Semiotic Implications of Medical Inquiry

Harley C. Shands and James D. Meltzer

In the nineteenth century, primarily in the western world, human beings pursued scientific method in a progressive acceleration of innovative research and development. This movement—Whitehead called it the invention of the method of invention—continues in our own period, with further acceleration.

At the beginning of the twentieth century there appeared a quite new movement that changed the focus from *object* to *method,* so that scientists began to develop a new kind of self-consciousness in the form of an interest in *methodology.* Planck had said that reality was approached through the use of symbols in inferential reasoning, but he emphasized that these symbols were like essential spectacles the optical properties of which were unknown. The various methodological or communicational or semiotic discoveries of the present century can metaphorically be described as oriented to understanding the structure of these "eye glasses."

Our principal interest for a number of years has been in the application of communicational-semiotic inquiry to the medical field (Shands and Meltzer, 1975). There the difference between objective and methodological inquiry is apparent as it is in natural science. Although it is obvious that psychiatry is the principal field in which human communication is the subject matter (in studying relations between persons, characteristic attitudes, orientations, and intellectual skills), investigation of human method has been hampered by the difficulty human beings have in objectifying "myself" and "my own" methods.

Recent epistemological discoveries, stemming primarily from Piaget's study of the developing intelligence of children in school, have allowed a new look at basic semiotic method. The application of some of these discoveries to psychiatric problems of traditional difficulty has given us a new understanding of some of them. In this discussion, the focus is upon the problem presented by the disability state exhibited by some workers following industrial accidents.

We have been able to identify a characteristic set of semiotic observations regularly found in these disabled workers, most of whom are uneducated, usually remarkably so in a country in which literacy is practically universal. In a very large proportion, the lack of education is explained by the immigrant status of the worker. We believe that the specific cognitive limitation preceded the illness, and that it constitutes a predisposition to develop the disability state. The conclusion repetitively reached is that the accident imposes a catastrophic strain on the limited integrative capacity of the worker so that his capacity to cope seems "fractured" in an irreversible way.

The unskilled laborer, "condemned" to his job by his lack of education (although many give the impression of a good "native" intellectual capacity) is at risk for further difficulty in adapting to an injury that radically changes the condition of his life. The fascinating observable is the worker's insistence that the "external" change has made a corresponding "internal" change that he can state but cannot describe or understand.

The characteristic complaint encountered is, "I am not the same person I was before the accident, it's just not me. I was always a good worker and enjoyed my work—now I can't enjoy anything. All I want is to be like I was before and go back to work." The problem immediately identified can be described as the loss of *identity*. This version, however, is very different from other identity losses in psychiatry because the claimant presents typically no evidence of neurotic or psychotic involvement.

We have found Piaget's notion of *conservation* precisely applicable. Piaget uses a variety of tests in which the crucial decision has to do with a conflict between qualitative and quantitative decision. The problem presented is that of how a change in *shape* is related to a change in *amount*. In traditional terms, the problem is that of appearance vs. "reality" (cf. Planck, above). When a ball of clay is rolled out into a sausage shape, it "looks different" while it is "really the same."

Piaget's *genetic epistemology* is a description of the sequential emergence of more sophisticated ways of processing the data of one's experience. The progression is characterized by partial "equilibria," stages of which appear as the ability to "conserve" in more and more complex contexts. Conservation of *mass* appears when the child of 8 is able to comprehend that a ball of clay rolled out into a sausage has changed its shape but not its mass; conservation of *weight* after apparent change in form appears at 10, but that of *volume* does not occur (in Piaget's norm) until about 12. At around this age, "reflective intelligence" appears and develops through the rest of adolescence. "Reflection" in this sense describes a putative equilibrium between the "inner" and the "outer" structure.

The idea that the universe is "reflected" in "the mind" is one that has long grasped the imagination of mankind. This idea describes an "equilibrium" that in the theoretical work of Newton established itself as dominant for two hundred years, one established as well in Marxism; it is a view now clearly the norm in common sense. The revolution in epistemology that has succeeded Newtonian mechanics in physics (in a "concrete" context involving inanimate matter) is one in which the influence of the means of communication upon that which is communicated has become a principal topic of inquiry. As the implications of this new approach have emerged, it has become clearer and clearer that the equilibrium implied in Newtonian theory is much easier to find in relation to "objects" the behavior of which is *regular*. The more complex the entity examined, the *less* regular and *more* unpredictable it appears and the more difficult equilibrium is to discover. The ultimate in unpredictability is to be found in human systems, in which the "subject matter" is the transactional relatedness between two persons seen as data-processing systems of the most astronomical complexity. If one measures "degrees of freedom" based upon the estimated number of single cells in the brain alone (without the humoral, the genetic and the immunological data-processing systems), the two together give a total of 10^{20} cells, each of which has as many as thousands of connections to many other cells.

With this number of potentialities, it is scarcely to be wondered that the twentieth-century revolution in *reflexive* (that is, self-reflective) human understanding should have been established by the demonstration of finite limits in the physical universe. Such finite limits powerfully support the establishment of conservation: Einstein's demonstration of the finite speed of light and Planck's demonstration of the finite mass of the quantum of action "set limits" to the human imagination. Modern semiotic inquiry has gone far toward establishing the conditions under which it is possible to describe anything (or anyone, including oneself), thus further promoting conservation through understanding human limitation.

Perhaps the most stringent of the formulations involved in the describing of description is that involved in the notion of the necessarily *dual* nature of any of the *signs* used by human beings in the idiosyncratic anthroposemiotic method. What then appears as a paradoxical measure of a grasp of reflexive "performance" is the human realization of human imperfection, of the trait C. S. Peirce refers to as "contrite fallibility." To a very considerable extent, the more the human being recognizes his own limitations, the more complex and sophisticated his data-processing development. The two outstanding examples of this relation appear in the principles of "uncertainty" and "complementarity" in which ambiguity is enshrined in modern physics.

Uses of Fallibility

The application of semiotic principles to the field of medicine is in its infancy, although it has long been clear that the physician's stock in trade is *interpretation*. The "reading of the entrails" practiced in ancient times on a magical basis has progressively given way to "objective" means of examining those same entrails in various of their formal (such as X ray) and abstractable characteristics such as the patterns made by electrical activity or the analysis of components of various fluids. Again we find the same metapattern in that the grasp of the "concrete" long precedes the grasp of the more complex.

In spite of the fact that madness is as old as man, it is only in the twentieth century that it has become possible to begin to understand the complicated semiotic relation between madness and the human condition. As recently as the middle of the last century, the principal American journal dedicated to the study of "insanity" showed in its first four volumes *no* indication that any of the savants then learnedly writing suspected that internal family relations had anything to do with madness—even though it was clear to Greek dramatists and to Shakespeare that this was the case (McPeak, 1976). It is an example of the purely "implicit" knowing of ancient times that Freud selected the term "Oedipus complex" to characterize a pattern he found first in relation to his own "neurosis"; it is a striking example of the "tunnel vision" of the genius that he did not adequately pay attention to the fact that many other "complexes" are to be found in the "family romance" of the Cadmus connection (that is, not only patricide and incest but suicide, fratricide, usurpation, human sacrifice, and self-sacrifice).

Again, it remains unclear to psychiatric theorizers as a group that the core of all the problems which human beings have in their relations with each other is to be found in the specific human method in which *meaning* is implicit in *consensus*—without being "rooted" in any "objective" context. The basic theme of human communication is clearly stated by the fragile Humpty Dumpty of *Alice in Wonderland* when he declares that a word means "just what I want it to mean": the only thing needed to make the statement quite accurate is to replace "I" with "we." Words mean what two or more members as a group "want them to mean," and it is this basic fact that makes human misunderstanding so prevalent. In a clear analysis of Einstein's basic philosophical achievement, Reichenbach has pointed out that he discovered that statements previously regarded as susceptible to demonstration of truth or falsity were in fact matters of definition, as most dramatically demonstrated in the differences in the perception of time described by observers in different frames of reference.

In the specific material we will present here, the influence of consensus is shown most dramatically in the differing use of the term "sign" in two dual units in two quite different frames of reference. In the *semiotic* context, *sign* as defined by Saussure is the composite of a *signifying* and a *signified*. The two participial forms indicate that the meaning is *in process,* even though the term "sign" seems to indicate a static form. Saussure defines the former as a "sound image," the latter as a "concept," but it is immediately apparent that the internal relatedness of such dual units goes far beyond that limited description. For example, as soon as written technology becomes available to human beings, the whole notion of signifying-signified achieves a different dimension. For the literate the primary referent of the spoken word is its written form: the literate person often asserts that he cannot "grasp" a word until and unless he sees it written, a clear indication of a shift in dominance in the influence of communicative method.

In actual practice, however, the relationship is reversed: if a written word is to "live" it must be spoken, either aloud or in the developed capacity of the literate for "inner speech." It is interesting to note that sophistication in literacy is indicated by the degree to which overt movements of the lips can be suppressed; on the subway in a metropolis it is not at all uncommon to see readers "mouthing" what they are reading—and only somewhat less common to note persons (with lip movements) "talking to themselves" in the process of silent thinking. Thus, with the advent of writing, the signifying-signified relation assumes a primacy while the referent "out there" assumes a secondary character.

It is in this context that it becomes clear that conservation is a term applying to the possibility of *abstracting* those consistent forms that endure (cf. Whitehead's "eternal objects") from the variability of the "appearances." The paradoxical human achievement is that of learning the human limitation involved in illusions that seem like realities. The sophisticated human being literally does *not* "believe his own eyes" when he performs the intellectual task of conserving. It is in the "neutral" context of various forms of numerical measurement that many of these illusions can be shown to be misleading—and it is the ease with which measurement can be shared that establishes its "objective" status. Thus we return to the central theme that all specific human meaning is established in consensus.

Medical "Signs"

Making now a sudden shift, the term "sign" is defined in an entirely different fashion in the specific usages it has in the *medical* context. In medicine, *sign* is the partner in a dual unit the other member of which is *symptom*. The latter term has a series of quite different meanings in philosophical context. In medicine, the two establish a subjective-objective dual unit: a symptom is formulated in a complaint, and the patient reports a *chief complaint* as the starting point of the written record known as a "history." The physical examination that succeeds the taking of a history is guided by the patient's complaints: the physician looks for observable signs corresponding to described symptoms. In the "typical" or "classical" instance, there are clear correspondences between the two; a dependable collection of signs and symptoms constitutes a *syndrome* from which the physician makes an overall *diagnosis* (a "knowing through" or knowing in depth) from which the treatment and the *prognosis* (or "fore-knowing") emerge by interpretation.

Semiotic Implications of "Progress"

The incredibly complex "armamentarium" (to use an ancient medical term) of the modern physician comprises both investigative and therapeutic modalities of many kinds. Since the model of natural science became dominant in American medicine in the early part of the twentieth century, the overwhelming emphasis in medicine has been given to research in the "basic sciences" of (principally) physiology and biochemistry, with their modern extensions into genetics and immunology. The emphasis has consistently been placed upon "objectivity" with the demonstration of signs more and more remote from the understanding of the unsophisticated. In the present day, the dialect of the specialist in internal medicine has become largely incomprehensible to the psychiatrist, for example, as the signs pursued have become more and more specialized.

Where the physician's interest focuses on those kinds of abstractings that can be quantified through more and more complex processes of instrumentation, the psychiatrist's concerns have pursued the analysis of behavior and of human relatedness, demonstrating the derivation of unusual or abnormal patterns of behavior from aberrant relationships within families in the past. In recent decades, in a number of new disciplines derived in part from psychiatric ways of inquiring, more sophisticated observational and experimental ways of examining relatedness have appeared. Ethologists examine animal groups as they live in the wild or in captivity; experimental ethologists observe the variations induced by experimental deprivation of "natural" relations (usually through depriving the infant of ordinary maternal care); psychiatrists-become-behaviorists have helped establish the new semiotic specializations of kinesics and paralinguistics. In all of these, the focus is upon the meaning of behavior as that meaning is derived through interpretation and established (or "ratified") through the consensus of observers.

The particular application of the general theme that forms the focus of this discussion is the examination of a number of aspects of the behavior of a group of persons formally identified as "psychiatric" patients in an esoteric context. A principal differentiating feature of this group of patients is their own rejection of that description: these persons agree, in a massive consensus, that "there is nothing wrong with my mind" or "with my nerves." The group has been seen for the evaluation of the degree and derivation of disability following industrial accidents. In two-thirds of a total of 120 claimants seen in about 10 years, the last hope of obtaining monetary compensation for extensive disability is in the establishment of a psychiatric diagnosis, but the claimant insists that although he/she is extensively or totally disabled, no psychiatric label applies. It is a peculiar demonstration of the "negative sign" that this (potentially financially self-destructive) assertion should become a significant part of the ultimate diagnostic syndrome.

What establishes the possibility of a psychiatric diagnosis by exclusion in the first instance is the demonstration of a lack of observable signs expected to go along with the kind of symptoms complained of by the claimant in such an inquiry. The claimant him/herself tends to assert that there is some as yet undiscovered organic illness, often with the notion of a displaced bone or vertebra or a "pinched nerve," explanations often offered by a chiropractor. An interesting complaint made by disabled persons in this group is that their symptoms become worse in bad weather, a complaint familiar in patients with organic types of arthritis. In this context, with no signs of arthritic involvement this symptom is another "negative" finding with a "positive" connotation.

A Cognitive Lesion?

What has made our inquiry into the syndrome we have termed "disproportionate disability" so intriguing is the manner in which our findings submit themselves to a semiotic-epistemological analysis, with the emergence (to us, anyhow) of hitherto unsuspected connections of significance between the level of development reached in Piaget's "time table" and the susceptibility or vulnerability to disability states. The question to which we have repeatedly returned is, "Can it be possible that certain entities in the broad psychiatric field are significantly related to ignorance?"

The lack of formal education that is the fate of the great majority of the world's population in undeveloped countries is clearly and closely related to the social "ill" of poverty, and to the prevalence in such countries of epidemic and communicable diseases, many of which depend for their transmission upon a widespread ignorance of so simple a set of factors as those involved in cleanliness. The startling possibility that has opened up in our investigation is that in the advanced country, the lack of personal development found in those functioning mostly as unskilled laborers (a proportion estimated in England as approximating 30% by Bernstein) is a significant part of predisposition that remains latent until and unless it becomes manifest in the context of two significant events. The first is the occurrence of an accident or injury at work under conditions justifying application for compensation benefits; the second is the involvement of the (now) claimant in the intricacies of bureaucratic process.

The most bizarre and compelling implication of our findings and interpretations is the "self-fulfilling" nature of the prophecy implied in compensation. In other words, and quite without any conscious intent as far as we can tell on the part of the disabled person or of the bureau, the shift in primary context from an ordinary occupational one to that of the bureaucratic maze plays a powerful, perhaps essential role in the genesis of that very disability the compensation board is designed to "treat." If our interpretation is correct, there is a clear analogue of "iatrogenesis" in this context: where in iatrogenic disease it is the pathological implication of the physician's "treatment" or the complications of his pharmacopeia that exaggerate or induce disease, in the compensation context it appears to be the activity of that bureau that, quite unconsciously on the part of all concerned, induces the chronic disability it "finds."

The explanation we have reached is a complex of negations or of falsifications of generally assumed hypotheses. The syndrome consistently found can be described in its several particulars. The principal semiotic interest lies in the total inability of the claimant to describe the "inner" components of his "feelings." He/she demonstrates pain and limitation of motion, often as noted above with the complaint of increased distress in bad weather; there are many complaints and symptoms. On the other hand, he/she cannot describe any of the emotional complications the psychiatrist expects to find in a patient examined by him.

The psychiatrist *expects* to find anxiety, depression, or anger, and in working in psychotherapy with "neurotic" patients, this expectation is routinely validated. It comes as a surprise to try to explore "feelings" of this sort, especially with reference to the "inner" correlates of visceral and proprioceptive sensations, only to encounter complete incomprehension on the part of the person interviewed in response to questions about such feeling states. As one listens carefully to many interviewees in this manner, it becomes clear that the expectation held by the disabled claimant is that emotional states are so standard that they do not need to be described. If the interviewer asks about feelings corresponding to postures or facial expressions exhibited, the claimant may agree that he feels "angry," but in answer to a question as to *how* that feeling is known, the answer is likely to be, "The same way anyone feels angry."

The implicit demonstration is that of the remoteness of "private" experience from the awareness of the unsophisticated, uneducated human being, and in turn this becomes a demonstration of some of the complexities of human consciousness and especially of human self-consciousness. Another instance of the ability of the disabled claimant to identify a difference without being able to specify the details of that difference is found in the self-description. The standard comment, in one or another version, is, "I'm just not the same person I was; it's just not me any more." The claimant is quite unable to describe "me" or a "self"—but he/she is able to report the major difference felt.

Again, as one explores the syndrome presented, the ability of such a claimant to report, as it were, from an "outside" point of view is remarkably different from his lack of ability to report inner or private experience except in terms of difference from before. He/she says consistently that there is no longer any feeling of enjoyment in any activity, nothing is any "fun" any more (including sexual activity for both sexes), there is no "interest" in social or religious activities of the accustomed variety. These routine comments appear to have a common origin in the fact that the human being has to have a central point of stability, a "place to stand" in Archimedes's phrase. Without the sense—no matter how "unconscious"—of being "me," there is no ability to "lose the self" in any activity, and without that ability to "forget myself" the human being does not experience the "absorption" basic to enjoyment. In our experience the claimant remains distressingly self-aware without in any way being able to describe the self, a truly paradoxical problem.

The explanatory suggestion that offers itself is that of the difference between context-dependence and context-independence. The basic problem is that of the abstraction—and conservation—of a *self* from the context of human relatedness in which one "exists." The claimant in our experience appears to demonstrate the condition of being "embedded" in, particularly, his occupational context so that when that context is lost (and is replaced by the mysterious context of a bureaucracy from which one may or may not expect to receive some partial monetary compensation, sometime, if certain undefined conditions are met), "myself"—otherwise unanalyzed—is radically different. The familiar phrase is appropriate; the claimant appears to feel "like a fish out of water"—but since the water has always been so much taken for granted and so little understood in any analytic sense, he/she obviously "does not know what hit him/her."

The further demonstrable regularly present in these instances is that the claimant shows a remarkable inadequacy in performing very simple cognitive operations, simple, that is, in terms of the development of the ideally "normal" school child studied by Piaget. The most routine demonstration of this cognitive deficit has been found in the similarities test, in which the subject is asked to supply a category in which two apparently different items are to be classed. The question is "What is similar about... ?", e.g., an apple and a banana, or a dog and a lion. The establishment of classes with which to organize experience is one of the first significant cognitive structurings; the claimant shows a remarkable inability to "get the point." The routine answer given is in terms of difference: he/she is likely to say that "an apple is round and red, a banana long and yellow."

This deficit, in the Piaget scheme, makes it clear that in the particular context, the subject is unable to perform the "operation" of forming classes. He is, in piagetian language, "pre-operational" in this matter, which means that he is functioning at a level corresponding to that of the 7-year-old child. In a similar demonstration of lack of development, the claimant is often quite unable to perform the seriation elicited by asking him/her to subtract 7 serially from 100; the claimant is likely to have to be asked "7 from 100?" then "7 from the remainder?" again and again: he/she is quite unable to take the instruction and "run" with it. Often his/her subtraction is poor. This indicates a lack of development in the construction not only of classes but of series. What is most startling is that these claimants, prior to the onset of the disability, have shown themselves capable of carrying the adult responsibilities of ordinary family relatedness, rearing children and supporting the family, not infrequently with the children going on to much higher levels of education than the parents were able to enjoy.

When this group is investigated in terms of their backgrounds of experience, what comes through as the most consistent finding is the paucity of formal education, often associated with an early life history of extreme deprivation. A remarkably high proportion of disabled claimants were immigrants, from Southern Europe, Puerto Rico, and from the deep south of the United

States, all of which consistently provided very little educational opportunity for the claimants, who tended consistently to come from poor families in which the previous generations were similarly poorly educated.

The poor state of educational achievement that has appeared as a predisposing factor to the development of disability does not seem to have that implication in the context of origin, i.e., in the "old country" or in the undeveloped social system. We have consistently been impressed with the contextual problem in this relation, since it seems that it is the *undeveloped* person in the *developed* country who is so much more at risk than is the developed person in the developed country or the undeveloped person in the undeveloped country. There seems to be a close relation to Pope's warning that "A little learning is a dangerous thing." The specific predisposition appears to have a high correlation with the experience of breakdown or failure in a context of marginal achievement. Where that marginality can be maintained, there is little or no evidence of the kind of symptoms associated with the disability state.

These observations appear to give a somewhat different coloring to the usual notion of the development of "objectivity." The significant problem is not so much that of "objectifying" in any simple sense but that of *abstracting* from a system the regularities that can be counted upon. In the reflexive process of human self-knowledge, the "regularities" involved in knowing oneself are those necessarily present with the "self," in whatever context, "portable regularities." This means that to continue to "know oneself" one must concentrate not upon the geographical or occupational or even familial regularities; instead one must "know" a *private world* derived by interpretation from those vague and poorly describable inner states in which the relevant sensory data come from visceral, muscular, and postural sources rather than from the traditional "five senses" primarily oriented to the "outer world." In "undeveloped" countries in which the human being is never alone, he does not need to "know himself" from inside out, he is always being given feedback by his associates. He does not need to have private feelings since every significant human activity (birth, death, marriage, puberty, and so on and on) is regulated and ritualized in overt manner in group activity. As Lévi-Strauss has emphasized, in the myths that present the ideologies of such "primitive" (that is, preliterate) societies, there are no authors or poets—even artistic activity is a collective process.

These observations support a number of other recent observations of major differences in personality style between persons of middle-class (especially upper-middle-class) and working-class status. The major difference between these groups is that of education; in the United States particularly it is common to find professional persons from working-class families of origin. Many of the claimants we have seen report that a son or daughter is in college;

this is especially probable in New York City where an emphasis upon higher free education has long been established. Our intuitive conclusion has been that there is no lack of "native" intelligence in these claimants (with some exceptions); there is instead a remarkable lack of formal education, with a clearly related intellectual incapacity.

In the present atmosphere of egalitarianism, differences of this sort are likely to be overlooked in part as an expression of an official commitment to "equal opportunity" in an interpretation that often means unequal coercion to employ less sophisticated persons. In our experience, however, without taking into account the educational-intellectual deficit in the claimants we have seen, the resulting disorder is completely mysterious.

In studying the literature of development, a theme that recurs time and again is that to become developed it is necessary to become independent of context (cf. Bernstein, 1964; Bruner, 1973) in many of the ways in which human beings have generally been comprehensively context-dependent. To develop as an "individual," one has to learn to dissociate himself from his family (especially his family of origin), to abandon traditional forms of religion, to adopt a democratic rather than an authoritarian political stance, to learn to regard the other sex as "equal" in striking opposition to traditional forms of enforced submission of women, and to learn to tolerate changes of residence, often repeated changes.

In our experience, we have come to believe that the disabled claimants we have seen have lost self-definition (although they had not developed any consciously formulated self) because of the loss of essential context. In other words, the transfer of self from occupational context to bureaucratic context changes the self in an apparently irreversible way. It then becomes more comprehensible that the claimant should believe preferentially that he has an undiscovered disease. Since he cannot change his own definition of "disease" he interprets symptoms that in a more sophisticated person might be perceived as grief or anxiety as related to "organic" disease. The absolute inability to process relevant data was shown in one case by a young man with a hysterically paralyzed arm and hand who insisted he had to see a "hand doctor." In the record there was a clear report of his having seen perhaps the most famous hand surgeon in the United States. The claimant had somehow managed to obliterate the fact that he had received precisely the kind of investigation he was demanding.

For us the most interesting aspect of this work is the implication that defining a world is an important part of constructing that world—and when the definition (no matter how poorly formulated) no longer is "in equilibrium" with the world as experienced, the result is not only a change in the world but an irreversible painful change (of a chronic nature) in the self. The demonstration is that the self and the universe are reciprocals, and that a massive change in one changes the other.

REFERENCES

Bernstein, Basil. 1964. "Social Class, Speech Systems and Psychotherapy." *Brit. Jour. Socio.* 15:54–64.

Bruner, Jerome S. 1973. *Beyond the Information Given.* New York: Norton.

Lévi-Strauss, Claude. 1966. *The Savage Mind.* Chicago: University of Chicago Press.

McPeak, William R. 1975. "Family Interactions as Etological Factors in Mental Disorders." *Am. J. Psych.* 132:1327.

Piaget, Jean. 1950. *The Psychology of Intelligence.* New York: Harcourt.

Planck, Max. 1949. *Scientific Autobiography and Other Papers,* trans. by F. Gaynor. New York: Philosophical Library.

Reichenbach, H. 1949. "The Philosophical Significance of the Theory of Relativity," in Schilpp, P., *Albert Einstein, Philosopher-Scientist.* New York: Harper.

de Saussure, F. 1966. *Course in General Linguistics.* New York: McGraw-Hill.

Shands, Harley C. and Meltzer, James D. 1975. "Disproportionate Disability: The Freud-Charcot Syndrome Rediscovered." *The Journal of Psychiatry and Law* 3:25–37.

Shands, Harley C. and Meltzer, James D. 1975. "Clinical Semiotics." *Language Sciences* 38:21–24. Bloomington, Ind.: Indiana University.

Whitehead, A. N. 1925. *Science and the Modern World.* New York: Mentor Books, 1960.

Semiotics and the Limits of Architecture

Diana Agrest and Mario Gandelsonas

Part I: The State of the Art.

INTRODUCTION

In the past fifteen years interest in the semiotics of architecture has grown in various parts of the world, as is shown by the publication of the Italian and English bibliographies prepared for the First International Congress of Semiotics in Milan (June 1974) and published in the journal *Versus* 8/9.[1] To this impressive number of works already published in English and Italian, an equally large Spanish bibliography will very soon be added. This great quantity of work is, however, not just a simple indication of the vitality of the field, but rather the result of a quite complex situation.

On the one hand, a great number of these works are part of developments in the behavioral sciences (psychology, sociology, etc.). This produces a situation in which the study of communication problems (transmission of meaning by means of sign systems) and moreover of signification (structures of such systems) is approached from presemiotic perspectives which have since been criticized and superseded by semiotics. On the other hand, in the proper semiotic works the dispersion of themes of analysis instead of the determination of the object of study, the disarticulation between empirical analysis and abstract generalizations, the quantitative expansion rather than the accumulative development of knowledge all become quite obvious.

Very few works have understood the sense and importance of the Saussurian gesture of the definition of the object of study[2] and developed their analysis in reference to a theoretical object previously defined. Very few are the works which may be considered theoretical developments in a strict sense, that is, hypothetic-deductive constructions, descriptions, or classifications which are explicitly inscribed within a given theoretical context, such as the work of M. Bense[3] or E. Garroni.[4] Finally, there are few works which propose a conceptual development of the problems stated in previous works; most works transpose models developed in another field (linguistic or semiotic) and cannot be considered the product of a consistent development of a more specifically architectural problematic. This situation is a product, in our view, of two major types of problems which a semiotics of architecture has to confront: those which have their origin in architecture and those which originate in semiotics itself.

TWO OBSTACLES: ARCHITECTURE AND SEMIOTICS

From the decade of the sixties architecture has been going through one of its periodic crises, due this time to several reasons: a) the failure of the massive interventions of post World War II and the corresponding collapse of the functionalist doctrine, the basic ideology of modern architecture; b) the increasing gap between the accelerated process of industrialization which affects the whole of the economic production and the craftslike character of the architectonic production; c) the expansion of the field of intervention, i.e., industrial design, architecture, urban design; d) the ever-growing distance between the figurative vocabulary and syntax created by modern architecture (simultaneous with cubism and neoplasticism) and the languages generated by mass media, in particular advertising, television, and film; e) the antihistoricist position of the modern movement and the fast consumption of formal vocabularies.

As a result of this crisis, discussions take place about the dubious architectural character of some realms of production. An example of this is the problem of housing which in certain contexts appears as "that" which opposes architecture—architecture versus housing—the latter representing the "death" of architecture. Parallel to this, the concern for the problem of industrialization displaces the architectural creativity from the design of buildings to the design of construction systems, of assembling, "montage," etc. The expansion of the field of intervention produces an hypertrophy of "architectonicity"; from the design of objects to the design of buildings and urban spaces, everything is considered architecture. Finally, the crisis and its results are manifested at the level of language in the form of eclecticism, a confusion of languages characterized by the use of figures and syntaxes belonging to heterogeneous and sometimes contradictory codes.

This set of circumstances acts as a first obstacle to the development of a semiotics of architecture, an obstacle which makes the identification of an object of analysis a very difficult task.

The development of semiotics has also gone through a succession of crises to the point of negating the validity of its own demarche.[5] The semiotic approach, which at this point is just beginning to expand, cannot be seen as a peaceful "factory" of models but as a field where many times antagonistic fights between different trends develop. We will mention some of the events that have been influential in the development of semiotics of architecture. a) The acceleration of semiotic analysis which took place in the 60s in France owed a great deal to the structuralist perspective, and adopted a theoretical and methodological outlook from the confluence of models drawn from structural linguistics and anthropology.[6] b) Strong criticism is directed from philosophy and epistemology centered on the empirical nature of the approach and on the problem of the absence of two notions: the subject and history.[7] The diffusion of theoretical hypothetic-deductive models from generative transformational linguistics reinforces the challenge to the empirical structural models. c) The theories of enunciation, of speech acts,[8] and the reaction against Chomsky's model influence the displacement of the semiotic problematic towards a pragmatics which introduces the problem of subjective and sociological determinations in language.[9] The analysis of text, on the one hand, opposes to Chomsky's Cartesian subject a more complex notion of subject drawn from psychoanalysis,[10] and, on the other hand, poses the problem of the articulation of the theory of meaning with history through the analysis of ideology considered as production of meaning.[11]

It is important to note that this schematic description of the sequence of events is applicable in particular to the semiotics of literature where since the Russian Formalism of the 1920s most work has been done. This is a field which received from the theory of literature and poetics an already structured theory, which had inventoried codes and specific systems with a high degree of sophistication. In the case of the semiotics of literature, we should seek the reason for these developments not so much in external factors (such as the rapid succession of various linguistic trends) as in the limitations of different analytical approaches which were made apparent by the result of such analysis.

This is not the case in the semiotic approach to architecture where, although a similar process takes place, most of the analyses are mechanical transcriptions of models which do not go beyond the general level. The changes in approach do not reflect a need or development provoked by the process of research itself but are instead a mere reflection of developments in other semiotics. This situation, which affects the possibility of producing specific models, acts as a second obstacle for the development of a Semiotic approach to architecture.

Nevertheless, it is possible to distinguish a number of works where a body of notions suggests—whether in an explicit or implicit way—the possible boundaries and the internal organization of the field of semiotics of architecture.

SEMIOTICS AND ARCHITECTURE: THE STATE OF THE ART

A panoramic view of these developments can be presented, classifying the works according to: a) their relationship with various approaches in linguistic theories which had a strong influence in the production of semiotic models; b) their relationship with different general semiotic perspectives, in particular those posited by the founders of this approach, F. de Saussure and C. S. Peirce.

The first attempts to develop a semiotic approach to architecture from a structuralist perspective center their effort in the definition of systems and the units of which they are composed, following the model of the sign.

From the impulse given to this approach by the works of C. Lévi-Strauss and R. Barthes Umberto Eco produced one of the first attempts to establish the basis for a semiotics of architecture.[12] This work develops in the field of architecture (defined in a wide sense which includes any man-made object with the exclusion of esthetic objects) the semiotic notion of sign, the function as first meaning of the form, the notion of connotation, the non-functional secondary meanings, the notion of code, the rules that establish equivalences and oppositions between forms and functions, and the diachronic transformation of primary and secondary meanings. It has also the virtue of reformulating previous theoretical attempts—such as communicational theories—and of introducing models from other disciplines, such as the anthropological analysis of space, which are then displaced and reelaborated within a problematic of signification.

Parallel to this work, other analyses are developed by R. de Fusco and M. L. Scalvini[13] which focus especially on architectural material in a more restrained way, that of the buildings designed according to a strict system of rules in different historical periods. In contrast with Eco's position the two aspects of the sign, signifier and signified, are considered at the level of configuration, as architectural shapes. The external configuration is considered as signifier which refers to an internal organization which becomes the signified. This particular definition of the architectural sign started a parochial controversy which involved E. Garroni, who has tried to show that these apparently antagonistic views do not exclude each other.[14]

The model of the sign has also been applied in the field of urbanism, an extension of the semiotic approach which is of major importance since the practice of architecture in our culture has been, since the Renaissance, associated with problems derived from the urban context. F. Choay's early works propose a typology of interpretative models of the city based on the analysis of texts.[15] She has further proposed the analysis of the city as a system of signification in terms of syntagmatic and paradigmatic relationships which define types of urban configurations.[16]

More recently, a more careful structural approach to architecture may be seen in the recognition and distinction among the different media (matters) in which architecture is manifested.[17] As a consequence there is a development of more specific theoretical models for their analysis.

The complexity of architecture—its heterogeneous nature—is revealed by the diversity of forms manifested by "architecture" in the various products of architectural practice, i.e., written, drawn, and/or built architecture. Traditionally the building has been considered as the "natural product" of architectural practice, while texts or drawings were seen as neutral means to achieve that product. However, not only is the main part of the creative process developed in the text and specifically in the drawing, but also on many occasions the process is interrupted at some of these levels without reaching the point of an effective realization of the building. The complex character of architecture has undoubtedly influenced the present tendencies to analyze these levels separately.

The development of techniques for the analysis of discourse has contributed to the accentuation of this emphasis on the analysis of texts. In particular M. Gandelsonas' work has centered on the analysis of a great number of theories developed since the Renaissance.[18] One of the most interesting characteristics of this material is that these theories are rewritings of a text, that of Vitruvius, written during the second century A.D. and resuscitated during the Renaissance, a fact which gives a certain unity to the material and facilitates the analytical work. These analyses, by artificially separating the normative texts from the other phases of the productive process—drawings and buildings—accentuate their differences.

The analysis of drawing in architecture as a system of representation and particularly as an instrument for creation has only recently begun and there is still much to do in this respect.[19] It is unquestionable that the creation of the system plan-elevation-section-perspective has contributed in great measure to the signifying complexity of architecture, both classic and modern.[20] This system of transformation of tri-dimensional space into two dimensions allows the play of symbolic relationships among the representational elements not completely noticeable in the building without the help of a mental reconstruction of plans or sections.[21]

The most complex problem has up to now been presented by those cases in which the analyst is confronted with a building without the possibility of access to a text or a two-dimensional representation. In such a case, the analyst confronts a situation which poses in a crude way the basic problems of a semiotics of architecture, that of the need for producing some notational system which would allow the description of the building by reducing the infinite figures that space and movement suggest, and also to find or generate a text which allows access to functional, figurative, or symbolic codes.[22]

The analyses developed by anthropologists like Lévi-Strauss[23] and Bourdieu[24] have not made this problem explicit. These analyses consist of the reconstruction of codes and rules based on a discourse and a graphic description provided by an informant, which are not considered as possible determinants of the results of the analysis but rather as neutral means containing information for the research. In more complex situations, such as the analysis of urban environments (historical or modern), the problem of description becomes insoluble for the structural approach; consequently the results are rather poor and schematic. This situation has forced the analyst to look for other modeling alternatives to which we will refer in the last section of this paper.

Finally, it would seem that the problem of the manifestation of architectural semiosis in different matters promotes not just different levels in the productive process (the process of design) but different languages; and what has been lost in this analytical schism is the problem of the relation between languages within the process of design, that is in the process of transformation from writing to drawing, from drawing to the building. This collision of languages is a determinant factor of the architectural semiosis; and in this sense the analysis of this problem might contribute to the construction of theories which describe the generation of meaning and forms in architecture and the "translation" of ideology into architectural formal codes and texts.[25]

At this point we would like to suggest some of the possible reasons for the almost exclusive development of structural models and the limited number of works based on generative models.

The production of architecture—as in the other artistic practices—is manifested in "works"; it is not the result of an infinite productivity controlled by more or less explicit rules as in the case of language. This fact makes it very difficult to apply the notion of grammaticality to an architectural "work." In this case the analyst could propose, at the most, criteria of acceptability which should be decided from the consideration of a set of notions which would include in particular gender, reader, or use. This might be one of the main reasons why most semiotic analyses are carried out from the structural perspective.

One of the first works within the generative approach is "Le statut de l'objet" by P. Boudon.[26] Boudon attempts to establish the basis for a very general theory of the production of objects elaborated on the basis of notions originated in anthropology, generative transformational linguistics, and philosophy of language. In later works Boudon has conducted his research with an anthropological emphasis manifested in his "Semiotique des lieux" or in his analysis of popular Arabic architecture.[27] The transposition of Chomsky's model has also been applied to the theorization of the process of design in terms of its operations as in Eisenman's work,[28] and to explain popular[29] and non-Western architectures.

There is a series of works of architectural semiotics which have been produced as part of a more general semiotic theory. Within this particular type of analysis, i.e., the structural approach, in addition to U. Eco we will mention L. Prieto's and E. Garroni's developments.

The interest of Prieto's work,[30] which takes E. Buyssens' notions as basic references for his developments, resides in the fact that his theory, in which objects and language occupy privileged positions based on the logic of classes, has given origin to developments which present interest at a taxonomic level such as in the case of the works of C. Jannello[31] and in the recent development by H. Pinon.[32]

Among the theories developed from general semiotics, one of the most interesting is that proposed by the Italian semiotician E. Garroni[33] who has not only indicated the validity, limitations, and complementarity of Eco's and de Fusco's approaches, but has also classified other approaches originating in architectural theories, such as typological analyses. In addition, he has proposed other theoretical alternatives for the analysis of architecture in terms of meaning, based on geometrical models and on Saumjan's generative and transformational grammar. The interest of these works, developed as part of a general semiotic theory, resides not only in their development of notions at a high level of abstraction but also in their potential production of newer and more powerful models. This might be the result of both their involvement with comparative analyses within a wider range of signifying systems and their distance to the more specific characteristics of such systems. Nevertheless, this distance is responsible for their limitations, which derive from their detachment with respect to the practice of architecture and their limited knowledge of indigenous theories—a detachment which makes difficult the testing of models and therefore the proposition of more "concrete theories," that is, theories that might produce more specific knowledge about architecture.

SEMIOTICS AND THE LIMITS OF ARCHITECTURE

The general aim of the semiotic approach to architecture is the production of knowledge of architecture seen as a system of signs, as a systematic and specific organization of forms and meanings. Similar objectives have been postulated by other theoretical and critical approaches to architecture. The basic difference between semiotics and these other approaches lies in the former's more specific and powerful models and therefore in its potential for a substantial contribution to the production of knowledge.

The problem is that most of the semiotic production has not fulfilled this potential role. In our opinion, the fulfillment of this role depends on a more critical position with respect to the following attitudes and notions:

a) The mechanical transference of models elaborated in other fields. Semiotics has been just one of the latest models in a long list of technical or scientific models used to develop new pseudo-theoretical approaches to architecture.

b) The two forms in which the traditional approaches to the problem of the relations between architecture and culture and society are manifested: first, architecture seen as an autonomous discipline with respect to other semiotic systems and second, architecture seen as a direct "representation" of political and economic instances.

c) The normative definition of architecture which separates a few buildings designed according to institutionalized rules from the rest of the man-made physical environment which is not given any consideration. U. Eco's definition of architecture involving the whole of the man-made environment has been postulated, precisely, as a critique of the traditional definition.[34] Nevertheless, it merely reflects a new ideological attitude developed in particular by the approach known as "Design Methods," where design is considered as a universal process which underlies every manmade object.

Our own work has been developed as a critique to these historically determined ideological notions. We consider that, inasmuch as they both acknowledge and distort pertinent questions, these notions should be taken as basic material for a theoretical analysis which in turn should displace them in order to develop a new and more productive theoretical problematic.

Instead of applying in a mechanical way linguistic or semiotic models, our analyses are based on, first, what C. Metz calls "indigenous" theories,[35] that is, theories developed through centuries by historians and critics of architecture; and second, on semiotic theoretical procedures developed for the analysis of other complex semiotic practices.

C. Lévi-Strauss has given two reasons why one cannot dispense with studying cultural "home-made" models. "First, these models might prove to be accurate or, at least, to provide some insight into the structure of the phenomena; after all each culture has its own theoreticians whose contributions deserve the same attention as that which the anthropologist gives to colleagues. And second, even if the models are biased or erroneous, the very and type of error are a part of the facts under study and probably rank among the most significant ones."[36]

An example of the efficacy of "indigenous" models coming from the theory and criticism of architecture is the work of Gian Carlo Argan on the notion of type.[37] This notion of type refers to a formal structure which implies the possibility of infinite formal variations. These types are basically configurational structures rather than functional ones. Argan relates this notion of type to the process of design in terms of two instances: on the one hand, what he calls the moment of typology, an instance associated to the configurational structures established in the past; on the other hand, the moment of invention, the instance of response to the demands of the contingent historical situation through criticism or subversion of past solutions sedimented and synthesized in the codification of the type.

In the elaboration of this notion Argan analyzes the same problem developed by C. Metz in relation to film semiotics, a problem that transcends this practice to become a fundamental question for semiotics of artistic facts: the consideration of a semiotic fact in terms of the notion of *language*—as a combinatory of codes—or as *text* produced following the rules established by codes and at the same time subverting them, a text written with and against language.

Architectural theories might not only provide "good models," as in the case of Argan's theory of type. Their close relationship with the practice of architecture might provide to semiotics a closer and more direct view of the problems that architects have tried or are trying to solve.

One of the central problems being discussed in the fields of history and criticism of architecture is the relation between architecture and the city. Of course, this is not a new problem, since architectural theories have always provided models and norms for the design and interpretation of urban spaces. These different models—the Renaissance city seen as a building-monument, the 19th-century garden city, the 20th-century futuristic city, or the recent "instant" city—have something in common: their simplistic, systematic nature. However, the city itself—and in particular the contemporary city—has developed in a manner which makes the application of these traditional or modern models difficult if not impossible. Therefore, the development of new interpretative theories and models for the understanding of the symbolic nature of new urban environments is not just a pertinent theoretical problem but also a practical demand.

We will mention two different analyses of this problem which might be of interest for a semiotic approach to architecture. First, Manfredo Tafuri's analysis of Piranesi's "Campus Martius"[38]—an anticipatory vision of the modern city—where architecture is seen as a systematic game with architectural rules, developed between the limits of redundancy and chaos, between the order of norms and the disorder and irrationality characteristic of the modern city. Second, Colin Rowe's thesis suggesting the use of "Villa Hadriana" as a model for the understanding of the meaning of modern urban spaces in terms of contextual relationships.[39] Villa Hadriana is an "architectural collage" in which fragments of architectures belonging to different periods and cultures are juxtaposed by means of operations in which the classical procedures (proportion, symmetry, balance) play a minor role and the relationships of juxtaposition and contiguity assume the major one.

The interest of these analyses is that they take as a reference complex graphic and/or built projects very different from those used as a reference in the traditional theories. However, these projects still imply an architectural or urban logic, inasmuch as the models derived from them allow the understanding of the traditional models of the environment as partial or simplified versions of the new models.

Of the different semiotic models developed for the analysis of complex practices, the models from both semiotics of culture and semiotics of film seem to be the most interesting ones to compare with architecture.

Architecture has been defined many times as the physical manifestation of a culture. This notion is implied since Vitruvius, when he prescribes that the architect's knowledge should be so vast that no aspect of culture is unknown to him. We have approached this question by placing less emphasis on the prescribed relationship between architecture and culture and more on the description of similarities between the analysis of architecture and the analysis of culture.

The analyst of architecture and the analyst of culture are confronted with a set of common problems, among which we mention the complexity conferred on it by its heterogeneous nature (a conglomerate of semiotic systems, of languages, of codes and texts), the articulation and transference of forms among the various systems involved, and the transformations which are produced either in the interior of each system simply by its coexistence with others, or in the movements of migration of forms between systems.

Among the most interesting approaches to the problem of culture from a semiotic standpoint is that of J. Lotman, who considers culture as significative information which can be seen either as a hierarchy of codes or as invested in texts which enter the public domain of society.[40]

This dual possibility of analysis, which has also been postulated and developed by Metz for the analysis of movies, has provided us a conceptual framework for the analysis of architecture in terms of codes belonging to different semiotic systems and in terms of the particular mode of articulation of these various codes in the architectural or urban texts.

The analysis of film is particularly interesting to compare with the analysis of architecture because both confront similar problems.[41] First is the interaction and articulation of different languages, a fact which is not immediately obvious in architecture where the various languages appear in sequence within the process of design and construction (and not juxtaposed as in the case of movies) and therefore the complexity does not show in the final product, the building. Second and related to this complexity is the notion of heterogeneity which applies to the different languages structured on the basis of different matters of expression (linguistic, two or three-dimensional scopic matters). Here, we should distinguish between internal and external heterogeneity: the former applies to the design process which has been analyzed in terms of codic differences or in terms of intertextual relationships between written, graphic, or built texts; the latter applies to the contextual relationships and to the process of interpretation of the building or its "reading." Third, the notion of specificity, which, as in semiotics of movies, should not be just applied to codes but also to the articulation of codes belonging to different semiotic systems. Furthermore, this notion seen from a diachronic point of view allows us to describe changes of the structure of articulation of codes through time and therefore to build a more dynamic model which accounts for the historical dimension of the production of meaning.

The notion of ideology, through the articulation of the theory of meaning with a theory of society, allows us to discuss the questions of autonomy of architecture and its relationships to other social instances overcoming banal and mechanical approaches.[42]

A strong criticism has been addressed to the so-called anti-historicist position of the semiotic approach to architecture in general and to the structuralist perspective in particular. It is important to notice that this criticism comes from the fields of architectural history and criticism, and that it refers to the emphasis on analyses of systematic characteristics of architecture that ignore the historical articulation between architecture and its social context.

In our opinion, structural and taxonomic procedures in the semiotic analysis of architecture are justified when they are just a stage of a more complex analysis which accounts for the articulation between symbolic, economic, and political instances. However, the historian's criticism is fair when addressed to those cases where the structural analysis (whether systematic or processual) of architecture is developed without making this wider theoretical framework explicit.

Architecture, more than any other practice analyzed by semiotics—perhaps with the exception of film—requires an enormous economical apparatus, and at the same time is submitted to tremendous political pressure. These economic and political forces influence in a very definite way both the structure and the production of meaning in architecture. Therefore, the artificial separation of the symbolic aspects of architecture from the economic and political determinations, which might be a productive procedure within a first analytical stage, should be followed by the development of models that account for more complex determinations.

The interest of the new approaches to the notion of ideology resides in the fact that they seem to offer the possibility of building such models, inasmuch as they try to interrelate the social theory of ideology and semiotic, the theory of the different systems of signs.[43] This notion of ideology concerns the different systems and processes of investment of meaning in different matters. These systems of operations define processes of production of meaning, the products of which are the different social texts, among them the architectural texts in a broad sense. However, ideology is not a property immanent to texts but rather a relationship between textual and extra-textual instances. The pertinency of an ideological analysis cannot be defined without considering the linkage between products (texts) and conditions of production (extra-textual instances, i.e., economic-political and/or subjective determinations). Therefore, in architecture, the ideological functions that characterize architectural notions—technical, cognitive, "masking," etc.—should be explained on the basis of analyses of the relationships among architectural text and extra-textual circumstances. An example of this kind of analysis can be seen in M. Gandelsonas' critique of the ideological notion of building, conceived as an unique and simple product of the design process—a notion related to the ideology of artistic creation—which excludes the notion of complex language and intermediary texts.[44]

The aim of semiotics is neither the acceptance of the ideological definition of architecture nor the proposition of new definitions, but rather displacement of the boundaries established by the ideological definitions. Within the practice of architecture, a first displacement of the definition of building as product of architecture, and therefore as object of analysis, has enabled us to show the importance of the analysis of texts and drawings as well as buildings.[45] With respect to the relation between architecture and the non-designed environment the displacement from the exclusive or inclusive definition of architecture has enabled us to show the need for considering their differences in terms of distinct semiotic systems and processes.[46]

The displacement of the limits established by traditional or modern definitions of architecture could be seen in our own work as a change of focus which is produced in two different directions: as a close-up that allows one to see a more complex internal structure within the process of design; or as a panoramic view that allows one to incorporate a wider physical and semiotic context in the process of "reading" the built environment.

Analysis of the intratext determined by the different languages that take part in the process of design allows the analysis of the specific characteristics of texts, the operations of meaning between texts, and their relationships with the intertext. First, each of the texts produced in the process of design and construction must be considered as a mixed text. The written texts are complemented with figures, the drawing with diagrams, written texts, and symbols; the built text has at least a double nature expressed in the opposition of two-dimensional figures versus volume and/or space. Second, in the relation between texts, there is a transmission, reduction, or expansion of meanings; for instance, the written text reduces the meanings opened by the graphic text, the built text acts as a condensed written text, etc. Third, the architectural complex intratext relates in a more direct manner with the intertext like the single texts of other practices, i.e., literature. The intervention of the intertext as a generator in architecture and the great number of "quotations" from texts external to architecture are some examples of this particular relationship which is caused by the impurity of the internal mixed texts which provide an easier access to external figures and signifiers.[47]

The analysis of the non-designed environment allows the theoretical development of the notion of productive reading, which is not the reproduction of a unique or complete sense of the built environment but rather a way of entering into the sequential mechanisms which are part of the production of that meaning, a meaning that society as a whole has put in the built world and not merely that imposed by the architect. A further important difference between reading in design and productive reading in the non-designed environment is the position of "direct reading" required by the latter. Instead of reading by following a previously written text, the reading of the non-designed environment starts from a first mark, not only towards an architectural text but towards other texts in culture, putting into play a force analogous to that of the mechanisms of the unconscious.

In the second part of this paper the semiotic problem of the relation between the designed and the non-designed environment will be developed. The focus on this specific theoretical problem will not exclude consideration of the other problems mentioned above—the relation between semiotics of architecture and other semiotic fields and the relation between theories of meaning and theory of ideology—but rather it will enable one to understand some of their interrelationships.

Part II: Design versus Non-Design.

INTRODUCTION

The specific relationship of architecture to ideology has been generally excluded from consideration in traditional architectural criticism. Concerned only to relate architecture formally, or internally, to itself, or at best to relate architecture externally to society in general, criticism has failed to truly incorporate the *cultural* problematic of architecture into its domain of concern. When the cultural dimension has been introduced, it has more often been as a simple explanation of architecture as "reflecting" a particular culture—the notion of style as the expression of the spirit of the age—than as a problem to be confronted independently from a consistent theoretical standpoint.

Practicing architects and critics of architecture have repeatedly emphasized the need to relate architecture to its social or cultural context. Positions have been developed around such concepts as "contextualism" and "ugly and ordinary" by writers like Colin Rowe and Denise Scott Brown and Robert Venturi. Rowe, for example, speaks of an architectural contextualism that situates the object of design or analysis in its physical-historical surroundings in terms of formal elements and relations; Venturi and Scott Brown speak of the need to recognize mass culture as *the* necessary cultural product of our time and as a new source of inspiration for designers. However, rather than attempting to appeal to the notion of collage—a familiar architectural strategy in periods of transition—or to the simulation of the objects of mass culture, this analysis will attempt to investigate the mechanisms of the built environment at this specific historical moment.

We wish to explore here these "external" or cultural relations of architecture—that is, between architecture and its social context—by means of a theoretical model that posits two distinct forms of cultural, or symbolic, production. The first, which we will call *design,* is that mode by which architecture relates to cultural systems outside itself; it is a normative process and embraces not only architectural but also urban design. The second, which is more properly called *non-design,* describes the way in which different cultural systems interrelate and give form to the built world; it is not a direct product of any institutionalized design practice but rather the result of a general process of culture.

In thus examining the mechanisms which relate architecture to culture— the processes by which meaning is produced, not only within architecture or design, but also in the domain of non-design—we are, of course, analyzing ideology itself. For ideology is no more than the social production of meaning. Thus, all cultural production, such as architecture, when articulated at the economic and political levels, manifests the ways by which ideology is produced as a part of a given social structure.[48]

In this sense, it is unnecessary to compare one type of architecture to any other type of architecture—as in the accepted mode of "formal," internal criticism—or to compare it to society in general. Rather, one must oppose the notion of architecture as *design* to the notion of a radically different kind of symbolic configuration—*non-design*. This opposition allows analysis of the built environmental in terms of the relationship between different cultural systems. Design and non-design, in fact, can be seen as two modes of social discourse; and to consider them in this way opens up the question of what might be called the "active relationship" between design, as one cultural system, and other cultural systems.

DESIGN AND CULTURE

Design, considered as both a practice and a product, is in effect a closed system—not only in relation to culture as a whole, but also in relation to other cultural systems such as literature, film, painting, philosophy, physics, geometry, etc. Properly defined, it is reductive, condensing and crystallizing general cultural notions within its own distinct parameters. Within the limits of this system, however, design constitutes a set of practices—architecture, urban design, and industrial design—unified with respect to certain normative theories. That is, it possesses specific characteristics that distinguish it from all other cultural practices and that establish a boundary between what is design and what is not. This boundary produces a kind of *closure* that acts to preserve and separate the ideological identity of design. This closure, however, does not preclude a certain level of permeability toward other cultural systems—a permeability which nevertheless is controlled and regulated in a precise way.

Culture, on the other hand, is understood to be a system of *social codes* that permit information to enter the public domain by means of appropriate signs. As a whole, culture can be seen as a hierarchy of these codes, manifested through various texts.[49]

The relationship between design and culture may, then, be stated as the mode by which design is articulated (as one cultural system) in relation to other cultural systems (at the level of codes). The transformations in these articulations are historically determined, and they display themselves as changes in the structures of meaning. Thus, the development of specific forms of articulation between design and other cultural systems can be seen as a dynamic process, the study of which opens up the problem of the production of meaning.

The relationship between design and other cultural systems is heightened and intensified at certain moments in this process, and its precise articulations become clearer. In architecture, this occurs when new economic, technical, functional, or symbolic problems force the production of new formal repertories, or the expansion and transformation of existing vocabularies.

Thus, during the French Enlightenment, elementary geometrical figures (the sphere, the pyramid, the cube, etc.) were introduced as the primary constituents of a new formal vocabulary by the "revolutionary" architects Boullée and Ledoux. For Ledoux these forms expressed the new notions of the *sublime,* while for Boullée they represented the universe and its scientific explanation developed in the context of profound social and political change.[50]

This recognition of articulations between design and other cultural systems also implies the recognition of differences between them—differences which may be understood through the notion of *specificity.*[51] This is a notion which permits the clarification of codes according to their relation to design or to other cultural systems.

Three types of codes regulate the interpretation and production of texts in design. First, there are those codes which may be seen as exclusive to design, such as codes establishing relationships between plans and elevations or plans and cross-sections. Second, there are those codes which are shared by various cultural systems, among which design is included (i.e., spatial, iconic). Third, there are those which, while they are crucial to one cultural system (such as rhythm to music), participate—albeit transformed—in another (such as architecture) by virtue of a shared characteristic, i.e., in the case of rhythm, the temporality of the sequence, audial in one case and visual in the other.[52] In a decreasing order of specificity, the first type of codes is specific to design, the second has a multiple specificity, and the third is non-specific.

The specificity of a signifying system is not, however, defined solely by the specificity of its codes, but also by the form in which those codes are articulated; that is to say, the combination of codes may be specific, although the codes themselves may or may not be specific to the system in question.[53] Examples of specific code articulation in architecture are found in classical theories of harmony that utilize the articulation of musical codes and arithmetical proportional series for the invention of specific *architectural* codes, which are then used to determine the proportions of and relationships between the different elements of a building.

Specificity manages to maintain the limits of architecture despite the apparent changes that occur under the pressures of history, technology, social action, or symbolic change. On the one hand, the most specific codes remain within the system of architecture; on the other hand, the less specific codes link design with other systems through the opening and closing of its limits. This mechanism allows for the articulation of design with some systems and not with others, a process which operates according to the "internal" determinations of design—that is, according to the rules of architectural language, to the logic of the configuration, and to the meaning proper to the "text" of design.[54]

The Mannerist inversion of the established architectural rules—by which each element is used in contradiction to what should be its prevailing ideological function—is an excellent example of such internal determination, in which the inversions so weaken the limits of architecture as to allow an opening to codes external to it; thus the "painterly" architecture of the sixteenth century in Italy.[55]

This process of articulation might, however, take place according to "external" determinations—to the forces of economics, politics, or other ideologies foreign to design. The influence of hermetic thought on the design of the Escorial Palace, for example, demonstrates the role of such external factors in architecture. Both the plan and the general configuration seem to have been derived from mystical or hermetic geometric regulating lines, based partly on parallel developments in quantitative mathematics, and partly on chapters eliminated from Renaissance editions of Vitruvius,[56] but not, as might be assumed, directly from classical architectural theory. Magic codes were thus substitutes for the Albertian geometric codes. Geometry, while represented by similar figures, was imbued with an entirely different meaning. At the same time, these geometric magic codes remained distinctly separate from other magic codes, such as those based on verbal or gestural practices, which never entered in their physical-spatial implications into architecture.

The concept of the closing and opening of limits introduces the notion of an ideological *filtering* in the production of design, which takes place by means of certain processes of symbolization. In this case an equivalence, or exchange, of sense is produced by restricting the access of certain codes and figures from other systems into architecture.

The notions of *metaphor* and *metonymy* allow for a more systematic analysis of this symbolic functioning. These should be considered as the mechanisms of opening and closure, ultimately revealing the way in which design maintains its limits in relation to culture and acts as a filter in relation to meaning.[57]

Metaphor and metonymy are, of course, notions that have been used principally in the analysis of discourse and text. Since in this context we are analyzing the *production* of meaning and not its structure, the reference in general will be to metaphoric or metonymic *operations* rather than to these figures as they applied to classical rhetoric.[58]

These tropes or rhetorical figures represent the most condensed expression of two basic kinds of relationship in discourse: the relation of similarity, which underlies the metaphor, and the relation of contiguity, which determines the metonymy. Each may exist in the relationship between the figure and the content or in the relation between figure and figure.

The development of any discourse (not necessarily a spoken one, and in this case the architectural discourse) may develop along two semantic-syntactic lines: one theme in the expression or content may lead to another either by means of similarity or by means of contiguity.[59] The most appropriate term for the former relation is "metaphoric," while the latter might be termed "metonymic."[60]

In its relationship to other cultural systems, which is a necessary condition for the regeneration of sense, architecture takes part in a game of substitutions which, thought of in terms of metaphoric or metonymic operations, explains, at the most specific level of form, the translation from extra-architectural to intra-architectural systems in a recoding which, by means of reducing meanings, maintains the limits of architecture.

The well-known nautical metaphor in Le Corbusier's Villa Savoye exemplifies this functioning. Here, two different signifying systems are related: dwelling and ocean liner. The necessary condition for this relationship is provided by the existence of an element common to both, in this case the window. Through a metaphoric operation, a figurative substitution of the signifying element common to both systems is produced (dwelling/window—liner/window), carrying and transferring codes from one system (liner) to the other (house). The new form is thus loaded with the new meanings required to translate into figures the proposed new architectural ideology.

The similarity of functions—in this case, both liner and house are forms of habitation—makes the metaphor possible.

To these metaphoric transpositions other metonymic operations are added—for example, the *promenade architecturale*—which also carry further meanings related to the liner.

At an urban scale, where the system of architectural design coexists with many others almost by definition, the role of the metaphor as a filtering device becomes particularly evident, especially in the functional approach to urban design.

At the moment when urbanism was constituted as an institutionalized practice in the first decade of this century, urban formal codes were developed on the basis of the prevailing architectural codification. From the set of possible systems that give meaning to form, the functional approach was emphasized almost exclusively. Le Corbusier may serve once more to exemplify the type of functionalism that is at work in a filtering operation in the substitutive relation between architecture and other systems.

In Le Corbusier's texts *Vers une Architecture* (1923) and *Urbanisme* (1925), these metaphoric operations function clearly as a mechanism for contact between different cultural systems and, on other levels, as a means to architectural recodification.[61] At the building scale, Le Corbusier establishes a connection between architectural systems and other systems, such as technology, tourism, sports, and geometry. This connection is established through a metaphor based on similarity of function.[62] Geometry, for example, had acted as an internal code for formal control from the classical period of Greek architecture. It had not, however, functioned as the provider of the formal vocabulary itself, geometric regulating lines being the "invisible" elements in the construction. For Le Corbusier, however, geometry became not only an instrument of formal control, but also the provider of the formal vocabulary itself in two and three dimensions. The instrument (tool) for representation, that is, drawing, became first the project itself, and then the construction, without alteration.

At the urban scale, Le Corbusier's metaphoric operation establishes a relation between geometry as a signifying system and the city by means of the common element of "order," which is manifested as a "grid"; a system of equivalences is established between the geometric grid with its connoted codes and the city grid with the set of values ascribed to it by Le Corbusier.

Thus, in *Urbanisme,* the existing city is seen as equivalent to disorder, chaos, illness, and irrationality. On the other hand, the grid, the geometric order, is seen as equivalent to order, health, beauty, reason, modernity, and progress. "Geometry is the foundation. . . . It is also the material basis on which we build those symbols which represent to us perfection and the divine. . . ."[63]

In the plans for the Ville Contemporaine, and later for the Ville Radieuse, Le Corbusier establishes the equivalence between those two systems by means of the common element of grid-order. The appropriate connoted codes of the geometric grid are transferred through a figurative substitution to the city plan and become the codes of the city itself.

It can be seen, in this case, that while there is an initial opening of the system, its closure is produced by means of a metaphorical equivalence by which the means of representation are imposed as ideological filters in order to develop an architectural recodification. In this substitution, meanings are limited and filtered by a system (geometry) which, while it may not be specific to architecture, will, in its recoding, become specific to urban design. This is made possible by the fact that a system such as geometry may participate in a double "game": symbolic at a formal-cultural level, and instrumental, or representative, at the level of the specific practice where physical configuration becomes the device that allows for translation and recoding.

The relationship between geometry as a symbolic system on the one hand, and as a basic organizational system on the other, is not, of course, a new problem and may be found at other points in the history of architecture. In the work of Piranesi, for example, the figurative and the geometric coexist, juxtaposed in a clear dialectical relationship. The rear of the altar of S. Maria del Priorato, for example, crudely displays the set of geometric volumes which serve as its support, while the face presents itself as almost pure allegory. The architectural contradiction between geometry and symbolism is here critically posed.[64]

When Boullée and Ledoux adopted geometry in itself as a formal system, the sacred symbology was substituted for a more secular symbology—that of man. In Le Corbusier, however, there is no longer a separation between the geometric and the symbolic; rather geometry itself represents the symbolic aspect of form, and carries with it an entire set of implicit values.

With the waning of the enthusiasm for functionalism in the late 1940s, a series of works appeared which, conscious of the cultural reductivism of the heroic period, were explicitly concerned with the cultural rather than the functional aspects of design. This cultural concern was demonstrated by an intention to make explicit the articulation between architecture and other cultural systems.[65] The work of the active members of Team 10 (Alison and Peter Smithson) reintroduce culture in this sense, and again new openings and closures are produced by means of metaphoric operations: openings to incorporate "the culture"; closures to preserve the specificity of the system.

However, while in Le Corbusier the metaphor was reductive in terms of the possible inclusion of other cultural systems—a product of the exclusive nature of geometry and its concomitant modernism—the intention of Team 10 was to establish relations between architecture and other systems. "Our hierarchy of associations," they stated, "is woven into a modulated continuum representing the true complexity of human associations.... *We must evolve an architecture from the fabric of life itself,* an equivalent of the complexity of our way of thought, of our passion for the natural world and our belief in the ability of man."[66]

This criticism addresses itself precisely to the functionalist reductivism of the 1920s and to its elimination of cultural aspects, here described as "human associations" and "the fabric of life itself." These aspects were considered as an intrinsic aspect of architecture by Team 10.

Once more, metaphor is being used as the substitutive operation to incorporate "vital" aspects into design. Two types of metaphor are used. The one, which accounts for urban form in general, resembles Le Corbusier's use of geometry at an urban scale. The other, which accounts for the realization of ideas at a building scale, is itself conceived as a fundamental element of urban design.

The first metaphoric operation links two systems through the common element "life," and thus relates the city to nature (a tree). Hence the plans for Golden Lane. The city is overlaid with the attributes of a tree and given qualities of growth, organicity, movement; at the level of form, the city is understood *as* a tree possessing a stem, branches, and leaves.

The second type of metaphoric operation articulates the relationship between design and life at the scale of the building and operates on the basis of a common function: circulation of people (street). In the proposal for Sheffield, the corridor is transformed through substitution into a street, carrying with it the urban codes which, when transferred to the building, give it "life."

Despite the explicit intent of Team 10 to open the system of architecture to culture, however, the result does not, in the end, differ much from the reductive system they criticize. The type of substitution utilized—the recodification of architecture by means of yet another formal analogy—is fundamentally similar to that effected by Le Corbusier. The process by which the Smithsons assimilate "life" to design is described exclusively in sociocultural terms, even though "nature" is invoked, while the form adopted is taken directly from nature, that is, from organic, physical life. The other systems to which architecture is supposed to be actively linked (in this case, life or nature) are, in this way, filtered and reduced through the metaphor of one system, that of architectural forms. Thus, there is little real difference between the street in the air and the open corridor; the symbolic functioning which would make an architecture "out of life itself" is in fact absent. We may now see that metaphoric operations, rather than functioning to open the design system beyond its limits, in fact operate as filtering mechanisms which precisely define those limits.

It is paradoxical that the metaphor which allows for the interrelation of different codes is here used as a closing mechanism. Design is once again a sieve which allows the passage of certain meanings and not others, while the metaphor, which is used as a translating device from other codes to architecture, provides a mechanism by which ideology operates through design. In the infinite field of signifying possibilities, the metaphor defines, by a complex process of selection, the field of "the possible," thus consolidating itself in different regions by means of a language or languages.

DESIGN/NON-DESIGN

There is, however, another possible way of stating the relationship between design and culture. Rather than seeing systems of culture from a point of view that imposes a hierarchical relationship in which architecture or design is dominant, we may posit a notion of the "non-designed" built environment—"social texts," as it were, produced by a given culture.

The act of placing design (that is, both architecture and urban design) in relation to the rest of the built environment—the non-designed environment—immediately changes the level at which the problem is formulated. While in the work of Team 10 the problem is stated as internal to a single cultural system (architecture or urban design)—the relating of architecture to the city in such a way that the former acquires the "life" of the latter, here the signifying function of design is considered to relate to and, in relating, to oppose the rest of the built environment. It is regarded as a problem *internal to culture,* and thus to an entire set of cultural systems.

In these terms, architecture is no longer either implicitly or explicitly seen as the dominant system, but simply *one* of many cultural systems, each of which, including architecture, may be closed or "designed." But it is the entire set of different cultural systems configurating the built environment, which we call non-design.

In the world of non-design, that no-man's-land of the symbolic, and the scene of social struggle, internal analysis of single systems is revealed as inadequate and impossible to apply. Here there is no unique producer, no subject, nor is there an established rhetorical system within a defined institutional framework. Instead there is a complex system of intertextual relationships.

The opposition between design and non-design is fundamentally defined by three questions: first, the problem of *institutionality;* second, the problem of *limits and specificity;* and third, the problem of the *subject.* While the first establishes the relationship between design and non-design, the second establishes their respective types of articulation within culture (ideology), and the third establishes the processes of symbolization.

Design may be defined as a social practice that functions by a set of socially sanctioned rules and norms—whether implicit or explicit—and therefore is constituted as an institution. Its institutional character is manifested in the normative writings and written texts of architecture, which fix its meaning and, therefore, its reading. These texts insure the recording of the codes of design and guarantee their performance as filters and preservers of unity. They assure the homogeneity and closure of the system and of the ideological role it plays. The absence of a normative written discourse in non-design, on the other hand, precludes defining it as an institution and makes possible the inscription of sense in a free and highly undetermined way; we are here presented with an aleatory play of meaning. Thus, while design maintains its limits and its specificity, these defining aspects are lost in the semiotically heterogeneous text of non-design.[67]

Non-design is the articulation—as an explicit form—between different cultural systems. This phenomenon may be approached in two ways: as empirical fact—the actual existence of such systems found, for example, in the street, where architecture, painting, music, gestures, advertising, etc. co-exist—and as a set of related codes. In the first instance, at the level of "texts," each system remains closed in itself, presenting juxtaposed manifestations rather than their relationships. At the level of codes, on the other hand, it is possible to discern the mode of articulation between the various systems and, in this way, to define the cultural and ideological overdetermination of the built environment, or rather the process by which culture is woven into it.[68] The predisposition of non-design to openness implies permeable limits and an always fluctuating or changing specificity.

Finally, if design is the production of an historically determined individual subject, which marks the work, non-design is the product of a social subject, the same subject which produces ideology. It manifests itself in the delirious, the carnivalesque, the oneiric, which are by and large excluded or repressed in design.

To study the reality of non-design and its symbolic production in relation to culture, it is necessary to perform an operation of "cutting"—"cutting" and not "deciphering," for while deciphering operates on "secret" marks and the possibility for discovering their *full* depth of meaning, cutting operates on a space of interrelations,[69] *empty* of meaning, in which codes substitute, exchange, replace, and represent each other, and in which history is seen as the form of a particular mode of symbolizing, determined by the double value of use and exchange of objects, and as a symbolic *modus operandi* which may be understood within the same logic of symbolic production and which is performed by the same social subject of ideology and the unconscious.[70]

The moment one object may be substituted for another beyond its "functional" use-value, it has a value added to it which is the value of exchange, and this value is nothing but symbolic. Our world of symbolic performances is comprised of a chain of such exchanges in meaning; that is how we operate within the realm of ideology. Non-design leaves this ideology in a "free-state," while design hides it.

The mode of analysis for these two phenomena of design and non-design (at least from the first moment that the difference between them is recognized) must therefore vary.

READING. MISE-EN-SÉQUENCE

As a complex social text, a semiotically heterogeneous object in which many different signifying matters and codes intervene, non-design has a disposition to be open to a situation which we will call here a *mise-en-séquence*.

We propose here for non-design a productive reading, not as the re-production of a unique or final sense, but as a way of retracing the mechanisms by which that sense was produced.[71] Productive reading corresponds to the expansive potential of non-design and permits access to the functioning of meaning as an intersection of codes. The object of analysis is not the "content," but the conditions of a content, not the "full" sense of design but, on the contrary, the "empty" sense which informs all works.[72] Instead of reading by following a previously written text, the reading starts from a "signifier of departure," not only toward an architectural text but toward other texts in culture, putting into play a force analogous to that of the unconscious, which also has the capacity to traverse and articulate different codes.

The metaphoric operation participates asymmetrically in both readings, design and non-design. While in design the metaphor is not only the point of departure but also the final point of the reading, in non-design the metaphoric and metonymic operations function similarly to dreams, as chains which permit access to meanings that have been repressed, thus acting as expansive forces. This expansive mechanism may be seen to be a device used for the purpose of criticism in the work of Piranesi. His opposition to the typological obsession of his time is an indication of his perception of the crisis of architecture and the consequent need for change and transformation. His Campo Marzio is a true architectural "explosion" that anticipates the destiny of our Western cities.[73] Piranesi's "explosive" vision comprises not just the architectural system *per se* but rather a system of relationships, of contiguity and substitution.

Non-design may also be seen as an explosive transformation of design. This kind of explosion implies in some way the dissolution of the limits of architecture, of the ideological limits which enclose different architectural practices.

In front of two drawings of Piranesi's Carceri, one of the Carcere Oscura of 1793 from the series of the Opere Varie and the other on the Carceri Oscure from the Ivenzioni, the Russian filmmaker Eisenstein makes a reading which may be considered as an example of this type of analysis. Eisenstein applies a cinematographic reading to the first prison, his reading producing displacements with respect to the limits imposed by pictorial and architectural codes, thereby making it "explode" in a kind of cinematographic sequence.[74] This is the starting point of a reading that travels across literary, political, musical, and historical codes, multiplying in this way perceptions which are potential in the Piranesian work. A proof of this potential lies in Eisenstein's reading of Piranesi's second engraving, done eighteen years later, in which Eisenstein finds that the second is actually an explosion of the first prison, done by Piranesi himself.[75] It should be noted that Eisenstein is here dealing with a closed cultural system, such as architecture or painting. What Eisenstein takes, however, is not just *any* closed work from these fields but rather the work of someone like Piranesi, who poses the problem of the explosion in form (or form as explosion) in his Carceri, or in his Campo Marzio, which is a delirium of typological chaining. Although this Piranesian strategy touches problems specific to architecture, it also comes very close to the problem of the explosion of sense in architecture, to the problem of meaning as signifying chaining. In creating this extreme situation, Piranesi is implicitly assessing the problem of the limits of architecture as a "language," that is, as a closed system.

"One evening, half asleep on a banquette in a bar, just for fun I tried to enumerate all the languages within earshot: music, conversations, the sounds of chairs, glasses, a whole stereophony of which a square in Tangiers (as described by Severo Sarduy) is the exemplary site. That too spoke within me, and this so-called 'interior' speech was very like the noise of the square, like that amassing of minor voices coming to me from the outside: I myself was a public square, a *sook;* through me passed words, tiny syntagms, bits of formulae, and *no sentence formed,* as though that were the law of such a language. This speech, at once very cultural and very savage, was above all lexical, sporadic; it set up in me, through its apparent flow, a definitive discontinuity: this *non-sentence* was in no way something that could not have acceded to the sentence, that might have been *before* the sentence; it was: what is eternally, splendidly, *outside the sentence.*"[76]

The built environment as the object of reading is not "seen" as a closed, simple unity but as a set of *fragments,* "units of readings." Each of these units may be replaced by others; each part may be taken for the whole. The dimension of the built environment, empirically determined, depends upon the density of meanings, the "semantic volume."

Since these fragments appear as an articulation of different texts belonging to various cultural systems—e.g., film, art, literature—it is possible to read them by starting from any of these systems, and not necessarily from design.

Certain types of configurations, like public places (streets, plazas, cafes, airports), are ideal "fragments of readings," not only for their "semantic volume," but also for the complexity they reveal as to the signifying mechanisms in non-design. They may be characterized as signifying "nodes," where multiple codes and physical matter are articulated, where design and non-design overlap, and where history and the present are juxtaposed.[77]

The reading that can be produced by these places is not a linear discourse but an infinite and spatialized text in which those levels of reading, organized along various codes, such as theater, film, fashion, politics, gesture, are combined and articulated. The reading example we choose to present below is in itself metaphorical. It is the metaphor of architecture as theater. It is not a specific detailed analysis, but rather it exemplifies the mechanisms of chains and shifters.

A metaphor begins to function by articulating the referential codes in relation to other codes by means of replacing the referential codes in the signifier of departure with another code. In this way, a *chain* linking the codes is developed. Once the intersemiotic metaphor, such as that between architecture and theater, is produced and a possible level of reading is established, the chain of signifiers along the codes and subcodes of that cultural system is organized by "natural association"—that is, metonymically.

Signifiers appear and disappear, sliding through other texts in a play that moves along the codes of, for instance, the theater (i.e., scenic, gestural, decorative, acting, textual, verbal, etc.) in an intertextual network. This play continues until some signifier becomes another departure signifier, opening the network toward new chains through what we have called the *mise-en-séquence,* thus starting other readings from other cultural systems like film, fashion, etc. These signifiers which open to other systems may be called *shifters.*[78]

SHIFTERS

Such a reading presents a symbolic structure of a "decondensed" kind. Here, by decondensation we refer to an operation which is the reverse of that in the elaboration of dreams. Condensation and displacement are the two basic operations in the work of elaboration of dreams. By them, the passage is produced from the latent level to the manifest level of the dream. These two operations of condensation and displacement are two ways of displacing meanings, or of overdetermining, or giving more than one meaning to, some elements; they are produced precisely by means of the two operations already discussed, namely metaphor and metonymy. The metaphor corresponds to condensation, and metonymy to displacement.[79] In this way, it is possible to see the relationship between ideology (cultural codes) and subject (of ideology and of the unconscious) in the logic of symbolic production in the environment as determined by a particular mode of production.

Some signifier fragments function as "condensers" from which decondensation is possible through a network of meanings. These will be called "shifters." A set of readings could be regarded as a musical staff in which various signifiers are situated in a polyphonic organization with each voice at a different level of reading. Certain of these signifiers organize several different readings and allow for the intercrossing of codes and for the shifting from one to the next. These are the shifters; they are part of a process of exchange of codes. They are the conditions of the probability of producing different readings; they are structures of transition, the organizers of symbolic space. These connective, condensing structures are the key to the understanding of the complexity of the built environment as an infinite text. They are not concerned with signification but with the linking of signifiers. They are the key to an intertext where meanings are displaced, thereby forming a network in which the subject of the reading, the laws of the unconscious, and the historico-cultural determinants are articulated. The importance of this notion of shifter is that it accounts for the process of configuration and for the dynamic aspect of a configuration, rather than for objects and functions. It accounts for the symbolic aspect of exchange. It provides an insight into the problem of the mode of operation of ideology within the built world. It allows us to enter into a mechanism of production of sense that corresponds to an ideology of exchange.

If the system of architecture and of design, even when we play with it, is always closed within a game of commentaries of language—a meta-lingual game—it is interesting to speculate on the outcome of a similar "game" of *non-design,* a game of the built world. For non-design is a non-language, and by comparison with a language, it is madness since it is outside language, and thus outside society. This non-language, this non-sense constitutes an explosion of the established language in relation to a sense already established (by conventions and repressive rules). It is symbolic of the built world outside the rules of design and their internal "linguistic" games. It permits us finally to understand another logic which informs the significance of building.

NOTES

1. *Versus 8/9* (Milan: Bompiani, 1974).

2. Ferdinand de Saussure, *Course in General Linguistics* (New York: McGraw-Hill, 1966).

3. Max Bense, "Semiotique, Esthetique et Design" in *L'architecture d'aujourd'hui 178* (Paris: Groupe Expansion, 1975).

4. Emilio Garroni, *Progetto di semiotica* (Bari: Laterza, 1972).

5. Tzvetan Todorov, "Semiotique," in Oswald Ducrot, Tzvetan Todorov, *Dictionnaire encyclopedique des sciences du langage* (Paris, Ed. du Seuil, 1972).

6. Roland Barthes, *Elements of Semiology* (New York: Hill and Wang, 1968).

7. Jean Dubois, *Grammaire structurale du français, la phrase et les transformations* (Paris: Larousse, 1969).

8. Tzvetan Todorov, "Problemes de l'enontiation" in *Langages 17, L'enonciation* (Paris: Didier/Larousse, 1970).

9. Eliseo Veron, "Vers uns Logique naturelle des mondes sociaux" in *Communications 20* (Paris: Ed. du Seuil, 1973).

10. Julia Kristeva, *Semeiotikè: Recherches pour une Sémanalyse* (Paris: Seuil, 1969).

11. *Communications 20,* op. cit.

12. Umberto Eco, *La struttura assente* (Milan: Bompiani, 1968).

13. Renato de Fusco, Maria Luis Scalvini, "Significanti e significati della Rotonda palladiana" in *OP. CIT.* 16, (Napoli: Ed. "1 centro," 1969).

14. Emilio Garroni, op. cit.

15. Francoise Choay, *L'urbanisme: utopies et realités* (Paris: Ed. du Seuil, 1965).

16. Francoise Choay, "Semiology and Urbanism" in *Meaning in Architecture* (New York: Braziller, 1970).

17. Mario Gandelsonas, "Linguistic and Semiotic Models in Architecture" in *Basic Questions of Design Theory* (New York: North Holland. 1975).

18. Ibid.

19. Groupe 107, *Pour une analyse semiotique du plan d'architecte* (Paris: 1974).

20. Erwin Panofsky, "Die perspektive als Symbolische Form" in *Vortrage der Bibliothek Wasburg* (Leipzig-Berlin: B. G. Teubner, 1927).

21. For example, it is impossible to understand the reason for the proportions of the different rooms or the shape and location of windows in a Palladian house without reconstructing the plan of the building which allows one to see the symmetrical allocation of rooms, or the relationship between elevation and internal organization.

22. Diana Agrest, "Designed versus non-designed public places," paper presented at the First Congress of the International Association of Semiotic Studies, Milan, 1974.

23. Claude Lévi-Strauss, "Do Dual Organizations Exist" in *Structural Anthropology* (New York: Anchor Books, Doubleday & Company, Inc., 1967).

24. Pierre Bourdieu, "La maison Kabouli" in *Echanges et Communications: Melanges offerts à Claude Lévi-Strauss à l'Occasion de son 60 Anniversaire* (Paris— The Hague: Mouton, 1970.

25. Mario Gandelsonas, "The Architectural Signifier," paper presented at the First Congress of the International Association of Semiotic Studies, Milan, 1974.

26. Pierre Boudon, "Sur une statut de l'objet: différer l'objet de l'objet," *Communications 13* pp. 65–87, 1969.

27. Pierre Boudon, "Re-lecture d'une ville: la Medina de Tunis," unpublished paper.

28. Peter Eisenman, "Notes on Conceptual Architecture II" in *Environmental Design Research,* Fourth International EDRA Conference (Pennsylvania: Dowden, Hutchinson & Ross, Inc., 1973).

29. Henry Glassie, "The variation of concepts in tradition: Barn building in Ostego County" in *Geoscience and Man* (New York: 1974).

30. Luis Prieto, *Mensajes y señales* (Barcelona: Seix y Barral, 1967).

31. Cesar Jannello, a series of papers published by the Facultad de Arquitectura y Urbanismo (Buenos Aires: FAU, 1970–1972).

32. Helio Piñon, *Aspectos de la significacion arquitectonica* (Barcelona: Escuela de Arquitectura, 1975).

33. Emilio Garroni, op. cit.

34. Umberto Eco, op. cit.

35. Christian Metz, *Langage et Cinema* (Paris: Larousse, 1969).

36. Claude Lévi-Strauss, op. cit.

37. Gian Carlo Argan, *Progetto e destino* (Milan: A. Mondadori Ed., 1965).

38. Manfredo Tafuri, *Progetto e Utopia* (Roma-Bari: Laterza, 1973).

39. Colin Rowe, "Collage City," unpublished text.

40. Juri Lotman, "Problemes de la typologie des cultures" in *Essays in Semiotics* (The Hague—Paris: Mouton, 1971).

41. Christian Metz, op. cit.

42. Diana Agrest, Mario Gandelsonas, "Semiotics and Architecture: ideological consumption or theoretical work" in *Oppositions 1* (New York: IAUS, 1973).

43. Eliseo Veron, "Remarques sur l'ideologique comme production de sens" in *Espaces et Societes*.

44. Mario Gandelsonas, "The Architectural Signifier," op. cit.

45. Mario Gandelsonas, "The Architectural Signifier," op. cit.

46. Diana Agrest, op. cit.

47. Mario Gandelsonas, "The Architectural Signifier," op. cit.

48. Accordingly, architecture itself must be approached as a particular form of cultural production—as a specific kind of overdetermined practice.

49. Jury Lotman, "Problèmes de la Typologie des Cultures," *Essays in Semiotics,* op. cit.

50. See Perouse de Montclos, *Etienne-Louis Boullée* (New York: George Braziller, Inc., 1974); Emil Kaufman, *Architecture in the Age of Reason* (Cambridge, Mass.: Harvard University Press, 1955).

51. See Christian Metz, *Langage et Cinéma,* op. cit. Emilio Garroni, *Progetto di Semiotica*, op. cit.

52. Ibid.

53. Christian Metz, "Spécificité des Codes et/ou spécificité des langages," *Semiotica,* I, no. 4, 1969.

54. The role of specificity in maintaining the limits of architecture becomes evident, for example, in the development of the steel industry in the nineteenth century, which determined the development of its own independent techniques according to a reason and coherence of its own (exemplified in works of such architects as Eiffel and Paxton), while the world of architectural forces developed according to a logic neatly dissociated from technology. Such technical-formal developments are absorbed through symbolic mechanisms that incorporate the structural system as one of the expressive elements of the architectonic vocabulary. This prevents the fusion of architecture with engineering and its disappearance as an autonomous practice.

55. Heinrich Wolfflin, *Renaissance and Baroque* (Ithaca: Cornell University Press, 1966).

56. Rene Taylor, "Architecture and Magic: Considerations on the Idea of the Escorial," *Essays in the History of Architecture presented to Rudolf Wittkower,* Douglas Fraser, Howard Hibbard, and Milton J. Lewine, eds. (New York: Phaidon Publishers, Inc., 1967).

57. The notions of closing and opening would allow rethinking of certain aspects of design at the level of meaning in a manner more systematic and specific than the traditional historical analysis which looks for the explanation of the meaning of formal architectural structures in the socio-cultural context in general and considers it as a problem of content.

58. Pierre Fontanier, *Les Figures du Discours* (1821) (Paris: Slammarion, 1968).

59. Roman Jakobson, *Studies on Child Language and Aphasia* (The Hague: Mouton, 1971).

60. This is developed by Mario Gandelsonas in "On Reading Architecture," *Progressive Architecture,* May 1972; idem, "Linguistics and Architecture," *Casabella,* 373, February 1973.

61. I refer in this article to the Corbusier of *Towards a New Architecture* and *The City of Tomorrow,* although it is possible to say that there are several Le Corbusiers.

62. Le Corbusier, *The City of Tomorrow* (London: John Rodker, 1929).

63. Ibid.

64. Manfredo Tafuri, *Giovan Battista Piranesi; L'Architettura comme "Utopia negativa"* (Turin: Accademia delle Scienze, 1972).

65. This articulation has, of course, always been present in architectural treatises from the Renaissance to Le Corbusier. But it is important here, however, to posit it in this functionalist context where the conception of culture is universalist, reductivist and imperialistic.

66. Alison Smithson, ed., *Team 10 Primer* (Cambridge, Mass.: The MIT Press, 1968).

67. See Diana Agrest and Mario Gandelsonas, "Critical Remarks in Semiotics and Architecture," *Semiotica,* IX, v. 3, 1973. For the problem of semiotic heterogeneity in art see Garroni, *Progetto di Semiotica.*

68. Diana Agrest, "Towards a Theory of Production of Sense in the Built Environment" (1968–1973), *On Streets,* Stanford Anderson, ed. (Cambridge, Mass.: The MIT Press, in print). Here I proposed considering the street as a signifying system.

69. Roland Barthes, *Sade/Fourier/Loyola* (Paris: Editions du Seuil, 1972).

A first type of cutting, and the most characteristic, is the architectural, which establishes a dividing line that implies a hierarchical order. The more systematized form of this approach is the typological analysis that tries to determine from the analysis of a set of buildings formal invariants in the distribution of architectural elements independent of their specific function, or to consider such a general distribution in relation to a function. The typological analysis may be seen in semiotic terms as a study centered particularly on two types of codes, formal and functional, within the limits of architecture. Although this kind of approach is necessary, it is not sufficient for the study of the (intertextual) articulation between design and other cultural systems given the problematic of the production of sense.

See the following works on architectural typology: Garroni, *Progetto di Semiotica;* Guilio Argan, "Sul concetto de tipologia architettonica," *Progetto e Destino,* Alberto Mondadori, ed. (1965); Aldo Rossi, *L'Architettura della Citta* (Padua: Marsilio Editori, 1966); Alan Colquhoun, "Typology and Design Method," *Meaning in Architecture,* Charles Jencks and George Baird, eds. (New York: George Braziller, Inc.: 1970), pp. 267–277.

70. See J. J. Goux, *Economie et Symbolique* (Paris: Editions du Seuil, 1973).

71. Roland Barthes, *S/Z* (Paris: Editions du Seuil, 1970).

72. An important difference between the reading of design and non-design is the existence or non-existence of a written text. In the case of design one may reconstruct a discourse in such a way as to illuminate its meaning by a previous reading. When we read Le Corbusier, we reconstruct a reading made by him. In the case of non-design, however, we must put ourselves in the position of direct reading.

73. Tafuri, *Giovan Battista Piranesi,* op. cit.

74. S. M. Eisenstein, "Piranesi, Eisenstein e la dialettica," *Rassegna Sovietica,* i–2, 1972.

75. Manfredo Tafuri, "Piranesi e la fluidita delle forme," *Rassegna Sovietica,* i–2, 1972.

76. Roland Barthes, *The Pleasure of the Text* (New York: Hill and Wang, 1975), p. 49.

77. These nodes, thought of as referents to non-design, permit a more precise formulation of its meaning and distinguish it from the term "place" with which we designate the signifying structure.

78. The notion of shifter or indexical sign had been developed by Roman Jakobson in "les Catégories verbales et le verbe Russe," *Essais de Linguistique Générale* (Paris: Editions Minuit). This notion has been also used by Lacan, and Barthes applied it in somewhat transformed form in *Systeme de la Mode* (Paris: Editions du Seuil, 1967) to describe those elements which allow the articulation between two different kinds of systems, written and graphic.

The shifter should not be mistaken as being in itself possessed of "double meaning," a notion which has become almost classical in architecture. It does not refer to language. Double meaning, on the contrary, refers to the issue of content, to the problem of ambiguity in relation to language and to metaphor. While the shifter accounts for the chaining of fragments, double meaning refers to a totality with different meanings. There is no chaining and no process involved in this notion.

79. Sigmund Freud, *Interpretation of Dreams* (London: G. Allen & Unwin, Ltd., 1961); idem., *Psychopathology of Everyday Life* (New York: Norton, 1966).

The Contribution of Musical Semiotics to the Semiotic Discussion in General

Jean-Jacques Nattiez

While in the first portion of this century semiotic research, essentially theoretic in approach, was the achievement of a few pioneers—Peirce, Saussure, Morris, Hjelmslev—and while it was slow, following the postwar years, at measuring its strength against empirical descriptions and concrete applications, in recent years the number of works placed explicitly under the semiotic banner has suddenly proliferated. The present North American Colloquium is caught in an irreversible movement of institutionalization which follows from this expansion of our discipline and finds expression through the creation of national associations and international meetings.

In the light of the present situation, the author of these lines does not hide his disquiet as these manifestations, far from representing a consensus on the object, the methods, and the limits of semiotics, display the often radically opposed orientations of theories and practices which have little in common aside from the affixed label. We know that it is impossible to list here all the arguments and the intellectual prerequisites which have led us to adopt our present stand. Instead of hoping to convince our reader, we have decided on an approach in which our previous stands, if today superseded, are revealed in

I wish to thank Gilles Naud for his invaluable assistance in translating this paper into English.

the hope that, by laying bare the doubts that we have encountered, our present position may be more easily comprehended.

Since 1967, we have been working on the construction of a musical semiotics[1] and our investigations have always been related to the search for a specificity of semiotics:[2] a general semiotics or a musical semiotics *sans rivage* would only constitute a scientific imposture. Let us therefore proceed in the manner of negative theology and examine, in turn, what musical semiotics is not. To do this, we will examine critically some of the ideas currently acknowledged in the literature on general semiotics.

Musical semiotics is the study of the signs of music. The strict etymological definition of our discipline—the science of signs—could lead one into thinking that a semiotics of music should seek the types of signs of which music is constituted. This type of investigation is not new: to quote but one example, the *Recherches sur l'analogie de la musique avec les arts qui ont pour objet l'imitation du langage* is a work by the musicologist Villoteau, who, in 1807, made the distinction between the expressive or imitative-expressive means "which move our soul," and the " 'meaningful signs' which cannot recall to us the idea or the memory of things without recourse to reason and to reflexion" (1807: 32–33).

Thus envisaged, a musical semiotics encounters a difficulty of general semiotics: the latter has never been able to provide any stable and universally accepted definition of the different types of signs. Why? From St-Augustin to Condillac, from Port-Royal to the Encyclopedia, from Peirce to Saussure, the *features* retained in order to define a semiotic category are not the same. With Saussure, the sign, properly speaking and by opposition to the symbol, is conventional and arbitrary, yet it is possible to dissociate these two aspects and show that there are signs established by convention where the link between signifier and signified is not arbitrary (as is the case of certain roadway signs); moreover, an arbitrary sign is not necessarily unmotivated, as Saussure himself points out: all the words that derive from the same root are, in some way, motivated.

This first difficulty, ascribable to the incapacity of general semiotics to recognize the semiotic difficulties inherent to the constitution of its definitions, invites yet another problem: a semiotic category, although defined with precision *in abstracto,* will not necessarily designate the same phenomenon in different fields of application. Take for instance the Saussurian symbol: the example, relating to language, given in the *Cours,* is the onomatopea. To distinguish, in music, between symbolic and non-symbolic facts amounts to a particularly delicate endeavor: the sequence of sounds which imitates the songs of birds, the crashing of waves can be considered symbolic, as can the evocation of movement, of feeling. But are the latter the result of a natural association—therefore conceivably understandable by anybody—or is it something acquired in the frame of a given musical culture? From a typological point of view, these sonic phenomena may be assigned to different categories according to these two alternatives. In fact the entire classificatory issue does little to help us comprehend how these musical references to movements or feelings function. And what more have we gained by calling the Wagnerian leitmotive a signal—after Prieto, for example—when we know that bugle or trumpet calls, which represent another semiotic genre, answer the same criterion of communicational intention?

We think, with Molino (1975:45), that a certain importance must be attributed to Roman Jakobson's remarks on the famous trichotomy of Peirce: "One of the most important features of the semiotic classification of Peirce resided in the perspicacity with which he has recognized that the difference between the three fundamental classes is nothing more than a difference of place assigned inside *an all-relative* hierarchy. It is not the absolute presence or absence of similitude or contiguity between the signifier and signified, nor the fact that the usual connection between these two constituents should be of the order of pure fact or of pure institutional order, which is at the basis of the division of the set of signs into icons, indices, symbols, *it is only the predominance of one of these factors over the others*" (1966:26).[3] As far as music is concerned, Molino has recently provided an illuminating illustration of this remark: "The sonic phenomena produced by music are indeed, at the same time, icons: they can imitate the clamors of the world and evoke them, or be simply the images of our feelings—a long tradition which cannot be so easily dismissed has considered them as such; indices: depending on the case, they may be the cause or the consequence or the simple concomitants of other phenomena which they evoke; symbols: in that they are entities defined and preserved through a social tradition and a consensus which endow them with the right to exist" (1975:45).

A semiotic approach to music made from the standpoint of sign typologies therefore seems ill-fated from the start, but the investigation is not lacking in positive facts:

1) first of all, it shows that the categories of semiotics are themselves symbolic constructions, in the general sense of the term[4]—i.e., an object which refers by association to some categories of thought which are not immediately given;[5] they are therefore appropriate to a semiotics;

2) the features that intervene in the definition of semiotic categories will change with the *hierarchical weights* conferred upon them by the theories and the various fields of application; it seems just to call such features *variables;*

3) what is true of the variables of semiotic categories could also be true of musical phenomena;

4) finally, if music can, in turn, be an icon, a signal, a symptom, a symbol, an image, or a sign, it is proof that music is first and foremost a *symbolic fact*.

If it is true that the sign—an "undefinable" category according to Granger (1971:72)—or, rather, the various types of signs have at least the common feature that they *refer to something else,* then we can envisage music as a symbolic phenomenon. In such a case, the goal of a musical semiotics is to inventory the types and modalities of symbolic references to which the music gives rise, and to elaborate an appropriate methodology to *describe* their symbolic functioning.

There cannot be a semiotics of music if musical meanings do not exist. The semiotic character of music has often been given a rather restrictive interpretation: a musical sign exists because it is a two-sided entity (signifier/ signified, expression/content); we must therefore unravel "what music is saying to us," and if, in the process, music is found to be an asemantic art, then we must concede the impossibility of a musical semiotics.

We believe that such reasoning harbors at least three major inaccuracies:

1) The musical signifier is conceived after the linguistic signifier. Now, perhaps, it is here that a study of music may bring a new element to our knowledge of other domains, linguistic or artistic. As Molino pointed out, "The root of the fallacy is, in fact, to believe that language constitutes the model of all symbolic phenomena. In this, the study of music brings forth a rectification and makes an essential contribution to our knowledge of the symbolic: there is more in the symbolic than just the phantasmal concept" (1975:45). By trying to reduce all forms of meaning to linguistic meaning alone, it is precisely the latter which we forbid ourselves to understand.

Works in experimental psychology have shown that in the musical domain we must take care not to identify the musical signified with the linguistic signified. When, in their experiments, Robert Francès and Michel Imberty ask their subjects to translate into verbal statements what the musical excerpts mean to them, they know quite well that the musical meanings reach their consciousness in the form of vague sensations which the verbal word exceeds, by and large: "While attempting to *say* what the music just heard means to them, the subjects add to its meaning some additional conceptualized and referenced meanings which exist only in verbal language" (Imberty 1975:91). It is interesting to note that these observations concur with the conclusions reached by René Lindekens from his research on the semiotics of the photographic image (1971). Insofar as the only way to find out how the semantic content of music is perceived is to proceed with verbalization, the musical signified, as such, can never be pinpointed accurately; but we may consider that the statistical character of the experimental methods allows for a good approximation of it.

2) We think that the position criticized here is also erroneous with regard to the conception it implies of the *symbolic nature* of music. At times music is considered an ineffable language, of divine essence, capable of expressing the inexpressible; at other times it is considered a purely formal game of sorts, and then it is judged capable of references to the exterior world. In order to understand a debate as old as philosophy itself, let us go back to Eduard Hanslick's famous essay, *Vom Musikalisch-Schönen* (1854). This author is often invoked when the issue is to deny music any power of evocation: "The beauty of a musical work is *specific to music,* meaning that it resides in the links between sounds, without any relation to a sphere of foreign extramusical ideas" (1854:10). Now, if we look more closely at the book, we find out that it is an "essay in the reform of musical aesthetics," in other words a booklet published after Richard Wagner's *Das Kunstwerk der Zukunft;* the purpose of Hanslick is *normative,* he defines what he thinks music must not be: as an art, it must not seek the essence of Beauty in the imitation and evocation of non-musical facts (think of the leitmotives!). But Hanslick does not deny for a moment that music can stimulate in us various impressions or feelings. It could even be argued that he anticipated the experimental approach to musical meaning: "Any feeling provoked by music must certainly be brought back to the manner—special to each feeling—in which the nerves are affected by an acoustic impression" (1854:85).

Also, we must not mistake a particular aesthetic conception, unique to an era or to a philosophy, with the *fact* that any music, once conceived, perceived, or analyzed, becomes the starting point for a series of symbolic *references.* Hanslick does not deny that music releases in us all sorts of associations; he asserts that musical Beauty *must* reside only in the sonic forms, and that the "pure and conscious contemplation of the musical work" will apply to nothing else but to that same formal organization.

Roman Jakobson sees in music a semiotic system in which the "introversive semiosis"—that is, the reference of each sonic element to the other elements to come—predominates over the "extroversive semiosis"—or the referential link with the exterior world (1973:99–100). It is our opinion that the concept of *dominance* used by Jakobson to characterize the semiotic specificity of poetry, figurative and abstract painting, pure and program music, must be extended to the aesthetic conceptions of these various artistic manifestations: then, the formal and asemantic theories of music proved in the works of Hanslick, Jakobson, Stravinsky, and Hindemith appear to be a cultural fact in which the extroversive semiosis has been minimized with respect to the internal interplay of sonic forms. This has not always been the case in music's history. When Fontenelle apostrophizes: "Sonate, que me veux-tu?" his question is symptomatic of the disarray in which the theorists of the classical period were thrown when they found themselves confronted with the dilemma of pure instrumental music[6]—and there are societies (like the African Dogon and the Mexican Tepehuas) where music plays the same role as speech in interhuman relations.[7] The symbolic character of music is a *semiotic fact* which can be ascertained everywhere, but to which the various aesthetic theories, the compositional concepts, or the strategies of perception bring a *variable or changing weight,* and assign it to various levels in the hierarchy of acoustic components, according to time and culture.

3) The position questioned here thus runs the risk of mistaking semiotics for semantics. If we refuse to identify the musical signified with the linguistic signified used at the time of verbalization, then what is our *general* concept of meaning?

We will say that an object, whatever (a sentence, a painting, a social conduct, a musical work...), takes on a meaning for an individual who perceives it when he relates the object to his *experience-domain,* or the set of all other objects, concepts, or data of the world which make up all or part of his experience. To be more direct: meanings are created when an object is related to a horizon or a background. Now is the time to use, in perhaps its more fruitful manner, the theoretic contribution of Peirce: in his *Essay on a Philosophy of Style* (1968:114), Granger describes this phenomenon by means of Peirce's semiotic triangle, which he schematizes as shown in Fig. 1.

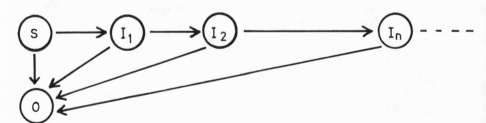

Figure 1

The sign S refers to an object O by means of an intermediate and *infinite chain of interpretants I.* These interpretants are the "atoms" of meaning by which we exercise our symbolic relation with the world.

The conceptual and verbalized meanings released in us upon listening to music are *but a part* of the interpretants associated with it. It is convenient here to use the expression "musical semantics" to describe the study of these interpretants are weighted. The objective of a musical semiotics is therefore sical experience—so long as we do not forget that a work of art is susceptible of many other types of references: when we analyze a musical score we favor such or such an aspect of the musical organization, we select this interpretant instead of that.[8] If we examine the Jakobsonian idea of a "musical introversive semiosis," a particularly positive idea will impose itself: when we establish relations of identity, equivalence, or contrast between the internal sonic phenomena of a work we are indeed calling into play a semiotic process—that is, an organization preferred by the composer, or by the performer, or by the listener, or by the musicologist, depending on the way in which certain interpretants are weighted. The objective of a musical semiotics is therefore not only to describe the semantic references *stricto sensu,* but to give an account of any type of symbolic association that takes place with the musical material.

Notwithstanding all of this, the fact remains that musical semantics represents an appreciable portion of the semiotic program in our domain. The perspectives in semantic research fall into three main categories.

The first of these we will call, after Spinoza, Granger, and Ricoeur, musical "hermeneutics." It is the *interpretation* of the meanings obtained from listening to music, the *exegetic* inspection of the proliferation of the interpretants, the establishment of subjective relations between the musical and individual experiences. As an example, think of the beautiful studies of Jankélévitch on Debussy (1968).

The second is *musicological reconstruction.* It deals with the construction of the relations between the meanings induced from the texts or situations in vocal or dramatic music, and the musical forms chosen. Such analyses tell us nothing about how the works are perceived; the musical lexicons developed in Lavignac's *Le voyage artistique à Bayreuth* (1897) or Chailley's *Passions de Bach* (1963) are typical of a composer's fancy. This type of research can be subdivided into more classes according to the methodology in use: the old studies of Pirro (1907), Schweitzer (1937), Lavignac, and more recently of Chailley, have in common that their authors conduct the analyses by going from the meanings to their musical embodiment; but it also proved necessary to proceed in the inverse manner, by going from signifier to signified, as in the works of Norma McLeod (1971) and Fritz Noske (1970). A synthesis of these onomasiological and semasiological orientations was proposed by Charles Boilès in his studies on Otomi music (1969). He later summarized the procedure as follows: "Two types of groupings were studied. The first grouping was arranged in sets according to designata common to all tunes placed in any given set. The other groupings were arranged in sets according to any musical similarities that seemed to be common to any set. Analysis of each group of tunes having common designata revealed certain phenomena that also occurred with great frequency in those tunes. The good fortune to discover musical vehicles that could be related to designata was further supported by results obtained from the second group'' (1973:39).

The last category is *experimental psychology,* to which we have already alluded; for Francès (1958) and Imberty (1975) it consists, among other things, in preferring free induction over guided induction in experiments on verbalization. This perspective has often been the object of some rather violent criticism: either all the interest—let alone its existence—of a musical semantics is denied, or else the claim is that it only leads to some already known results. But no experiment has ever brought out total agreement in the answers obtained, and for this reason the individual testimony, profound, rich, and subdued though it may be, cannot present the same scientific warranties as an experiment, however regional and limited.

Its overall epistemological validity is not a safeguard against some serious difficulties. The inquiries are usually conducted over fragments of musical works, some very short in duration, in other words *artifacts* extracted from the musical flux: we fear that the answers obtained will not correspond to a true listening situation, and as far as we can detect, there is still no complete experimental semantic analysis of a complete work.

In these researches, the correspondence between the meanings presented and the musical material as such is never abandoned, but it is an aspect which has never been tackled systematically. The works in experimental psychology have at least established an important principle: ''In the end, the features of the musical structures are pertinent to one determined (semantic) factor only, although they may also be observed in others'' (Imberty 1970:92). This means that there is no stable relation between a particular musical feature and a given meaning; the relation is always the result of some complex combinations of variables.

A semiotics of music is constructed with the help of linguistic models. During the 1960s and especially in Europe, the semiotic project, reactivated most visibly by Barthes in 1964—even if other scholars (Buyssens, Prieto, Mounin) were already working on it, albeit more discreetly—manifested itself in joint relation to linguistics. Today, it is not at all obvious that linguistics should be a determining factor in the construction of any particular semiotics, and in order to understand how this pertains to musical semiotics, it may be useful to go back in time.

It is quite independently from Peirce that Saussure places the semiotic project in line with semiotics with a few famous quotes from his *Cours de linguistique générale.* But we must not forget that when he writes: ''Linguistics can become the master-pattern of all semiotics, although language is only a particular system'' (1922:101), it is because he envisages a synchronic linguistics which depends on the *arbitrary* character of the linguistic signs, and because, according to him, semiotics should first of all attend to the arbitrary signs.

From Sechehaye, an authorized interpreter of Saussure since he was an editor of the *Cours,* we can see in the *C.L.G.* a true course in general semiotics: *"Language is only a particular case—albeit perhaps the most important—of a general case, and the problems concerning it must be considered before all as problems of semiotics* (. . . .) What is the special character of semiotics? . . . Any semiotics is essentially a science of values" (1917:13–14). Now this is the same notion of value[9] which, in the *Cours,* informs all the famous dichotomies: internal/external linguistics, signifier/signified, synchrony/diachrony, language/speech, syntagm/paradigm (Molino 1969: 341).

This interpretation of the *Cours* is similar to the semiotic conception of Hjelmslev. For him, the concepts of the *Prolegomena to a Theory of Language* "have a universal character and are valid for the system of signs in general (or for the system of figures which serve to form the signs)" (1943:130). For Hjelmslev, "language" is not limited to human language; it includes the set of *all* languages.[10]

With the publication of No. 4 of *Communication* (1964), Roland Barthes adds a new argument: semiotics constructs itself from linguistics because, in the past half century, the latter has developed tremendously while the former has remained essentially programmatic. The 1962 position of Mounin is more or less identical: "Even if not formally constituted, this semiotics of the future delimits and defines itself little by little with respect to the notional discoveries of recent linguistics. And as the latter brings into display, scientifically, the defining characters of natural languages, we can verify whether these same characters are valid or not with respect to the definition of systems of signs other than natural languages" (1970:68)—although an essential difference remains: in order to justify "the reversal of the Saussurian conception," Barthes does not hesitate to consider *a priori* all the systems of signs as languages, whereas, with Mounin, this comparative work is "propaedeutical," or preparatory to assessing the true importance of the functional linguistic model. But in both cases the objective is semiotic: the objects studied by Barthes are languages constituted of two-sided signs, those of Mounin are signals produced with an intent to communicate.

The question is whether, in this recourse to linguistics, the semiotic character of the object has been preserved. In much of the European research in semiotics, including our own articles on musical semiotics up to 1973, it seemed that the fact of using the abstract categories elaborated by linguistics in order to describe languages was judged enough to turn any object into a language. We thus ran the "ontological" risk, so well denounced by François Latraverse, which "consists of inferring the worth of a method from the nature of what it manipulates" (1974:70).

Gino Stefani's statement at the Belgrade Congress on musical semiotics in 1973, which bore a remarkable similarity to our thesis, defended in the same year, seems significant of this first stage in the development of musical semiotics: "The major influence on the new semiotic current in musicology can be imputed, up to now, to structural linguistics" (1975:12). "The more consistent contributions to a semiotics of music come from the application to music of linguistic methods and perspectives" (1975:13). Now, at the same time that general semiotics appealed to linguistics in order to free itself from the theoretical state in which it found itself, the linguistic models available in 1964 were perhaps not necessarily the best ones with which to analyze the linguistic and non-linguistic domains as symbolic facts. When Barthes asserted that "the development of mass media communications, today, contributes greatly to an actualization of this vast field of *meaning,* at the very time when the success of disciplines like linguistics, information theory, formal logic and structural anthropology provide *semantic analysis*[11] with new tools" (1964a:1), he was only deluding himself since:

a) While the concepts of signifier and signified, expression and content, can be used to operate a distinction in the domain, they are of little help in conducting a conclusive *analysis*.

b) The concepts of denotation and connotation, in the interpretation of Barthes, led him to a form of social psychoanalysis which certainly could do without linguistic concepts.[12]

c) The preferred linguistic model at the time in France was phonology, a model which did little to describe a particularly *symbolic* aspect of language.

d) As for information theory, Bar-Hillel has shown that it is inadequate to solve problems of semantics.

e) As for structural anthropology, today we can quote Dan Sperber: "In structural research the symbolic signifier, freed from the signified, is not much of a signifier except by a doubtful metaphor whose only merit is to elude the problem of the nature of symbolism, not to solve it" (1974:64). It seems difficult today to maintain an "identity of perspective between structuralism and semiotics" (Tremblay-Querido 1973:9).

f) There remains the question of the decomposition of the object studied according to the paradigmatic and syntagmatic axes: "These operations," Barthes claims, "represent an important aspect of the semiotic enterprise" (1964b:109). "Essentially, a semiotic analysis consists of distributing the facts inventoried according to these two axes" (1964b:116). Indeed, we think that this operation brings to light some fundamentally semiotic phenomena—

to which we shall later return—but if we re-read the context of these same two lines in *Eléments de sémiologie,* we realize that the semiotic justification is provided by recourse to the Saussurian model, not by the symbolic aspect which it brings into focus.

Then, the ontological illusion may well be succeeded by a sort of scientific illusion: the use of linguistics is no longer justified on the grounds that it effects a direct link with a semiotic fact, but because it fills a void (Barthes) and figures as a pilot science for the human sciences. In 1973, Stefani could say: "Any work on musical texts does not automatically belong to the realm of semiotics. Without mentioning other characters we feel that a dominant feature of our research is indeed the rigor which contributes to making semiotics into a science" (1975:9–10). We do not complain, but rigor alone cannot transform any musicological discourse into a semiotic object unless we identify science with semiotics, as Gardin suggested after Morris (1975:75) and as we thought for a time.[13] But in that case, as Ruwet pointed out (1975:33), there is no need for the term semiotics. In fact, there is a semiotic process in every scientific description (as we will show about music), but no science identifies itself with semiotics for that reason. The semiotic character must be *thematized:* this small difference is fundamental.

Now that the "dissemination" of semiotics is, today, at a maximum, a history of semiotic theories and practices should evaluate, for all the different domains, the manner in which the symbolic character of the objects studied has been brought to light and evidenced by recourse to linguistic models. Quite possibly, as we will see, such a venture may take place despite all facts and not because a linguistic model has been used. Today, the divorce between linguistics and semiotics is consummated; it is only unfortunate that this separation was made on account of fashion—structuralism, said Lévi-Strauss, died in 1968—and not for epistemological reasons. Whereas in 1966 Nicolas Ruwet could write: "I will treat music as a semiotic system which shares a certain number of common features—such as the existence of a syntax—with language and other systems of signs" (1972:100), a little less than 10 years thereafter he does not hesitate to say: "I don't particularly like the expression 'musical semiotics,' which I consider useless and perhaps even dangerous" (1975:33). This last assertion is undoubtedly excessive and unjust, but we ourselves have experienced this separation: when we set out to work, in 1967, by far the most vigorous example was the beautiful article by Christian Metz, "Le cinéma, langue ou langage?" First of all, we asked ourselves: "Is music a language?"—which is effectively a semiotic question—and this in turn led us to compare music and language; this "comparative semiotics," as we proposed calling it, thus served as a propedeutical or preparatory basis to control the transplantation, into musicology, of the linguistic models.

Later on, we will show explicitly how the use of a particular model can contribute to the specifically semiotic description of a musical work. Insofar as these borrowings have been more or less closely related to the semiotic project—at least in Europe[14]—our discipline can certainly benefit from their positive contributions:

1.) The comparison between music and language. On this subject, both the scattered (Dufrenne 1967, Schaeffer 1966) and the systematic (Springer 1956, Nattiez 1975e:2nd part) remarks available today favor a better understanding of the specificity of music and language. Besides the fact that it serves as a basis for the importation of linguistic models (Nettl 1958, Bright 1963, Becker 1973), this comparison contributes to a new form of classification of the Beaux-Arts (Nattiez 1973b:184). With the development of a systematic knowledge of music, we can hope, as Molino once suggested (1975:59), that the comparison will no longer be conducted one-way only (from language to music) but will also proceed from music to language. For example, it seems that what has been said of musical meaning could help examine in a different light the problem of linguistic semantics; of course, musical meaning is more connotative than denotative when compared to verbal meaning, but if we consider only the "core," or the "cognitive" part of meaning, the one which lexicologists set up with degrees of variations from one dictionary to the next, thereby indicating the existence of a certain laxity, do we not prevent ourselves from grasping the specificity of verbal communication, which, more often than not, remains an absence of communicaton?

2.) The functional models. First, the application of the functional models: given the analogy between the note and the phoneme brought about by comparative semiotics (Jakobson 1936), some phonological principles may be used in order to reconstitute extra-occidental music systems (Nettl 1958; Bright 1963), or to analyze the structure of a dance (Kaeppler 1972); up to this date, the best elaborated methodology is that of Vida Chenoweth (1973), based on Pike's tagmemic model. We agree with Stefani (1975:13) that the attempts to apply the Prague model to the analysis of musical works (Mâche 1971) remain rather vague.

Next, the functional point of view, in a more general way: this includes the attempts to apply Jakobson's grid of linguistic functions (1963) to music (Lévi-Strauss 1964, Stefani 1969, 1972), as well as what Stefani (1975:13) aptly calls the socio-cultural functionalism (Bogatyrev 1936, Kluge 1967, Sychra 1948), where the influence of Mukarovsky's functional aesthetics prevails. Finally, although their reference to the concepts of the Prague School is not always explicit, some American works (McLeod 1971, Boilès 1973) also enter this category.

3.) The distributional model. From the linguistics of Harris it can be said that Ruwet drew the fundamental principle of making explicit the analytical criteria (1966) and the idea of a taxonomic classification of a musical work (1962, 1966, 1967), which he relates to the paradigmatic procedures of analysis used by Lévi-Strauss in anthropology (1958) and by Jakobson in poetry (1963). Here we must distinguish between the parsing techniques, which are of linguistic origin, and the properly structural treatment of the units thereby obtained, which is of Lévi-Straussian inspiration—this being especially obvious in the analysis of the Prélude to *Pélléas* (but also in the recent analysis, by Lévi-Strauss, of Ravel's *Boléro* [1971:590–96]).

When we apply Ruwet's method of analysis to the analysis of monodies, we engage in the parsing of the musical syntagm into units which are paradigmatically associated, if identical or transformed according to a series of well-defined rules. If we look at it more closely, it will be seen that the procedure raises a number of questions, which have been tackled in various critical contributions (Arom 1969, Nattiez 1974c, Lidov 1975); these testify to the interest of the method. Being especially concerned with the question of making explicit every analytical gesture or criterion, we have developed this first aspect of Ruwet's enterprise[15] by applying it to the analysis of *Intégrales* by Varèse, the *Intermezzo* Op. 119 No. 3 by Brahms, *Syrinx* by Debussy (Nattiez 1975e: part 3, chapter II), and to *Density 21.5* by Varèse (1975d). The same perspective can also be ascertained in the works of Arom (1969, 1970) and Levy (1975) on non-European music, Stefani (1973) and Morin (1976) on J. S. Bach, Guertin on Messiaen (1975), and Hirbour-Paquette on Debussy (1975).

4.) The generative-transformational model. If we except a recent study, still unpublished, on the tonal harmonic system (Jackendoff and Lerdhal 1975) and a grammar of the melodic aspect of J. S. Bach chorales (Baroni-Jacoboni 1975), most applications of the Chomskian model are restricted to the analysis of folk and non-European music. We cannot fail, however, to note the number of works which indulge in the metaphorical use of certain Chomskian concepts: deep and surface structures (Blacking 1971), transformations (Herndon 1975, Cooper 1973), phrase or kernel sentences (Bent 1974:43, Treitler 1974:66). Generally, the generative ventures fan out in two directions: for generating pieces that belong to a given style (Sapir 1969; Lindblom and Sundberg 1970, 1973, 1975; Sundberg 1975; Asch 1972; Becker 1974), or to formalize musical theories verified according to an hypothetico-deductive procedure (Lidov 1975, Ruwet 1975).

Since the time of the first articles by Ruwet (1962), and given the influence of linguistics since then, we can consider that an autonomous current of research and musical analysis has abundantly developed, representing an original perspective in contemporary musicology.

A semiotics of music must be based on the acknowledgment of the symbolic character of the musical phenomena. It is still largely questionable whether the use of such linguistic models fosters a specifically semiotic approach to musical works, however. Speaking about "examples of semiotic analyses" Stefani specifies "analyses that are based on making explicit criteria rigorously adhered to" (1975a:15). If the explication of the criteria is indeed a necessary condition of scientific seriousness, is it enough to make semiotic objects out of musical works?

In the first paragraph, our conclusion was that a sign, or a symbolic fact, exists when there is some kind of *reference* or "renvoi." The very fact that a work or a human conduct becomes the object of an analysis implies that we have associated it with a certain number of interpretants. Simply put, the analyst is a specially attentive manipulator of interpretants, but one who, operating in the isolation of his workroom, should in principle be conscious of the fact that the scientific prehension of the object studied is not immediate, that in the passage from the work to its meta-language many aspects have been left aside. The composer, the performer, the listener also organize for themselves the interpretants of the work which is created, played, or listened to in a specific manner, and this without their being necessarily aware that a symbolic process is at work.

By making explicit the criteria of a musical analysis, the latter is transformed into a semiotic enterprise from the fact that it now enables us to describe and show, through such an analysis, just which interpretants have been retained, and how.

But the same enterprise is also semiotic in another way: created by an individual, the work is transmitted—at least in occidental music—by means of a written document, the musical score, to a performer who interprets it, translates it for the benefit of listeners. In this way, "a network of exchanges takes place between individuals" (Molino): the work cannot be dissociated from the one who produces it and the one who receives it. This is why "it is impossible to analyze, to reduce to units and organize a symbolic 'object' without going back to the three dimensions which the object necessarily presents" (Molino 1975:47). Molino calls these three aspects, after Gilson and Valery's terminology, the *poietic* (production pole), the *esthesic* (pole of reception), and the *neutral* (level of the *material* object, as heard and produced) aspects of a work.

As soon as an analysis explicates its own criteria, it cannot fail to encounter these three dimensions, because the reasons for considering particular units of a musical work to be paradigmatically equivalent are based on a phenomenon of perceptive association, on a knowledge of the equivalences allowed by the composer, or on both at the same time. One may wonder, then, about the necessity for a "neutral" description of the object, especially when the analysis is being referred constantly to the two extreme poles of the trichotomy. In fact, the poietic and the esthesic dimensions are not necessarily bound to correspond, and it is one of the contemporary myths of semiotics to conceive as normal a state of equilibrium between both. The aim of a neutral level is to inventory, as exhaustively as possible, the set of all possible configurations: bear in mind that a work is never perceived in the same manner from one time to the next, let alone by two individuals at the same time.

In this sense, Ruwet's principle of paradigmatic parsing, based on the dialectic repetition/transformation, is semiotic, less because it is inspired by linguistic procedures than because it helps inventory all possible relations between the units of the same piece. When he stressed the "impossibility of representing the structure of a musical piece by means of a unique diagram" (Ruwet 1972:134), he was not only raising a technical and material problem of analysis, but also showing that the multiplicity (properly infinite) of interpretants attached to a work forces us to present many different configurations or possible modes of organization of that work, *according to the explicit criteria that have been defined.*

Hence, when Stefani cautions us in a recent article (1976:49) to adhere to a monoplanar semiotics and deal only with the signifier, thereby leaving semiotics aside, he is only the victim of a semiotic concept still confined in the scheme expression/content, and even if the functional aspects of his analyses are not exactly comparable to concepts, they are not very far indeed from the Saussurian signified. Now, we think that Peirce's semiotic triangle breaks up the Saussurian dichotomy since, in the process of apprehending symbolically the musical material, the classical signifier is itself sprinkled with interpretants.

We will now give an example (Fig. 2) of the necessity for examining an object from the point of view of the three dimensions. The example is borrowed from an article by one of our collaborators, Gilles Naud, on Xenakis' composition: *Nomos Alpha*. The work was selected because Xenakis has published the mathematical program which served to compose the work. The following passage (Naud 1975:71) is poietically divided by Xenakis into two objects: s2a and s3a. The neutral analysis, conducted on the basis of paradigmatic principles, identifies three distinct objects: α, β, and γ. The (esthesic) experiments on the auditive perception of this piece show that the same passage was categorized by a first category of listeners into objects (1), (2), and (3), which concur with the neutral segmentations. A second group of listeners identified objects (4) and (5), which coincide with the poietic data; a third group of listeners identified (6) only, and thus did not distinguish be-

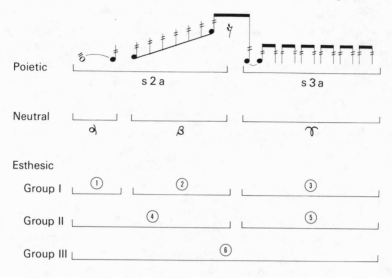

Figure 2

tween objects α, β, and γ. Had we preoccupied ourselves with only the poietic data, it would have been impossible to explain groups I and III of listeners, and a minimal neutral segmentation is also necessary in order to explain group I's perception.

This theory of the neutral level has met with much opposition, and, surprisingly, on behalf of researchers who should appreciate its necessity. During the past fifty years, linguistics has multiplied the modalities of an *immanent* description of languages. What happens today, after so many years of neutral descriptions, is that we can no longer remain at a stage where the phenomena are tackled "in themselves and for themselves," as Saussure would have it: they must now be envisaged in their relation to the poietic and the esthesic poles. An essential difference, however, with the reducing attempts (social character, psychology of the sign) denounced by Saussure in a famous page of his *Cours,* is that the only way to relate a poietic and an esthesic characterization to the works studied is through a neutral and immanent description of the object—this has been the fundamental attainment of structuralism—and for two principal reasons:

1) the musical works have an autonomous material reality which cannot be reduced to the poietic and esthesic aspects;

2) the *links* between the works and the strategies of production and of reception cannot be specified unless we first dispose of a *description* of the work itself.

Now, we may assign to their proper place in our semiotics the techniques imported from linguistics into musicology—not to mention the semiotic character of the inventories of paradigmatic equivalences: they provide models for inventorying, classifying, and organizing the constitutive elements of a work on the neutral level, such that the latter may in turn supply a basis from which the relations to the poietic and the esthesic dimensions can be effected. The external data supplied at these two extreme poles may then reilluminate or organize differently the combination proposed at the neutral level. It is easy to see that a work of art is never static, but is part of an unending process: and a semiotics of music must especially endeavor to bring out this *symbolic dynamism,* this swirl of interpretants.

Conclusion

Today, we can assess the attainments and perspectives of musical semiotics:

a) From the linguistic point of view, the essential comparison between language and music has been made. The task of reversing the perspective of comparative semiotics still remains, however.

b) Musical semantics will have to develop new methods in order to deal with musical works in their entirety, and make emphatically explicit the links between musical material and the meanings inventoried.

c) Ruwet's method had to be reevaluated on account of some difficulties it presented, but if it now can serve to classify and describe the units of a given work, it must also fulfill two further programs: it must be used in conjunction with the poietic and the esthesic poles of the analysis, as already mentioned; and it must set grounds for an integration of the isolated work to a series or corpus, by showing how it pertains stylistically to that series, while at the same time manifesting its own stylistic originality.[16]

d) We have shown why clarification of analytical criteria deserves a choice place in our semiotic project: it is equally important to reconstitute the criteria of already existing analyses.[17] Through a comparison of different analyses of the same work, we can extend the semiotic perspective on musical works to the discourse on the works themselves, and try to seek out and explain reasons for the differences between musicologists, or specify the non-explicated criteria which separate the various schools of musicology. The pedagogical importance of this perspective, at a time when musical semiotics is both the ferment and the symptom of a contest of the more uncertain aspects of the musicological discourse,[18] will escape no one.

NOTES

1. In its latest formulation: *Fondements d'une sémiologie de la musique* (1975e).

2. On this question, see our recent articles: 1974a, 1975b, 1975c.

3. Emphasis added.

4. Care must be taken not to mistake, in the remainder of this essay, *symbol,* a particular type of sign, for the symbolic function and facts, as defined here and which semiotics must study.

5. Let us give Ricoeur's definition of the symbolic function: "the general function of mediation by means of which the spirit, or conscience, builds up all its universes of perception and discourse" (1965:19).

6. Concerning this problem, see the article of Roland-Manuel (1963).

7. With regard to these two musical civilizations, cf. respectively Calame-Griaule (1965:527–43) and Boilès (1967).

8. Here we have an indication as to how a sociology devoid of allegorism could be created. Stefani's formulation concurs with our conceptions on this matter (Nattiez 1974b): "It would be important (and specifically semiotic) to establish through which specific mediations the semantic assertions (of musical sociology) are based on musical texts, or in other words, to find out how the interpretants of Peirce, which a musical work suggests to the receptors of the musical signs according to determinations which are specific to the given cultural systems (economics, language, politics, musical systems . . .), are articulated" (Stefani 1975a:16).

9. An unsolved problem which will not be examined here is the following: in order to account for the object as a symbolic fact, how important is it to make a description based on the notion of value?

10. Which is also a source of problems, for his definition of languages (1947) is based, quite evidently, on the characteristics of the human language.

11. Emphasis added.

12. Gardin has clearly shown how Barthes, in his article "Rhétorique de l'image," had used a certain linguistic vocabulary without subscribing to one of the requirements of phonology which confers most of its seriousness: to make explicit a procedure (commutation) by which we already know how the results of an analysis are obtained (1974: chapter II).

13. In the first version—today out of print—of our analysis of *Syrinx* (1975a), upon which Ruwet based his formulation of the criticism mentioned here. For our "retractatio," cf. Nattiez 1974a:5.

14. It is characteristic that the term of semiotics is never invoked in the linguistically-inspired works of American musicologists, much in the same way as Peirce and Morris develop their theories, not on linguistics, but on logic.

15. For a criticism of its Lévi-Straussian counterpart, cf. Nattiez 1973a:77–79.

16. We have often emphasized, elsewhere, the importance of stylistic characterization in our semiotic project (Nattiez 1971, 1975a, 1975e); we did not mention it here, but it is absolutely fundamental.

17. Concerning the theory of such a perspective, cf. Gardin 1974: chapter I; for musical illustrations: Nattiez-Paquette 1973, Nattiez 1975d.

18. Music analysis has become, lately, the *object* of musicological preoccupations, which is the sign of a certain disquiet. Particularly revealing is the publication in Germany of a history of musical analysis (Beck 1974) and a partially overlapping collection of music analysis (Schuhmacher 1974), and the article by Marcia Herndon (1974) in which she analyzes the same piece, belong to the music of oral tradition, in the manner of different musicologists.

REFERENCES

Arom, S. 1969. "Essai d'une notation des monodies à des fins d'analyse," *Revue de musicologie,* LV/2, 172–216.

———. 1970. *Conte et chantefables Ngbaka ma'bo,* Paris, Bibliothèque de la S.E.L.A.F., no. 21.

Asch, M. 1972. "A Grammar of Slavey Drum Dance Music: An Application of Linguistic Methodology to Music Analysis," annual meeting of the Society for Ethnomusicology (Toronto), mimeogr.

Baroni, M., and C. Jacoboni. 1975. "Analysis and Generation of Bach's Choral Melodies," *Actes du 1er congrès international de sémiotique musicale,* Pesaro, Centro di Iniziativa Culturale, 125–149.

———. 1976. *Verso una grammatica della melodia,* Bologna, Antiquae Musicae Italicae Studiosi, Università Studi di Bologna.

Barthes, R. 1964a. "Présentation," *Communications,* no. 4, 1–2.

———. 1964b. "Eléments de sémiologie," *Communications,* no. 4, 91–135.

Beck, H. 1974. *Methoden der Werkanalyse in Musikgeschichte und Gegenwart,* Wilhelmhaven, Heinrichofen's Verlag.

Becker, A. 1973. "A Grammar of Musical Genre: Rules for a Javanese Srepegan," communication at the annual congress of the S.E.M. (Urbana) (unpublished).

Bent, I. 1973. "Current Methods in Stylistic Analysis," *Report of the 11th congress of the I.M.S.* (Copenhagen, 1972), t. I, Copenhagen, Hensen, 42–3.

Blacking, J. 1971. "Deep and Surface Structures in Venda Music," *Yearbook of the International Folk Music Council,* III, 69–98.

Bogatyrev, P. 1936. "La chanson populaire du point de vue fonctionnel," *Travaux du Cercle linguistique de Prague,* VI, 222–234 (Neudeln, Krauss Reprint, 1968).

Boilès, C. 1967. "Tepehua Thought-Song: a Case of Semantic Signaling," *Ethnomusicology,* XI/3, 267–291.

———. 1969. Otomi Cult Music, Ph.D. dissertation, Tulane University.

———. 1973. "Sémiotique de l'ethnomusicologie," *Musique en Jeu,* no. 10, 34–41.

Bright, W. 1963. "Language and Music: Areas for Cooperation," *Ethnomusicology,* VII, 26–32.

Calame-Griaule, G. 1965. *Ethnologie et langage, la parole chez les Dogon,* Paris, Gallimard, Bibl. des sciences humaines.

Chailley, J. 1963. *Les Passions de Bach,* Paris, P.U.F.

Chenoweth, V. 1972. *Melodic Analysis and Perception,* Papua, New-Guinea, Summer Institute of Linguistics.

Cooper, R. 1973. "Propositions pour un modèle transformationnel de description musicale," *Musique en Jeu,* no. 10, 70–88.

Dufrenne, M. 1967. "L'art est-il un langage?" *Esthétique et philosophie,* Paris, Klincksieck, 74–122.

Francès, R. 1958. *La perception de la musique,* Paris, Vrin.

Gardin, J. C. 1974. *Les analyses de discours,* Neuchâtel, Delaschaux et Niestlé.

Granger, G. G. 1968. *Essai d'une philosophie du style,* Paris, Colin.

———. 1971. "Langue et systèmes formels," *Langages,* no. 21, 71–87.

Guertin, M. 1975. Analyse d' "Ile de feu II" de Messiaen du point de vue sémiologique, M.A. dissertation, unpublished.

Hanslick, E. 1854. *Vom Musikalisch-Schönen,* quoted from the 2nd French edition of 1893, Paris, Maquet.

Herndon, M. 1974. "Analysis: the Herding of Sacred Cows?" *Ethnomusicology,* XVIII/2, 219–262.

———. 1975. "Le modèle transformationnel en linguistique: ses implications pour l'étude de la musique," *Semiotica* XV/1, 71–82.

Hirbour-Paquette, L. 1975. Les Préludes pour le piano de Claude Debussy, Ph.D. dissertation, unpublished.

Hjelmslev, L. 1943. *Prolégomènes à une théorie du langage,* quoted from the French edition, Paris, Minuit, 1971.

———. 1947. "La structure fondamentale du langage," in *Prolégomènes à une théorie du langage,* Paris, Minuit, 1971, 179–231.

Imberty, M. 1970. "Polysémie et cohérence sémantique du langage musical: I. La polysémie dans les réponses verbales associées à la musique et la construction d'une échelle circulaire des expressivités musicales," *Sciences de L'Art,* VII/1–2, 77–93.

———. 1975. "Perspectives nouvelles de la sémantique musicale expérimentale," *Musique en Jeu,* no 17, 87–109.

Jackendoff, F. and F. Lerdahl. 1974. "Toward a Formal Theory of Tonal Music," colloquium Musique-Linguistique, I.R.C.A.M., Paris, unpublished.

Jakobson, R. 1963. "Linguistique et poétique," in *Essais de linguistique générale,* Paris, Minuit, 209–248.

———. 1966. "A la recherche de l'essence du langage," in *Problèmes du langage,* Paris, Gallimard, 22–38.

———. 1973. "Le langage en relation avec les autres systèmes de communication," in *Essais de linguistique générale II,* Paris, Minuit, 91–112.

Jankelevitch, V. 1968. *La Vie et la Mort dans la Musique de Debussy,* Neuchâtel, La Baconnière.

Kaeppler, A. 1972. "Method and Theory in Analysing Dance Structure with an Analysis of Tougan Dance," *Ethnomusicology,* XVI/2, 173–217.

Kluge, R. 1967. "Typ, Funktion, Bedeutung, Bemerkungen zur semantischen Analytik musikalischen Typen," *Beiträge zur Musikwissenschaft,* IX/2, 98–104.

Latraverse, F. 1974. "Théorie stratificationnelle et sémiologie," *Langages,* no. 35, 70–81.

Lavignac, A. 1897. *Le voyage artistique à Bayreuth,* Paris, Delagrave.

Lévi-Strauss, C. 1958. "La structures des mythes," in *Anthropologie structurale,* Paris, Plon, 227–255.

———. 1964. *Le Cru et le Cuit,* Paris, Plon.

———. 1971. *L'homme nu,* Paris, Plon.

Levy, M. 1975. "On the Problem of Defining Musical Units," *Actes du 1er congrès international de sémiotique musicale,* Pesaro, Centro di Iniziativa Culturale, 135–149.

Lidov, D. 1975. *On Musical Phrase,* Monographs on semiotics and musical analyses, I, Université de Montréal.

Lindblom, B. and J. Sundberg. 1970. "Toward a Generative Theory of Melody," *Swedish Journal of Musicology,* vol. 52, 71–87.

———. 1973. "Music composed by a computer program," *STL-QPS4* no 4, Royal Academy of Science, Stockholm.

———. 1975. "A Generative Theory of Swedish Nursery Tunes," *Actes du 1er congrès international de sémiotique musicale,* Pesaro, Centro di Iniziativa Culturale, 111–124.

Lindekens, R. 1971. *Eléments pour une sémiotique de la photographie,* Bruxelles-Paris, AIMAV-Didier.

McLeod, N. 1971. "The Semantic Parameter in Music: the Blanket Rite of the Lower Kutenai," *Yearbook for Inter-American Musical Research,* VII, 83–101.

Mâche, F. B. 1971. "Méthodes linguistiques et musicologie," *Musique en Jeu,* no 5, 75–91.

Molino, J. 1969. "Linguistique et économie politique: sur un modèle épistémologique du *Cours* de Saussure," *L'Age de la Science,* II/18, 335–49.

———. 1975. "Fait musical et sémiologie de la musique," *Musique en Jeu,* no 17, 37–62.

Morin, E. 1975. "Analyse sémiologique de la Fugue no 7 en mi bémol du 1er livre du *Clavecin bien tempéré,*" Université de Montréal, unpublished.

Mounin, G. 1970. *Introduction à la sémiologie,* Paris, Minuit.

Nattiez, J. J. 1971. "Situation de la sémiologie musicale," *Musique en Jeu,* no 5, 3–17.

———. 1973a. "Analyse musicale et sémiologie: le structuralisme de Lévi-Strauss," *Musique en Jeu,* no. 12, 59–79.

———. 1973b. "Quelques problèmes de la sémiologie fonctionelle," *Semiotica,* IX/2, 157–190.

———. 1974a. "Pour une définition de la sémiologie," *Langages,* no. 35, 3–13.

———. 1974b. "Sur les relations entre sociologie et sémiologie musicales," *International Review of the Aesthetics and Sociology of Music,* V/1, 61–75.

———. 1974c. "Problèmes de sémiologie musicale et de poétique structurale," *Semiotica,* XI/3, 247–268.

———. 1975a. "From Taxonomic Analysis to Stylistic Characterization: Debussy's *Syrinx,*" *Actes du 1er congrès international de sémiotique musicale,* Pesaro, Centro di Iniziativa Culturale, 83–110.

———. 1975b. "Le point de vue sémiologique," *Cahiers de linguistique de l'UQAM,* no. 5, 49–76.

———. 1975c. "Sémiologie générale et concepts linguistiques," *Hommage à Georges Mounin pour son 65e anniversaire, Cahiers de linguistique d'orientalisme et de slavistique,* nos 5–6, 297–312.

———. 1975d. *"Densité 21.5" de Varèse: essai d'analyse sémiologique,* Monographs on semiotics and musical analyses, II, Université de Montréal.

———. 1975e. *Fondements d'une sémiologie de la musique,* Paris, 10/18.

Nattiez, J. J., and L. Hirbour-Paquette. 1973. "Analyse musicale et sémiologie: à propos du *Prélude* de *Pelléas,*" *Musique en Jeu,* no 10, 42–69.

Naud, G. 1975. "Aperçus d'une analyse sémiologique de *Nomos Alpha,*" *Musique en Jeu,* no 17, 63–72.

Nettl, B. 1958. "Some Linguistic Approaches to Musical Analysis," *Journal of the International Folk Music Council,* X, 37–41.

Noske, F. 1970. "Don Giovanni: Musical Affinities and Dramatic Structure," *Studia Musicologica,* XII, 167–203.

Pirro, A. 1907. *L'esthétique de J. S. Bach,* Paris, Fischbacher.

Ricoeur, P. 1965. *De l'interprétation,* Paris, Seuil.

Roland-Manuel, 1963. "Le classicisme français et le problème de l'expression musicale," in *Histoire de la Musique*, Encyclopédie de la Pléiade, t. II, Paris, Gallimard, 82–93.

Ruwet, N. 1962. "Note sur les duplications dans l'oeuvre de Claude Debussy," *Revue belge de musicologie*, XVI, 57–70; in Ruwet 1972:70–99.

――――. 1966. "Méthodes d'analyse en musicologie," *Revue belge de musicologie*, XIX/1, 65–90; in Ruwet 1972:100–134.

――――. 1967. "Quelques remarques sur le rôle de la répétition dans la syntaxe musicale," in *To Honour Roman Jakobson*, La Haye, Mouton, 1693–1703; in Ruwet 1972:135–150.

――――. 1972. *Langage, musique, poésie*, Paris, Seuil.

――――. 1975. "Théorie et méthodes dans les études musicales: quelques remarques rétrospectives et préliminaires," *Musique en Jeu*, no 17, 11–36.

Sapir, J. D. 1969. "Diola-Fogny Funeral Songs and the Native Critic," *African Language Review*, 8, 176–191.

Saussure, F. de. 1922. *Cours de linguistique générale*, Paris, Payot.

Schaeffer, P. 1966. *Traité des objets musicaux*, Paris, Seuil.

Schuhmacher, G. (ed.). 1974. *Zur musikalischen Analyse*, Darmstadt, Wissenschaftliche Buchgesellschaft.

Schweitzer, A. 1973. *J. S. Bach, le musicien-poète*, Lausanne, M. et P. Foetich.

Sechehaye, A. 1917. "Les problèmes de la langue à la lumiére d'une théorie nouvelle," *Revue philosophique*, LXXXIV, 1–30.

Sperber, D. 1974. *Le symbolisme en général*, Paris, Hermann.

Springer, G. 1956. "Language and Music: Parallel and Divergencies," in *For Roman Jakobson*, La Haye, Mouton, 504–613.

Stefani, G. 1969. *Communications sonores dans la liturgie*, Paris, Institut Catholique (xeroxed).

――――. 1972. "Caro Mozart," *Nuova Rivista Musicale Italiana*, VI/1, 102–199.

――――. 1973. *La ripetizione in Bach: i preludi "ad arpeggio" del Clavicembalo*, Centro Internazionale di Semiotica e di Linguistica, Urbino, Documenti e prepublicazioni E/22, 1973.

――――. 1975. "Situation de la sémiotique musicale," *Actes du 1er congrès international de sémiotique musicale*, Pesaro, Centro di Iniziativa Culturale, 9–25.

――――. 1976. "Analisi, semiosi, semiotica" in *Introduzione alla Semiotica della Musica*, Palermo, Sellerio Editore, 36–49.

Sundberg, J. 1975. "Linguistic Methods in Music Description," *Colloque Musique et Linguistique*, Centre Beaubourg, Paris (unpublished).

Sychra, A. 1948. "La chanson folklorique du point de vue sémiologique" (translated from Czech), *Musique en Jeu*, 1973, no. 10, 12–33.

Treitler, L. 1974. "Methods, Style, Analysis," *Report of the 11th Congress of the I.M.S.* (Copenhagen, 1972), t. I, Copenhagen, Hansen, 61–70.

Tremblay-Querido, C. 1973. "Vers une science des systèmes symboliques?" *Sociologie et sociétés*, V/2, 3–15.

Villoteau, G. 1807. *Recherches sur l'analogie de la musique avec les arts qui ont pour objet l'imitation du langage*, Slatkine Reprints, 1970, 2 vol.

Semiotics and Spectacles: The Circus Institution and Representations

Paul Bouissac

Any spectacle implies an *Institution* which provides the means for recurrent displays of collective representations. By the word "means," we understand not only the structure of the physical channel or the medium used and the nature of the underlying social organization, but also the specific code involved in any category of performance. This code makes possible the expression-communication and occasionally the creation-communication of these collective representations. In addition, it determines the conditions of their circulation in a given society. Therefore, in the study of spectacles we should carefully avoid restricting our attention exclusively to the performances themselves and attempting to analyze them independently from the institutions through which they are produced. True enough, institutions cannot usually be experienced as such and must be inferred from particular instances, but when we refer to the theatre, the cinema, the television, the circus, we refer in fact to such institutions although we possibly have the impression of referring merely to particular categories of performances in general, somewhat in the same manner as when we refer to French, Chinese, or Swahili as languages. *Institution* is understood here in the sense suggested

This research was supported by a John Simon Guggenheim Memorial Foundation Fellowship (1973–74).

by John Searle (1969, p. 33), who distinguishes *regulative rules* from *constitutive rules* and defines the latter as the condition of possibility of some category of phenomena which we call "institutional facts" as opposed to "brute facts." It seems conspicuous that circus or theatre performances are institutional facts and that their very existence is conditioned by institutions, i.e., by "systems of constitutive rules" of the type "X counts as Y in context C." Therefore, it seems that spectacles as institutions can legitimately be considered as grammars. These grammars have to be learned by the members of the societies where they are observed in order for them to acquire the capability of participating with appropriateness as producers or consumers in the circulation of the messages involved. It is noticeable, in this respect, that the celebrated interest of children in the circus is the result of education rather than a spontaneous phenomenon. We not infrequently witness the fright of a young child which has been taken to the show by its parents and protests loudly against a situation which is obviously a traumatic experience. It is significant, on the other hand, that circus performers usually loathe audiences which are primarily made up of children because they cannot "appreciate" the skill of their feats and the complexity of their act as a whole and "react indiscriminately" to whatever happens in the ring. In other words, children possess only a partial knowledge of the code involved, they still have to learn the rules and to master the grammar and poetics of the art. This is the case for any type of spectacle.

These grammars not only enable us to form and understand messages of a special kind but also to construct specific contexts for these messages. They include at least some topological rules, proxemic rules, chronemic rules, social behavior patterning rules, coding rules, syntactical rules, situation patterning rules, and performing rules. Approximately in the same way as M. A. K. Halliday (1971) contends that "syntax enunciates the theme," we could say that the institution, as a set of implicitly known constitutive rules, provides more information than any of the actual performances it produces. Without raising the interesting problem of the acquisition of such a competence, we can observe that "circus" refers to more than a collection of past experiences and that it creates an expectation which does not exclude a certain amount of novelty. This is why an exclusive concern for the performances observed leads to statements redundant with the situation of the spectator, a pitfall which is not always overcome by students of the performing arts. It is a methodological necessity to include as parts of our object of study not only both terms of the communication process, i.e., the *Sender* and the *Receiver,* but also to investigate the specific conditions of possibility of such a process and to engage deliberately in a meta-communicative analysis fundamentally different from a mere exegesis.

This approach to spectacles would have been impossible without the conceptual tools provided by semiotics. Even though some perfectionists claim that nothing should be undertaken until an irreproachable theory has been created, it is a fact that during the last two decades the semiotic methodology has set forth with great clarity, through its confrontation with specific domains of research at the operational level, a certain number of complementary relations involved in any expression-communication process. The variety of tendencies, terminologies, and theoretical claims as well as occasional ideological skirmishes and personality clashes must not obliterate the fact that a relative consensus has been reached and this epistemological minimum lays the basis for a discipline. In other words it provides an original mapping of our experience of our natural and cultural environment and consistent procedures to negotiate this experience on a scientific or quasi-scientific level. The present colloquium demonstrates this inasmuch as, even though dissents are expressed, the issues are formulated in approximately the same terms, and a rich dialogue can develop on the basis of a common understanding of such concepts as "signs," "semiosis," "communication," "information," "translatability" and so on. The object construed by semiotics, the semiotic model, is indeed a very powerful one because it encompasses the universals of communication and at the same time can account for particular instances by providing criteria for distinguishing constants from variables and for expressing specific functions.

In the field of spectacles examples of such achievements are already numerous but special mention should be made of Ivo Osolsobě's (1974) major contribution to the semiotics of the theatre, Vilmo Voigt's (1974) analysis of public celebrations, Solomon Marcus's (1970) formalistic treatment of theatrical texts, Mariane Mesnil's (1974) studies of folkloristic performances, and Zoltan Kovecses's (1975) attempt to set forth a semiotic theory of sports.

The selection of the circus as the subject matter of this brief paper provides us with a very familiar object of experience practically untouched by traditional aesthetics. The circus is somewhat relegated to the half-respectability of the marginal category of folklore and popular culture, although it constitutes one of the most vivid themes of our cultural environment and one of the most profitable industries prospering in our society. As I have in other circumstances tentatively dealt at length with particular types of circus acts (Bouissac, 1976), I will try here to set forth some specific features of the circus as an institution and show how it relates to the contextual culture in which it is observed.

Let us consider first the topological determinations which underlie the physical setting of circus performances. An arbitrary circle differentiates, temporally or permanently, a space within the proxemic continuum of the city. This space is somewhat neutralized or desemantized with respect to the surrounding topological and proxemic systems. It contains nothing except a uniform soil made of sawdust, wood chips, or a rough mat. It creates a parenthesis. It is important to point out that were this first operation not done, it would be impossible to produce a circus act. This indeed requires precisely a semantically neutral ground in order to construct upon it, and within it, its own finite system, and to manipulate its components in an absolute void or noiseless milieu. It has no corners, no orientation, no intrinsic structuration, with the exception naturally of the central versus peripheral categories; but this opposition is not actualized as long as the circle remains empty. Incidentally, this potential topological differentiation of the circle serves to articulate various oppositions such as male (center)/female (periphery) in the Bororo villages (Lévi-Strauss, 1958, p. 156). I have shown elsewhere (Bouissac, 1974, p. 9) that, in horse acts, it contributes to the contrast between collective and individualistic values. By the same token another space is defined: the surrounding "crown" reserved to the audience. Moreover, each of these differentiated spaces is connected to respectively differentiated outside spaces: on the one hand the back stage from which the acts emerge and into which they disappear, and on the other hand, the world where the spectators live. This topological disjunction relates at the same time the two differentiated spaces and creates a communication situation ascribing respective positions to the addressers and the addressees. As Osolsobě says about the theatre, "There is no art whose communication basis would be more conspicuous than dramatic art: communication is the basic purpose of theatre buildings and the whole special organization and equipment of those buildings serves this purpose." But he adds later on that "This kind of dialogue is, however, regulated by special implicit rules enabling the audience only a limited set of responses" (1970). The whole communicative situation is characterized as complementary or even meta-complementary and is opposed to symmetrical communication in Gregory Bateson's (1958, p. 176) terms.

In the case of the circus the peripheral situation of the spectators indicates that the messages produced are not uni-directional, they are not primarily of a linguistic or ritualistic social-behavioral nature, but that it is the totality of the patterned behavior performed which is what essentially constitutes the message. This is a feature which is more important than it might sound because it entails not only specific performing rules but also coding rules in contradistinction to the theatre, the mime or the cinema. Notably, it excludes face to face interaction as its primary signified, and focuses on the general biological aspects of the situation which are displayed.

In addition performances are scheduled outside of the regular working hours. This cannot be simply accounted for by the fact that it is the only way for a circus to have enough spectators. It also entails consequences of a semiotic nature, i.e., the activities displayed in the ring are not commonly and spontaneously viewed by the audience as real work but something that is done outside of the regular working time. This has a disconnective effect with respect to social reality and operates a chronemic neutralization similar to the subsequent oversemantized actions, the circus acts, which take place in this blank space and time throughout the performance. But above all, the temporal form of the events taking place in the ring is circulatory because it suggests a universe in which an element would return to its initial state after having undergone a certain number of transformations. Of course, it may happen from time to time that the linear time upsets dramatically the presentation of an act in the form of an accident. In those conditions, we move from the circus to the drama of real life. Let us note, in passing, that the theme of circus is generally used by literary works only inasmuch as it provides opportunities for dramatic accidents.

A further characteristic feature is that each circus act constructs its own situation, its own immediate context. During a given act, there is nothing in the ring which is not the result of a deliberate selection and combination. These decisions reflect the personality of the actors involved only within the boundaries determined by the constitutive rules of the circus. The wild animal trainer is not thrown to the lions. The construction of the steel or nylon enclosure, the disposition of stools and other accessories, and the presence of the lions are not imposed upon the man by accidental circumstances or by malevolent humans or superhumans as the case would be in a novel or a film. However, this situation includes in its system a potential disturbance able to transform it drastically but is conserved through successive controls demonstrating a specific skill which must be assessed in view of the given context. This articulatory level of the circus act must be completed by the semantic operations which are performed in the process and account for the meaningfulness that such circus acts convey to their audience. This is true of animal acts and acrobatic acts as well as clown acts, but in the first two the articulatory level is fundamentally of a biological nature, and can be expressed by cybernetic models (Ashby, 1957, p. 77; Bouissac, 1973, p. 200), whereas the latter is primarily of a socio-cultural nature. In fact, we should speak of emphasis rather than clearcut dichotomies since these two poles are seldom actualized exclusively in one act. Indeed, social cultural signs are present in acrobatic and animal acts as well as biological signs in clown acts; nonetheless, they all can be formalized in the same way. The formalization is all the easier because the elements or terms collocated in a circus act are already somewhat formalized: they can be considered as *iconic signs* (Bouissac, 1974, p. 5). They stand for classes and relations. They are selective strings of features relevant to the operations performed. But given the fact that all these elements (horse, dog, ladder, ropes, human beings, actions, etc.) are in the case of the circus at the same time natural and functional objects, they undergo a process of stylization or rather iconization consisting of the suppression of the *noise* which they naturally contain and the adjunction of supplementary elements for the sake of *redundancy:* animals are groomed, normalized, decorated, placed on pedestals, the gestures of the trainers and acrobats are stylicized and stereotyped, music contributes to the iconization of movements, etc. Backstage, these modifications involve considerable daily work such as painting the accessories at regular intervals, brushing the elephants, washing the horses, etc. The liberty taken with the plain truth which is sometimes reproached to circus folk is often a consequence of the necessity of such operations. For instance, if I may strike an autobiographical note and refer to a time when I was a circus manager, one of our cats was a castrated male lion which consequently had lost his mane and looked like a female as long as he was facing the audience. We used to introduce him as a female in an act in which he was wrestling with his male trainer. This was presented as a side show and the display was visible from one side only. The point of distorting the plain truth was that this act was based upon the conjunction of danger and love. In fact the animal was playful and friendly, extremely fond of his trainer, and his natural aggressive drive had been considerably reduced by the surgery mentioned above. The misleading description I was giving of the situation reinforced the iconization process inasmuch as it oriented the perceptions of the viewers by suggesting a selection of the ambiguous features which were so transformed into relevant ones. In addition, as I was standing in front of the cage, I used to wave my hat whenever the animal accidentally turned his backside toward the public. This was designed to prevent anyone from *seeing* that the animal's anatomy was not exactly female-like. Such an element would have been *noise* with respect to the intended picture. I can now rationalize my behavior retroactively by saying that I was *iconizing* rather than lying.

We must also take into consideration the fact that the colorful drawings pictured in the posters and programs as well as in illustrated books educate the perception of the spectators and reinforce the iconic aspects of the circus visual "lexicon." As a result each term of the text is well defined. Its componential features are easily identified and it can appropriately express nonambiguous relations. The recurrence of such features or complementary ones which are present in other terms of the text have a functional redundancy. The relation posited between these terms are nonambiguous and the successive operations which are applied to them are displayed in ideal conditions for intelligibility, because the situation itself is an iconic sign.

Therefore, given the space and time setting which creates a disconnection with the continuum of reality and given the fact that each act constructs its own situation by formulating some relations between iconic signs and effectuates some operations upon these relations, it seems legitimate to consider that a circus act is a sort of *semiotic formula displaying a logical operation.* The signs are unequivocally manipulated in a primarily visual meta-discourse. I would like to say tentatively that they give semiosis to be enjoyed by giving meta-semiosis to be experienced and that this discourse is concretely rooted in what is the most significant in our environment, i.e., the constitutive rules of our cultural reality. There are indeed no legitimate reasons to assume that the enjoyment of logical operations is restricted to a handful of logicians; meta-discursive activities are a general property of mankind, as Lévi-Strauss's analysis of myths demonstrates, and even some animal species seem to engage in meta-communicative behavior (Bateson, 1955).

I would like now to illustrate this hypothesis with three brief examples. The first one is of a particular meta-communicative nature because it deals with some constitutive rules of the circus itself. We have pointed out earlier that the communication situation in the circus is nonsymmetrical and that the public response is strictly codified. Moreover, the space of the performance and the space of the audience are no less strictly differentiated. The following sequence, observed in Paris during the summer of 1974,* operates a controlled transgression of these two rules and by so doing makes them manifest. A musician-clown enters the ring playing a short tune on a saxophone and bows to the public which responds by moderate applause as it is an introductory sequence. An individual in the public keeps clapping his hands and shouting "Bravo! bravo!" after everybody has stopped. The musician-clown, who by the way is the authoritative character, turns toward him and engages in a dialogue aimed at reducing to silence this troublemaker. It becomes rapidly clear that the troublemaker is another clown and that this argument, based on the transgression of the complementary rule, constitutes a part of their act. I will not take into consideration here the actual content of their dialogue. It consists of an interesting game of words involving mainly pronouns and "yes" and "no" answers, with some instances of echolalia. Instead, I will focus our attention on the fact that by stealing the show and outsmarting his partner the transgressor manipulates the implicit rules not only by substituting a symmetrical relation for the complementary one but eventually by inverting the direction of the complementariness for the greatest enjoyment of the public. The next sequence in this act deals with the qualification of the audience as such because the rightfulness of the situation of the troublemaker

*Cirque Gruss. The clowns were Dédé and Alexis Gruss.

is questioned and he has to give evidence that he is a lawful spectator. Eventually, the clown leaves his seat and joins his partner in the ring *where he belongs*. It could be noted that practically every circus program includes an operation of this sort either in the form of a performer emerging from the audience or in the form of the activities of the circus being expanded into the audience beyond the boundaries of the ring. Such sequences are clearly of a meta-discursive nature.

The second and third examples will be from observations made in the summer of 1975 at the Circus Hall of Fame in Sarasota. Two clowns are engaged in a sort of magic competition, each one trying to outsmart his companion by performing a better trick. We shall examine here only one of these tricks. The clown takes a scarf, puts it on his half-raised left hand and says to the audience several times with insistence "Watch! watch! watch!" implying that something extraordinary is going to happen. Then suddenly changing his intonation slightly he says "Watch" again as he takes away the scarf and shows that he is holding a watch in his hand.

Clowns are primarily manipulators of cultural objects and of their constitutive rules, i.e., institutions, social behaviors, artifacts, words, etc. This example in its simplicity and effectiveness performs a meta-linguistic statement which amounts to a formulation of the context sensitiveness of morphemes as an identical morpheme takes successively two meanings through an instant transformation of the immediate context. We could even go further and say that it formulates a relation between identity and difference, identity having been transformed into alterity *by sleight of hand*.

Similar operations take place also in animal acts. In the same program, the announcer introduces the great equestrian Mrs. Canastrelli and her Lippizan named Enchanter. The lady trainer enters the ring with a small black pony, harnessed as a Viennese Lippizan, performing unmounted exercises of "basse et haute école." The announcer protests that this is not a Lippizan but to be sure he asks the pony "Are you a Lippizan?" By an emphatic movement of the head the pony answers "yes." The unbelieving announcer repeats the question. The answer is unmistakably "yes." Then the pony performs successively in order of increasing difficulty five different tricks identical to those performed by Lippizaner of the famed Austrian riding school. It takes a bow to the public and leaves the ring. This short act performs a micro-narrative, consisting in one transformation which could be formulated as follows: a non-Lippizan (because indeed the pony is characterized by two qualities, blackness and shortness, which are the contrary of the two specific qualities which define a Lippizan in the opinion of the public, whiteness and height), claims to be what he does not appear to be. In addition, it should be noted that on the one hand a Lippizan has such aristocratic connotations as pure breed, royal stables, historical significance, etc., and on the other hand the little black pony usually has in the circus code the status of transgressor possibly through an analogy with the black sheep. Nevertheless, our pony lives up to his claim and performs successfully the qualifying test. He exits with a hero status. There are at least two levels of the formulation of this act according to what value is ascribed to the difference: one is sociological, the other is logical. Either social inferiority is transformed into social equality (the little guy made it) or more abstractly, alterity has been transformed into identity. This is all the more significant if it is placed in the context of the general function of horses in the circus code. It seems that they are indeed the privileged logical tool to actualize the fundamental antinomy between collective and individualistic values. If one thinks of all the issues involving identity and alterity in society or small groups, one easily sees what content such a formulation articulates visually for the audience.

The choice of the circus as a semiotic investigation is not, on my part, only the effect of mania. It is conspicuous indeed that on the one hand this particular object confronts us with problems narrowly related to those encountered in all performing arts as well as in visual arts. I should add that I take art in the sense of technique and not in the sense of aesthetics. Moreover, it is impossible to elucidate ''what is going on in a circus act'' unless we relate its operations to the contextual culture in which it is observed. For any art, *to be is to be performed* and to perform necessarily refers us to the constitutive rules of a culture. I have tried to show that any given circus act can be construed as a formula displaying at least one operation effectuated on relations constitutive of its cultural context or even of its own code. This formula has the particularity of being expressed by modified natural and cultural objects and by context and actions which are performed in mutual relation. Therefore, it seems possible to contend that the circus as an institution produces particular sets of formulae which all have certain features in common. It should be possible to construct a meta-formula, a formula of the formulae, which would be an adequate description of the institution. It would simply make explicit what is implicit in the practice of the circus as performer or spectator. But this would be necessary if we want to enjoy the meta-enjoyment and fully understand our understanding of a circus act. So far I have devoted my efforts to local semi-formalizations with the help of semiotics. These tentative results it seems at least provide a guide to observation and a tentative meta-language which makes this something more than a mere exegesis.

REFERENCES

W. R. Ashby. 1957. *An Introduction to Cybernetics,* New York, Wiley and Sons.
G. Bateson. 1955. ''A Theory of Play and Fantasy,'' *A.P.A. Psychiatric Research Reports* II.

————. 1958. *Navem,* 2nd ed. Stanford, Stanford University Press.

P. Bouissac. 1973. *La Mesure des gestes,* The Hague-Paris, Mouton.

————. 1974. "Circus performances as Texts: a Matter of Poetic Competence," *Folklore Preprint Series* Vol. 2, No. 3, Bloomington, Indiana University.

————. 1976. *Circus and Culture, a Semiotic Approach,* Bloomington, Indiana University Press.

M. A. K. Halliday. 1971. "Linguistic Function and Literary Style" in S. Chatman (ed.) *Literary Style: a Symposium,* New York, Oxford University Press.

Z. Kovecses. 1975. Ms. "The Semiotics of Sports," LSA 1975 Linguistic Institute, Tampa.

C. Lévi-Strauss. 1958. *Anthropologie structurale,* Paris, Plon.

S. Marcus. 1970. *Poetica Matematică,* Bucharest, Editura Acad. Rep. Soc. Romania.

M. Mesnil. 1974. *Trois Essais sur la fête: du folklore à l'ethno-sémiotique,* Brussels, Editions de l'Université de Bruxelles.

I. Osolsobě. 1970. "Dramatic art as communication through communication about communication," *Otazky Divadla a Filmu-Theatralia et Cinematographica* I, Brno.

————. 1974. *Divaldo Které Mluví zpívá a Tančí* (The theatre which speaks, sings and dances) with a summary in English, Prague, Editio Supraphon.

J. R. Searle. 1969. *Speech Acts,* Cambridge University Press.

V. Voigt. 1974. Ms. "The Semiotics of May Day Study in Hungary," a paper read at the First Congress of the International Association of Semiotic Studies, Milan, June 2–6.

Semiotics and Culture

Erik Schwimmer

Historically, semiotics and anthropology have developed independently. Semiotics was first conceived by philosophers and linguists, without any thought of solving problems arising out of man's cultural diversity. Conversely, anthropology and the study of culture have very diffuse origins. Those who contributed to its earliest development were sometimes philosophers, sometimes historians, geographers, biologists as well as sociologists, psychologists, while we cannot ignore the important amateur contributions of travellers, poets, artists, missionaries. Perhaps the most illuminating recent interpretation of the history of anthropology is that of K.O.L. Burridge, *Encountering Aborigines* (1973), in which anthropology is shown to be essentially a product of theological and philosophical questioning arising out of the European renaissance. Burridge thus, very appropriately, describes anthropology in a manner consistent with anthropological method: not as an area of objective knowledge as much as a mental activity inaugurated by certain occidental cultures in a specific stage of their development, an activity serving purposes specific to those cultures and to a specific period in time.

I acknowledge gratefully the financial support of the Canada Council (a leave fellowship for 1975) which enabled me to do the research for this paper.

In considering the relationship between semiotics and culture, Burridge's book is thus a useful starting point. It traces the history of western man's reflections and investigations in one particular, but pivotal, cultural field, that of the Australian aborigines. It traces the history of the questions westerners asked about Aborigines, and the relation between these questions and the basic religio-philosophic and political issues of the centuries under consideration. For Burridge, this historically and environmentally determined set of questions (not a system but a set), this unorganized agglomeration, is the sum of anthropology.

Not all anthropologists would agree with such a view; nor do I entirely agree with it. Few, however, would fault Burridge's description of the inventory. It leaves open several controversial questions: does the inventory form a system? If so, is it basically biological? Basically semiotic? Or again, is it an ideological system, without a counterpart in objective reality?

Our first question should be: taking Burridge's inventory as our starting point, how is it related to semiotics? Secondly, if we survey the chief contemporary theories of anthropology, i.e., the various attempts inductively to make a system out of the inventory, or deductively to make a system using the inventory, how do such systems relate to semiotics? Our last, and perhaps most fruitful, question should be: what anthropological studies have opened up perspectives for semiotics?

Burridge (page 153) summarizes his inventory in a diagram in which anthropological activity comprises six stages of rationalization. At the first stage, we have those made by indigenous informants, who interconnect the inventory of actions and events of their own culture into a "homemade model." At the second stage, the outside observer "has attempted to understand them in the only terms he has available: his own." At the third stage, the two initial models are related together: homemade models and investigators' models are made to "interact and modify each other." When an anthropologist talks about his "data," it is the rationalizations of this third stage that he is, according to Burridge, mostly referring to.

When Burridge outlines the three further stages of anthropological activity, his presentation becomes a little more controversial as it is anchored in the British functionalist school of social anthropology—it bases its theories exclusively on descriptive generalization. It is not the purpose of the present paper to confront this method of analysis with the axiomatic theory of some schools of anthropology (cultural ecologists, followers of Popper) or the transformational theory of some other schools (French structuralists, some "cognitive" anthropologists). Let us therefore merely say that, by one method or another, the "data" have to be critically examined for coherence and intelligibility, after which they become the subject of a "monograph."[1] This monograph

Stages of Rationalization in Ethnography

First stage:
Indigenous informants report actions and events, and construct explanatory theories, and sometimes homemade models (to interrelate such theories): Text I
Second stage:
Initial theories of investigator: Text II
Hard data: observations and measurements by investigator: Text III
Third stage:
Synthesis of stages 1 and 2. Rationalization of the DATA as homemade models, investigator's models, and hard data "interact and modify each other"
Fourth stage:
Analysis of the DATA which are accounted for in the form of a MONOGRAPH, containing models which make the data coherent and intelligible, in the framework of a THEORY which might be, for instance: functionalist, or axiomatic, or transformational.
Fifth and Sixth Stages:

MODALITIES	METHODS	
	Fifth stage:	Sixth stage:
Functionalist:	Objectivization on the basis of descriptive generalizations	Mathematical formalization
Axiomatic:	Nomothetic theory	Evolutionary, etc., taxonomy
Transformational:	Elaboration of increasingly general paradigms by structural analysis	Synchronic and diachronic taxonomy

must then be subjected to comparison with other monographs so as to establish relationships between the various existing monographs and express understanding of cultural phenomena in a language that is apposite to a plurality of cultures, and—at least in principle—for all cultures. At some stage, such a language should be formalized and objectivized into a set of propositions about what Burridge calls "*a priori* relations, capable of containing all possible kinds of empirical relations." The approaches of the principal schools have been summarized in the accompanying diagram.

At what points in this enterprise do we find a relation with semiotics? Burridge's first two stages—the construction of the homemade and the investigator's models—are comparable to the starting point of a semiotic investigation, for both are in fact largely "texts." The basis of the homemade model is a text written down, ideally, at the dictation of an indigenous informant, and the investigator's model is based on his notebook of observations. The construction of the homemade model out of informants' verbal statements is fundamentally a semantic exercise. The notebook will normally also contain a list of events recorded, objects described, and hypotheses by the field worker as to relationships between statements, events, and objects. Such hypotheses often lead to the recording of further statements, events, and objects, and notebooks should ideally indicate the logic of the investigation. One of the characteristics peculiar to such ethnographic texts is the intertwining of empirical and logical elements. From one viewpoint, informants' statements and investigator's observations are a disconnected set of notes; from another they are full of unstated logical presuppositions, as the statements are in general answers to questions asked (explicitly or implicitly) by the investigator. The observations are likewise answers to unstated questions, many of which are to be found in works of anthropological theory, or even in fieldwork manuals. The investigator's notebooks, therefore, are texts suitable for semiotic analysis, and one may say that when Burridge talks of an investigator's "model," he assumes that the investigator has carried on his own semiotic analysis on the text to obtain his model.

By thus explaining the anthropologist's fieldwork activity to semioticists, I am glossing over the unsystematic nature of most notebooks anthropologists have actually compiled. Partly they are unsystematic, no doubt, because fieldwork is a taxing activity and in practice the ethnographer has little time to think about academic niceties while he is recording data in the field. Partly also, they are unsystematic because it is only in the last few years that anthropologists have been able to look upon their fieldwork activity from an explicitly semiotic point of view. Indeed, this may have been an innovation of the ethnoscientists and cognitive anthropologists of the 1960s.[2] Even these last mentioned did not have the benefit of our present knowledge of semiotics; if we regard as semiotics only those operations explicitly derivable from Peirce or Saussure, there is little "semiotics" in anthropology: it developed independently.[3]

A very rigorous distinction must always be made, in analysis, between informants' statements and investigator's observations. The former are analyzable semantically—they are linguistic phenomena—whereas the latter, insofar as they describe actions and events, are analyzable in parts as semiotic texts. They have, however, a further dimension, namely a totally objective quality independent of the viewpoint of the investigator. If I describe, for instance, material culture, supporting my description by diagrams and photographs, and by measurements made with the aid of instruments, observer's bias may for practical purposes be disregarded. Similarly, even in the description of events certain elements must be regarded as totally objective (timing, for instance, if I look at my watch).

Summarizing, we may say that in the first two stages of rationalization, we find semantic analysis of informants' texts and semiotic analysis of investigators' texts, but we must recognize that texts of the latter type contain many statements which are, at least in principle, unquestionable objective records about the culture under investigation. One may add that unless many such statements were recorded, the field worker would not be recognized as an anthropologist by his colleagues, and if he was trying to write a doctoral thesis, he might well fail his thesis examination because of deficiencies in his "data." I am making this point in order to stress that a certain kind of objectivity is a strict formal requirement for entry into the profession, and therefore an integral part of the discipline of anthropology. This objectivity aspect is as important in anthropology as in medical semiotics where Shands (1975) uses the term "symptom" for informant's (patient's) statement and "sign" for objective facts about the patient's condition. In contrast, a purely semiotic investigation of the field-notes (in terms of Eco's semiotic theory) could well be made—could be made *just* as well—if there was not a single objective fact in the notebook.

The difference between semiotics and anthropology becomes clearer in what Burridge calls the third stage of rationalization, in which the homemade and the investigator's models are made to "interact and modify each other." For it is at this stage that we notice that there are discrepancies between informants' statements and our objective measurements. Informants may state some rule of behavior which is often contravened in our record of events, or there may be conflicts in descriptions of the same events, offered by different informants. Our demographic data, our physical measurements, our seemingly unequivocal observations may call into question elements of the informants' model, while again the informants' model may lead us to question passages in our field record. Very often, the discrepancy is not merely due to error, but to our imperfect understanding either of events or of informants' statements. At this third stage, therefore, an important semantic and semiotic activity is taking place, namely the critical examination of certain indigenous concepts when the investigator finds inconsistencies in his record due to his limited understanding of such concepts; and of explanations of behavior when these do not account for the established facts. At the same time, however, the third stage of rationalization does much to refine the objective records, the degree of conformity of the records to the facts about the culture. Very often, at this stage, discrepancies are discovered which require the systematic collection of a very objective type of data to test hypotheses. Thus, in my own investigation of plant emblems among the Orokaiva, I found that my theory about them did not explain the facts. I decided, in order to clarify the situation, that I should ask every adult in the village to give me a complete list of his/her plant emblems and of the parental plant emblems, including the third generation as well wherever possible. There is no doubt that I thus increased the degree of objectivity of my investigation. One cannot collect every fact imaginable, but one has to collect facts in an area of confusion as long as there is any chance that further facts will lessen that confusion. Again, this objectivizing activity is not part of a strictly semiotic investigation; it has to do with the descriptive requirements of a kind of natural science.

When we come to the establishment of coherence and intelligibility required in an anthropological monograph, we find that the culture we attempt to describe has to be interpreted simultaneously in two seemingly contradictory ways: as a system of signs, intelligible in its conceptual coherence, and at the same time as a viable economic, political, and social system, with contradictions which are managed by an appropriate superstructure. This kind of interdependence is formulated differently by the various schools of anthropology, but there will be little disagreement that anthropological intelligibility in principle incorporates physical as well as mental elements. The cultural ecology school and some narrowly Marxist anthropologists might hold that the mental is always and everywhere an epiphenomenon of the physical, but even so both kinds of elements (whatever their relationship) form an integral part of their work.[4]

Whether there are any recognized schools of anthropology who teach, or have ever taught, that mental elements in culture, i.e., systems of signs, determine its techno-economic infrastructure is most doubtful. Marvin Harris imputed such a viewpoint to Lévi-Strauss, and Robert Murphy (1972) appears to support such an imputation. For anyone who has taken a look at what the French structuralists are actually doing in anthropology, and who has observed the great similarity between their practical preoccupations and those of their colleagues across the Channel, the Harris-Murphy account of French "mentalism" and "Hegelianism" is almost a fairy tale. There is today very little difference between the French and British way of collecting field data, in other words their operations in what Burridge calls the first three stages of rationalization. These schools view infrastructure as an integral part of the data that have to be made intelligible and coherent in the preparation of monographs.

A more subtle question, relating to "mentalism," might be raised in connection with some highly important American schools of anthropology, described variously as ethnoscience, cognitive anthropology, the new ethnography, or ethnography of communication. It is these schools that led Harris to give a central position to a distinction between the "etic" and "emic" study of culture, a distinction which was developed within the ethnoscience school itself, after a linguistic analogy (cf. Pike 1966). I do not myself think that the "etic"-"emic" distinction was intended by the ethnoscience school as the basis of any general theory of culture; their dominant preoccupation was plainly methodological.

The problem they raised is one which semioticists will have no difficulty in understanding. It is quite independent from any general question as to whether we may equate culture with semiotics, in other words, whether culture can be exhaustively described as essentially reducible to a system of signs. We have already seen that anthropologists do not normally work on such an assumption. If therefore Frake, Conklin, Lounsbury, Burling, Metzger held such a view it would have been somewhat revolutionary. Certainly nobody would have taken notice unless they had clearly stated it.

What they did say, and in much detail, was that anthropological fieldwork was greatly deficient in methodology. While they did not reduce anthropology explicitly or implicitly to semiotics, they did emphasize that semiotics is an important component of anthropology, i.e., that all field workers, as part of their task, are preoccupied with the analysis of semiotic domains in culture. Yet this tended to be done with variable degrees of rigor. Even British anthropologists of the Oxford school, traditionally most precise in the delineation of indigenous systems of thought, tended to think of the "understanding" or "translating" of such systems in anthropological terms as an art rather than a science. I doubt whether the work of the various schools of the new American ethnography was essentially better than that of the Oxford school, but it was certainly more systematic in describing its method, hence more "teachable" under the conditions of the American university system. Typical examples of "new ethnography" are analyses of color categories, "categories of eating," the diagnosis of disease, the use of kinship terminology. Rules for the conduct of specific rituals such as weddings or offerings to supernaturals were painstakingly elicited and checked against behavior by a systematic question and answer method. The methods of eliciting data and analyzing the resulting texts were basically semiotic. Yet these practitioners could not and would not claim that they were thus analyzing the whole of culture; their method applied only to specific domains.

Certain theoreticians belonging to this school, of whom I would mention especially Goodenough (1970) and Keesing (1971), went one step further and believed that culture could be equated to a summation of a large but finite number of semiotic domains. As they argued, the domains can be analyzed so as to intersect, or in practice always do intersect, so that as the number of domains increases, and especially if one chooses the domains with such intersections in view, finally somehow the whole of culture can be accounted for. I must confess that such a mechanical construction of culture out of semiotic domains feels to me like a *deus ex machina* theory; I would not be inclined to defend it against Marvin Harris' assaults.

By no means all ethnoscience practitioners have followed the lines of Goodenough and Keesing; I shall summarize their various attempts below. Thus Berlin (1970, 1971) attempted no less than "a universalist-evolutionary approach to ethnographic semantics.'' Having analyzed a specific semiotic domain (plant taxonomies) in various cultures, he posited some universal characteristics of plant taxonomies and some variations that would hold universally in accordance with various stages of evolution. I have seen one detailed test of the theory, in some British Columbia Indian cultures, and this test did not support the theory very well (Nancy Turner, n.d.). Nonetheless, it is clear that once semiotic domains have been analyzed (which is necessarily done by "emic" methods), the resulting model can serve almost any theory of culture the investigator happens to hold. In anthropology, semiotic analysis is a useful, often indispensable, method, but it does not presuppose or entail any specific theory of culture.

We have seen that there is little support for a reduction of anthropology to a domain of semiotics. It is true that Lévi-Strauss, in 1960, made a suggestion to this effect, building on an earlier stray remark by Saussure (Lévi-Strauss 1973: chap. I), but as over the last decade or so semiotics developed in France as a serious discipline (dominated by figures like Greimas, Barthes, Kristeva), it soon became clear that the approaches were fundamentally different. As Lévi-Strauss was, during the 1960s, mainly preoccupied with myth analysis (Lévi-Strauss 1964, 1966, 1968, 1971), it is there that we can see the diverging of the paths, especially with regard to the treatment of text corpora. While Greimas (1970), Bremond (1973), and the others analyzed their texts purely from evidence internal to the closed corpora, using ideally all the evidence the corpora contained, Lévi-Strauss and others of his school (as well as Hymes [1971] and a few others in the United States) introduced issues of culture history, ecology, social relations, establishing contradictions an ethnologist would find in the cultures. Such contradictions would enter freely into the interpretation of the texts. Clearly Greimas and Lévi-Strauss have entirely different ideas as to the kind of intelligibility that should be produced by analysis.[5] It seems therefore most convenient to abandon Lévi-Strauss's earlier suggestion and distinguish between anthropological intelligibility (as in Lévi-Strauss) and semiotic intelligibility (as in Greimas).

One might conceivably argue that one ought to proceed in steps by first analyzing texts by purely semiotic techniques, and then try a later stage to clarify why a particular culture, at a particular point in time, elaborated the system we have established by semiotic analysis. Thus one could divide neatly into a semiotic and a purely anthropological stage of a cultural investigation. In practice, however, it does not generally happen that purely semiotic techniques make even a specific domain of culture intelligible as a system.

Thus, Bulmer found in an ethnozoological study of the Karam of New Guinea (1967) that the carefully elicited Karam rules for the classification of animals did not predict the primary taxon in which an important game animal, the cassowary, should be included. The only way in which this anomaly could be made intelligible was by introducing data on the ecological, social, economic, and ritual levels of the culture. The symbol "cassowary" is an integral part of many Karam semiotic domains, and its position in one domain is determined in part by its position in the others. Certainly one can start in one domain, but ultimately the anthropologist cannot abandon his role of detective, following whatever clues, in any cultural domain, will clear up the problems raised by anomalies.

This brings us to the key question how we can conceive of the relationship of semiotic domains and culture. I have already referred to the cultural ecology school which views meaning as produced, fully and directly, by ecological and technological factors. In other words, in that school of anthropology it is not necessary to inquire how people think about what they do, as their actions, and their thoughts as well, are determined by ecological and technological factors alone. Clearly, this kind of theory is non-falsifiable as it is always possible to construct some techno-ecological explanation to account for any action. We need not consider it further here, as the cultural ecology school places semiotics outside the field of anthropology, except insofar as the production of meaning (ideology) can be apparently accounted for by attaching to it some techno-ecological explanation.

Other anthropological schools have rarely, whatever their theories, in practice managed to avoid semiotic analysis, and some have explicitly advocated it, though mostly not as the ultimate objective of their discipline. A crucial question that concerned anthropologists was how they should regard indigenous informants' statements of "belief." One of the great ancestors of social and cultural anthropology, Tylor, held that "the beliefs of savages are the result of attempts to *understand* natural facts." This view implied that the analysis of indigenous statements of such beliefs would yield valuable insight. Tylor's view led to several decades of anthropology during which vast quantities of such statements of belief were collected, compared, compiled, and organized in works, the most famous of which has remained Frazer's *Golden Bough*.

The British functionalist school was a reaction to this kind of exegesis. Radcliffe Brown, its chief theoretician, compared the mental processes underlying indigenous statements of belief to "those that are found in dreams and in art" (1933). Hence, he did not believe that by analyzing them he would learn anything about social reality, except inasmuch as myths provide "charters" for social action. Thus, functionalists considered it fruitless to ask what a myth meant, but useful to recognize what institution it justified, legitimized, was a "charter" for. If British social anthropologists have made a considerable contribution to our understanding of the "semiotics" of culture—and I think they have—it is because they collected excellent, very detailed data on social institutions, and their monographs sought to present these coherently and intelligibly. In constructing models of the charters of social institutions, they in practice analyzed semiotic domains, with punctilious attention to linguistic aspects and to comprehensive coverage of the domains. If this is true for Malinowski and Firth,[6] and even for Radcliffe Brown, as Leach has shown in a recent essay (1971), it is even more true for later British social anthropologists such as Fortes and Goody, and for the Oxford school of anthropology.

Fortes's essay on Oedipus and Job (1959) is a good example of the way the British school both contributed to and took its distance from semiotic analysis. The essay reduces Tale religious thought to two basic contradictory statements: (1) we are punished because we are guilty; (2) we are punished even though we are innocent. This reduction is achieved after systematic semiotic analysis of a vast body of data. But then these findings are related to Fortes's analysis of Tale kinship—his theory of "complementary filiation." According to this theory, Tale society is organized around a basic contradiction between agnatic and uterine power. This contradiction between actual sources of power is expressed by a contradiction between sources of misfortune. But in the end, Fortes argues, the contradictions are necessary for the maintenance of and the functioning of Tale society. It is to make this, to him, basic point that he engages in his brilliant semiotic exercise. The point I wish to make is that though Fortes does not aim at semiotic analysis, he is very good at it, and some readers like myself find his analysis far more exciting than the conclusion to which it leads him.

The Oxford school is less concerned with the explanation of the functioning and maintenance of society and more programmatic about its semiotic objectives. Evans Pritchard proposed a theory according to which anthropology is essentially "translation," by which he meant that the field worker's data are cast essentially in the conceptual system of the culture under study (as perceived by the investigator), and the task of analysis (leading to the "monograph") consists in translating this conceptual system into a language comprehensible to a reader of a different (viz., the scientist's) cultural background. This seems, on the surface, a purely semantic activity; or rather, insofar as the field worker's data are records of indigenous behavior as well as verbal statements, a semiotic activity. But we cannot ignore a substratum of functional theory even in the works of the Oxford school: Evans Pritchard's works about ecology, politics, kinship, and religion are interconnected by the assumption that each kind of institution serves the others, is determined by the others in its form and content. The work of translation to some extent serves the purpose of demonstrating this system of interrelations.

Yet it is significant that Evans Pritchard and his school[7] placed anthropology among the humanities rather than the (social or other) sciences. The coherence and intelligibility this school pursued was essentially of an historiographical type. While functionalism, in its classical form, viewed the social system after the analogy of a biological organism, the Oxford school—and in a different way, perhaps also the American anthropologists Kroeber and Eggan—viewed it as a coherent intelligible formation produced in an environmental and historical context, and as such approachable only as unique and incomparable (except insofar as other such formations could be brought into an environmental and historical relation to it).

We are thus concerned not merely with one atemporal semiotic system (as exemplified by Evans Pritchard's books about the Nuer [1940, 1951, 1965]) but with the transformations of such a system over time, as exemplified by Evans Pritchard's essays about the Azande and his book about the Sanusi of Cyrenaica (1949), and by Burridge's books about millennial movements. Burridge's views about anthropological theory, discussed in the opening pages of this essay, are another instance of the same kind of transformational model.

Not too far removed from this Oxford school are the theories of those who view culture as equivalent to information. This view is exemplified by the work of Gregory Bateson and by that of Claude Lévi-Strauss and his followers. While Lévi-Strauss in the end has become most fully identified with this type of theory, we must not forget that Bateson was the first to see its possibilities.

In his monograph about the Iatmul (*Naven,* 1936), he divided his analysis into two aspects of culture he called ethos and eidos. Ethos is defined as "a culturally standardized system of organization of the instincts and emotions of individuals" and eidos as "a standardization of the cognitive aspects of the personality of individuals." Eidos is cognitive organization which pervades every aspect of the culture and gives support to every cultural activity. In later works, Bateson referred to eidos as a "codification system," organized by contradictions in the culture by a process to which Bateson gave the name "schismogenesis." For Bateson (1966, 1972), the "codification system" *is* the culture.

If the analysis of a culture can be reduced to analyzing the codification system, then indeed it almost seems that anthropology becomes a purely semiotic activity. Yet the test for such a proposition does not lie only in Bateson's own later studies in psychiatry and metacommunication, but also in ethnographic work, viz., in the book *Naven* itself. From an anthropological viewpoint, the most vital concept in this book is *schismogenesis,* i.e., the location of a basic contradiction in the social system, as the various attitudes a man develops towards his maternal kin are not logically reconcilable. They must be acted out in ritual or neutralized in the fantasy world of myth. Thus *Naven* is not merely concerned with codification, but also with the ways man finds for coping with the basic contradictions in his life. And these contradictions arise, as Bateson shows very well, in all aspects of life, including the economic and sociological as well as the developmental. Thus, Bateson has not genuinely eliminated infrastructure from the study of culture. He has merely shifted infrastructure to the field of information itself, mapping out an "ecology of mind" and thus postulating a natural basis for symbolism. There is no theoretical charter for excluding infrastructure from the study of schismogenesis.

Both Bateson and Lévi-Strauss, in studying culture as an information system, took a deliberate step away from empirical reality by concentrating on discontinuities in culture. Both Bateson's schismogenesis and Lévi-Strauss' binary oppositions reduce the fluidities and continuities of everyday life into what one may call codable units, i.e., structures of which the elements are constituted by a series of either/or choices. The theory that culture is information really amounts to a proposition that culture is codable by some such method. I do not think that it is essential to the theory that the oppositions should be *binary;* there are many other possible ways of constructing a code—and Lévi-Strauss has used them too, e.g., triads, Kleinian groups, in *Mythologiques* (esp. 1968, 1971)—but binaries are the simplest form, and very pervasive in culture.

From a purely methodological viewpoint, it is not the use of binary oppositions and other oppositions that set Lévi-Strauss apart from many other contemporary anthropologists. More distinctive is his use of a structuralist comparative method, by the construction of families of models known as combinatories. The argument, put briefly, is that any given body of anthropological data is codable in many different ways. In principle, there is no way of deciding what is the "right" or "wrong" coding. In practice, three kinds of verification are possible. One may collect further data, and see whether they are consistent with the various codings that have been suggested. One may test the various codings for internal logical consistency, often revealing "anomalies" (such as in Bulmer's instance of the cassowary referred to above) and thus opening up further areas of empirical investigation. Finally, and most importantly, one may test the codings—which, it should be remembered, are all "emic," i.e., expressed in terms of indigenous categories of thought—on some assumption that they correspond to something in objective reality.

It is this third kind of verification that has made Lévi-Strauss a very controversial figure. The theoretical justification for it is highly complex and has been best analyzed, in my opinion, by Valerio Valeri in a little-known essay. Valeri explains: "Social reality always implies organization: it is a mediated system of signs. And signs can function in a communication system only insofar as they are finite in number. Otherwise, we could not have communication which is based on combination and recurrence: on repeatability as against unrepeatability, which is incommunicable" (1970:355). To put it briefly, social reality, like the natural world, is the product of a limited number of combinations, regulated by a code. The systems of thought reconstructed by anthropologists form part of this basic "combinatory" and in this sense have objective reality.

But as so many codings of any body of data are possible, how can we decide which of them have this objective quality and which may be purely subjective, such as those (to refer back to Radcliffe Brown) "found in dreams and in art"? A coding is objectively true only insofar as it can be shown to be part of the basic combinatory of social reality.

How can this ever be shown? First of all, it can never be completely shown. Thus, no model ever constructed by an anthropologist can be claimed to correspond completely to social reality. This is a qualification of the highest importance; it puts Lévi-Strauss in a category apart from the phenomenologists. But the truth of a coding can be partially tested by methods of "internal" and "external" comparison. If it can be shown that one particular coding of a cultural domain stands in a relation of transformation to models of other domains of the same culture, so that the models of all the domains form, as it were, a "family of models" between which relations of transformation hold, then such a coding is in principle to be preferred to a coding that seems unrelated to other domains in the culture. This assumption is not entirely an invention of Lévi-Strauss; we find it also in Ruth Benedict's theory of "patterns of culture." But Lévi-Strauss tends to give primacy to those levels of culture Marxists would call "infrastructure," as generating basic contradictions which are apt to reverberate on other levels, even though we cannot—in his view—assume *a priori* that they will do so.[8] We can apply the same method to external comparisons, i.e., we can compare the coding of a domain in one culture with codings of the same domain in other cultures, starting with those which are geographically contiguous or historically related, but not necessarily confining ourselves to these. Where geographic and historical relations exist, few anthropologists will dispute the aptness of believing that a coding which emphasizes the relations existing within a culture area is in principle more credible than a coding totally obscuring such relations. Normally, the relations that are found are not of identity but of transformation, and such transformation can in principle be historically reconstructed. As soon as we extend the method beyond this, we have to rely on a theory such as that whereby intellectual categories are based on the natural structure of perceptive categories, i.e., their aesthetics.

As Valeri interprets Lévi-Strauss, "Logic is based on aesthetics, and aesthetics on properties of physical nature," such as for instance the neurophysiology of the brain. Such a theory would justify using the structural comparative method irrespective of what the geographical and historical distance between different cultures may be.

I do not wish to examine this theory critically, as it has never really been systematically presented by Lévi-Strauss himself. It is a reconstruction by Valeri, and by others, and I assume that if Lévi-Strauss attached importance to such reasoning, he could have developed it more fully in his own writings.

Mercifully, Lévi-Strauss has not stretched it to its limits: he works preferably within a "combinatory" where historical or geographical relations can be assumed, and does not rely for essential demonstrations on the more remote relations he has sometimes explored. In practice it is unimportant to an anthropologist whether symbolism has a natural basis. If in the analysis of New Guinean mythology, someone suggests to me that a South American or Polynesian parallel may help me to interpret a particular myth, I do not reverently accept such a suggestion because of any supposed unity of mankind; nor do I throw it out as anathema. If the suggestion helps me to interpret a considerable body of New Guinean myths, and if that interpretation can be strongly corroborated from data internal to my culture area, I would call it helpful. If I find that numerous suggestions, say from Polynesian sources, are helpful in Melanesia, then this merely leads me to the thought that we ought to try finding relations between the culture areas of Melanesia and Polynesia. The theory of the unity of mankind does not provide me with a shortcut in empirical research. It is merely a speculation arising out of striking similarities in systems of thought of widely separated peoples. Though an anthropologist may sometimes give himself over to such speculation, he should not let it interfere with his work, which requires the analysis of diversity as well as similarity.

The use of "combinatories" is one of the most sophisticated methods in anthropology, where the relationship with semiotics is evident. It is not really, as some have assumed, merely an extension of Jakobsonian linguistics to the field of culture, but is closer to the transformationalism of Lamb and—with important reservations—that of Chomsky. The main difference between

Lévi-Strauss and Chomsky, as I understand it, is that the latter believes in a method of discovering a universal "deep" structure by examining one particular language, whereas Lévi-Strauss uses a comparative method in which the "depth" of the structures discovered increases as the scope of the investigation spreads out over an increasing number of cultures. A "combinatory" covering only South and North America would therefore be less "deep" than a combinatory that would account for, say, Oceanic or European data as well. The difference in approach between the two scholars is directly related to their ideas as to the kind of knowledge provided by their investigations. Chomsky believes he can obtain exhaustive knowledge of at least one language, his own, whereas Lévi-Strauss distrusts the objectivity an anthropologist would achieve in studying his own culture; and as for other cultures, knowledge is always bound to remain very fragmentary, just like the knowledge of an astronomer of other planets.

I have dwelt on French structuralism at some length because of its complexity, but must refer also to highly important American schools of anthropology deeply concerned with semiotics. These schools have been unanimous in rejecting Lévi-Strauss's use of combinatories. They have usually not attempted to develop new methods of external intercultural comparison.

The most interesting leading figures, such as Clifford Geertz, David M. Schneider, and Victor Turner, have tended to work intensively in single cultures and relate their results directly to universal propositions. They have not been specifically concerned with cultural diversity as an epistemological tool for discovering the nature of man. Geertz, in his theoretical statements, tends to relate cultural symbols to institutions which in turn are related to ecological variables (as in his work on "agricultural involution"). In that respect, little would seem to divide him from the British Oxford school, but he relies far more on psychological explanations (of religion, etc.), and on information theory (like Bateson's idea of *eidos*). He does not appear to view his sophisticated analysis of symbolic action as an end in itself, but as a necessary preliminary to the analysis of aspects of social life where their role is important. When he calls his concept of culture "essentially a semiotic one" (1973) he seems to ignore much of his own previous work, or else may be using the term "essentially" a little loosely.[9]

Both Schneider and Turner have more specifically used a philosophical kind of psychological explanation as a basis for their theoretical work, thus replacing Lévi-Strauss' concept of "combinatories" by a rival explanatory construct. At first sight, we find little to choose between their claim that sentiment logically precedes structure and Lévi-Strauss' argument, presented in attempted rebuttal (1971), that structure or cognition precedes sentiment. Precedence depends, of course, on the nature of the question under investigation. Symbols derive patently both from sentiments and from cognitive structure. Yet, it is clear that, having rejected the notion of combinatories, Schneider and Turner had to put something in their place, unless they were to remain imprisoned in the exegesis of semiotic domains in specific cultures. When they speak of sentiments, it is because certain experiences of the nuclear family are patently universal, hence objective facts usable in the interpretation of symbols in any culture.

Schneider's work on kinship (see esp. Schneider 1967, 1968, 1972) and Turner's on ritual (see esp. 1964, 1967 a b, 1969, 1971, 1973) consists, in practice, largely of a kind of semiotic analysis of unusual thoroughness, very systematic in identifying the different levels of meaning. But like other anthropologists, they seek an anchor in some kind of objectivity, a direct relation to the referent; the reality of the culture under consideration. Schneider has described his approach as one of "psychological reductionism"; moreover, he has argued that Lévi-Strauss is likewise a psychological reductionist inasmuch as he, too, rests his analysis not infrequently on certain universal experiences of the nuclear family. We cannot inquire here into the justice of this claim, nor into the question whether, theoretically, the method of "combinatories" is possible in the absence of "psychological reduction." All that concerns us is that such reduction is basically a device for giving anthropology a dimension of objectivity in its analysis of symbol systems.

I have called the psychology of Geertz, Schneider, and Turner a "philosophical psychology." I intended to suggest by this that it is not based on any scientific school of psychology but on general psychological assumptions about human nature. Other anthropologists, of course, have based their work on more specific theories of behavioral evolution, structure of the personality, perception, cognition, and so forth.[10] Piaget has provided a "genetic structuralist" model, on a psychological basis, which emphasizes the importance of the transformation of structures over time. In anthropology, one of its most interesting products has been the work of Bourdieu (1972) based on fieldwork among the Berber, specifically his essays on the sense of honor, the house as a reversed model of the universe, and patrilineal parallel cousin marriage. The emphasis on process in these basically structuralist investigations makes them akin to the "post-structural" movement now current at Oxford University.[11]

In this survey of different ways of utilizing semiotic methods for analyzing cultures, I have left out many highly important figures merely because their methodology and theory have to be viewed as an amalgam or synthesis of several directions I have already summarized. Edmund Leach and Rodney Needham are among them; they have affinities with the various British schools mentioned as well as with Lévi-Straussian structuralism. They also exemplify one kind of semiotics now beginning to become important in anthropology, namely that based on the philosophical investigations of Wittgenstein.[12]

We must finally consider the Marxist critique of the various methods whereby anthropologists have tried to relate semiotics to natural science. Classical anthropological analysis fully includes the concept that whatever statements informants make about their social or religious system or about the meaning of symbols are determined by the informants' own best interests whether as individuals or as members of certain families or certain communities (as opposed to others). Raymond Firth has gone to the trouble of devoting an entire book to show the ideological basis of Tikopian myths in terms of clan interests (1967). If Lévi-Strauss believes that symbolism has a natural basis; he recognizes also as a matter of course that it is continually manipulated for ideological purposes.

The Marxist critique arises out of the argument that if infrastructure, in the last instance, determines history, then it also determines, in the last instance, the formation of symbol systems. In that case, symbol systems have meaning only insofar as they are seen as part of a total dialectical system related to infrastructure, or—to use Marxist terminology—if they are "totalized." Now we have seen that all anthropologists tend to engage in devices of "totalization," but that they do not all start from modes of production as explanatory constructs "in the last instance."

Can we start on a Marxist basis and still inquire into the meaning of symbol systems in the cultures anthropologists study? Several French anthropologists have tried it, relying for their theoretical underpinning on philosophers such as Althusser, Maurice Godelier (1967, 1973) being perhaps the best known of these. Godelier has formulated a theory of economic anthropology which avoids the snares of being entirely "emic" or substantivist, and also of being entirely "etic" or formalist. He tends to obtain interesting semiotic analysis of the "emics" of economic systems while placing these in a vaster "etic" evolutionary scheme, based on varieties in modes of production. This method is supported by an argument whereby in non-literate societies the mode of production is such as to draw various other levels of structure (kinship, politics, religion) into the sphere of infrastructure from which they became separated during later evolutionary stages.

In practice, certain American anthropologists such as Sahlins (1972) and Murra (1972–1974) work along lines very similar to Godelier, though they have not felt the need to reconcile what they do with Marxist doctrine.

After this brief survey, can we say what perspectives anthropology and semiotics have opened up for each other? I think it will be clear that the contemporary anthropologist engages in semiotics a good deal of the time. It will also be clear that he does not do so very systematically. Finally it is clear that all anthropological schools have reasons why their study is not reducible to semiotics, but the reasons are all different and agree in nothing except a desire to totalize.

Umberto Eco (1972) has drawn a neat distinction between what semioticists do with texts, and what biologists (natural scientists) do with the reality to which the texts refer.[13] I have tried to show that Eco's argument cuts through the middle of anthropology, dismembering the subject into biology and semiotics, while rejecting as a hopeless enterprise the attempt to relate them together. My survey has shown that if the enterprise is not wholly hopeless, it is very nearly so; we must therefore answer Eco with caution.

We have seen, in this essay, that numerous anthropological schools, though starting their investigations from the viewpoint of basically biological kinds of theory, were forced to build into their methodological equipment ever more sophisticated semiotic techniques. Conversely, those who started off with a basically semiotic or linguistic viewpoint, such as sociolinguists, cognitive anthropologists, ethnoscientists, in order to work on the "ethnography of communication," have tended to become increasingly enmeshed in the kind of anomalies of which we saw one example when discussing Bulmer's cassowary.[14]

Veron (1973) has put forward a similar argument about the relations between linguistics and sociology: both disciplines have the tendency to formulate fundamental problems that can be resolved only by the other. He asked how such questions, that seem to circulate by being tossed from the one discipline to the other, can ever be satisfactorily dealt with. They can be dealt with only in a universe of discourse of greater generality that would be simultaneously semiotic and biological. Veron finds this universe of discourse in what he terms "ideology"—the "social production of meaning."

Though Veron elaborated this concept in a later paper (1974), it remains somewhat sketchy from the viewpoint of the social sciences. It may be usefully supplemented by a recent work by the sociologist Fernand Dumont (1974) who proposes a science of ideology, in which ideologies may be studied from two conflicting viewpoints: (a) from an objective natural-science viewpoint, as a "residue" from infrastructure; or (b) from the viewpoint of the subject, a construction of a meaningful ideational schema by which external world and self-identity are structured. He described these conflicting viewpoints as "un conflit des pratiques de l'interprétation: ce pourrait bien être, à tout prendre, une définition opératoire de la société, une définition de l'objet de la sociologie" (1974:171).

Such views of the concept *ideology* differ considerably from those proposed by Hjelmslev (1963) and Barthes (1964), who relegate ideology to a secondary "connotative" level of meaning, separable from a "denotative" level. Whether we prefer to follow Veron and Dumont or Hjelmslev and Barthes depends on our whole philosophy of society, but it seems to me also that the Hjelmslev-Barthes approach would lead the field anthropologist into serious practical difficulties. When I analyzed four explanations offered by the Orokaiva tribe of the Northern District of Papua to account for a disastrous volcanic eruption, I discovered (Schwimmer 1975b) that, in fact, the distinction between denotation and connotation was hard to make: denotation (objective explanation of the phenomena) is inseparable from connotation (ideological claims of tribal superiority and the like). All one could say is that some explanations the Orokaiva offered did greater violence to facts they ought to have known than did others; in other words, some explanations were more scientifically credible; but this is not quite the distinction suggested by Hjelmslev.

In the first part of the present paper we found that Burridge, in effect, treated the discipline of anthropology entirely as an historical phenomenon. In the second part of the paper I attempted to show that this history pertains partly to semiotics, partly to various forms of "totalization." I am now arguing that these two constituents of the discipline can cohere only if we view anthropology as a study of processes of social production of meaning. Thus, the study of infrastructure is relevant to anthropology insofar as infrastructure produces meaning; and meaning systems are relevant insofar as they are related to social production.[15]

This view, if applied to the *history* of anthropology, leads directly to Burridge's implication that the discipline's development is inseparable from the reflections arising out of colonial relationships entered upon by European powers. When seeking the "meaning" of anthropology, Burridge actually made it manifest by presenting it as a process of social production. Is there any more satisfactory way of saying what anthropology means? Certainly, other theorists have been far more ambitious than Burridge; they have tried to provide anthropology with an *ontological* meaning, as though it were supposed to answer the question: What is man? But in making such ambitious attempts they failed to recognize that the question "What is man?" has no anthropological meaning, unless we also answer with the retort: Why do you ask that question?

Thus we are led back to the recognition that anthropology is an ideological science, in the sense of Veron and Dumont. It contains within it both semiotics and biology. A very specific example of the problems with which an ideological science can deal is offered by the many excellent studies made of religious movements over the last two decades. They contain a fine analysis of the systems of "meaning," the doctrines, taught by the various movements involved; thus, they depend on semiotic techniques. But at the same time, they deal with objective reality insofar as it produced the movements—real economic and political contradictions, in a framework of social relations. They deal with structural transformations, and with the real genesis of these transformations. But they do not become "nomothetic" except in respect of methodology or epistemology: anthropology is in fact a non-science, except insofar as it reflects upon the ideological production of meaning.

It is for semioticists to say whether this makes anthropology generically different from other domains in semiotics, or generically the same.

NOTES

1. For a recent "structuralist" view of the high importance of "monographs," see Lévi-Strauss 1975.

2. The "ethnoscience" school was concerned with the meticulous establishment of rules of culturally appropriate behavior and with folk classifications; for examples of "ethnoscientific" analysis, see Berlin (1967), Burling (1965, 1970), Conklin (1954, 1955, 1969), Frake (1961), Goodenough (1956, 1965), Lounsbury (1956, 1964a and b), Metzger and Williams (1963a and b, 1966, 1967), Pike (1966), Tyler (1965, 1969). Cognitive anthropology was a later movement involving many of the same scholars, but drawing on new developments in linguistics, such as transformational grammar and formal semantic analysis. Apart from cultural classifications in a variety of domains, these schools led to important advances in kinship studies, both in respect of the semiotics of culturally recognized categories of thought (see esp. Keesing 1967, 1968, 1969, 1970) and in respect of mathematization and the construction of adequate rewrite rules (see the surveys in Buchler and Selby 1968, Douglas R. White, 1973). Here the advances were in processual analysis, optimatization analysis, graph theory, matrix analysis and various kinds of mathematical modelling; they were, as White remarks (1973:418) spurred by "the clear separation of culture as a symbolic system from behaviour as a biosocial/physical system."

3. Margaret Mead (1964) introduced the term "semiotics" into anthropology. Neither she nor any other prominent practitioners of the semiotic art in anthropology have availed themselves greatly of concepts and terminology derived directly from Peirce (1965–66) and Saussure (1916). Instead, they all created their own, e.g., Geertz 1973, Schneider 1967, 1972, Turner 1971, 1969.

4. I refer especially to efforts by Rappaport (1967) and others to present ecological circumstances as a necessary and sufficient "efficient cause" of ritual behavior.

5. The place of semiotics in anthropological folkloristics has been left out of this paper entirely. I discussed this subject in detail in a very recent paper (Schwimmer 1975a).

6. In his recent book on symbolism, Raymond Firth (1973) has shown that the framework of British social anthropology can accommodate most anthropological methods that have been developed in the study of symbolism. Firth's experiments with proxemics were especially interesting. His work is a good illustration of my contention

that the use of semiotic methods is compatible with a wide range of theoretical viewpoints in anthropology.

7. It is difficult to state the precise boundaries of this "school," as it never became an orthodoxy and many whose first inspiration came from Evans Pritchard are now known for their original contributions rather than their attachment to an Oxford "school." For a good account, see Jensen 1975. Examples of its semiotic concerns: Evans Pritchard 1956, 1967; Beattie 1964; Beidelman 1961, 1963, 1966, 1968, 1974; Burridge 1960, 1969a and b, 1973; Douglas 1966, 1973; Lienhardt 1961, 1975; Middleton 1960; Turner 1961, 1964, 1967a and b, 1968, 1969a and b, 1971, 1973; Willis 1967, 1975.

8. For general expositions of the structural comparative method, see Lévi-Strauss 1958, 1962a and b, 1973; Pouillon 1975; Pouwer 1966a and b. When Althusser (1974) accuses Lévi-Strauss of ignoring primacy of the infrastructure, he rests his criticism on a few isolated pronouncements rather than on Lévi-Strauss' habitual anthropological practice.

9. I am aware that Geertz (1973) makes some claims of having developed a semiotic theory of culture. Yet even this volume mostly contains ethnographic analyses rooted in the institutional and ecological emphases of the American anthropological tradition. Geertz is not concerned only with "meaning," as he sometimes suggests, but also with the teleology of institutions (Geertz 1957, 1964a and b) and the adaptation to environments (Geertz 1963, 1966). In the context of American anthropology, his intention is perhaps polemical rather than purely theoretical. He believes semiotics has traditionally been underemphasized and seeks to restore the balance. He is successful in his efforts inasmuch as he has provided some splendid demonstrations of the power of anthropological semiotics.

10. Semiotic analysis is not very prevalent in this literature, but we find interesting Freud-inspired instances in the Herskovits' *Dahomean Narrative* (1958), Bettelheim's *Symbolic Wounds,* Anne Parsons' study of an unexpected South Italian variant of the Oedipus complex (1964). Erika Bourguignon (1973) argues for fuller semiotic analysis in personality studies, after demonstrating its value in her own work with Haitian peasants (1959). The Ortigues (1966), using Lacan's methodology, did an illuminating analysis of the "oedipal problem" in a non-Western population.

11. For a survey of this movement see Hastrup in *Yearbook of Symbolic Anthropology I,* 1976, ed. E. G. Schwimmer; also Hastrup 1975:82–88.

12. See for instance: Bulmer 1967, 1970; Leach 1964, 1969, 1972; Needham 1963, 1971, 1972, 1973; Rigby 1968; Robinson 1968; Andrew and Marilyn Strathern 1968; Tambiah 1968. Among the authors I very much wished to discuss in the present survey, as all have contributed signally to "semiotic anthropology," I have to reserve the following for treatment in a later paper: Clastres 1974, De Heusch 1971, 1972, Griaule 1948, Mabuchi 1967, Munn 1969, 1973, Oppitz 1974, Peacock 1971, Retel-Laurentin 1974, Vogt 1970, Zahan 1969, 1975, Zimmermann 1974.

13. According to Sebeok (1975), Eco takes a more flexible view of boundaries in a new work (Eco, 1975) not available when the present paper was written. It is tempting to quote Bachelard (1970:80): "tracer nettement une frontière, c'est déjà la dépasser."

14. The theoretical implications of such anomalies are well demonstrated in Bulmer 1970. Though I agree with Bulmer on all material points, I wonder whether the kind of classification he calls "logical" might not be better called "ideological."

15. Sperber (1974) demonstrates that we cannot interpret meaning systems out-

side the context of their social production. When he turns this into an argument *against semiotics*, we suspect he thinks of what Sebeok (1975) calls "semiology" rather than of what Sebeok calls "semiotics," or at least, of "semiotics," as discussed in the present paper.

REFERENCES

Althusser, Louis, 1974. *Eléments d'Autocritique*. Hachette Littérature.

Bachelard, G. 1970. *Etudes*. Paris: Vlin.

Barthes, Roland. 1964. "Eléments de Sémiologie," in *Communications* 4:91–144.

Bateson, Gregory. 1936. *Naven*. Cambridge: Harvard University Press.

———. 1966. "Information, Codification and Communication," in *Communication and Culture*, A. G. Smith, ed. New York: Holt, Rinehart and Winston.

———. 1972. *Steps to an Ecology of Mind*. New York: Ballantine.

Beidelman, Thomas A. 1961a. "Hyena and Rabbit: A Kaguru Representation of Matrilineal Relations," *Africa* 31:61–74.

———. 1961b. "Right and Left Hand Among the Kaguru: A Note on Symbolic Classification," *Africa* 31:250–6.

———. 1963. "Further Adventures of Hyena and Rabbit: The Folktale as a Sociological Model," *Africa* 33:54–69.

———. 1966. "The Ox and Nuer Sacrifice," *Man* 1:453–67.

———. 1968. "Some Nuer Notions of Nakedness, Nudity and Sexuality," *Africa* 38:114–31.

———. 1974. "Sir Edward Evan Evans Pritchard (1902–1973): An Appreciation," *Anthropos* 69:553–567.

Berlin, Brent. 1967. "Categories of Eating in Tzeltal and Navaho," *International Journal of American Linguistics* 33:1.

———. 1970. "An Universalist-Evolutionary Approach to Ethnographic Semantics," in *Current Directions in Anthropology*, Ann Fischer, ed., pp. 3–18, American Anthropological Association *Bulletin* no. 3, pt. 2.

———. 1971. "Speculations on the Growth of Ethnobotanical Nomenclature," *Working Paper* no. 39, Berkeley: Language-Behavior Research Laboratory.

Bettelheim, Bruno. 1954. *Symbolic Wounds*. New York: The Free Press.

Bourdieu, Pierre. 1972. *Esquisse d'une théorie de la pratique*. Genève: Droz.

Bourguignon, Erika. 1959. "The Persistence of Folk Belief: Some Notes on Cannibalism and Zombis in Haiti," *Journal of American Folklore* 72:36–46.

———. 1973. "Psychological Anthropology," in *Handbook of Cultural Anthropology*, J. J. Honigman, ed., pp. 1073–1118.

Bremond, C. 1973. *Logique du récit*. Paris: Seuil.

Buchler, Ira R. and Henry A. Selby. 1968. *Kinship and Social Organization*. New York: Macmillan.

Bulmer, Ralph. 1967. "Why a Cassowary Is Not a Bird," *Man* 2:5–25.

———. 1970. "Which Came First, the Chicken or the Egg-Head?" *Echanges et Communications*, J. Pouillon et P. Maranda, eds., pp. 1169–1191. Mouton.

Burling, Robbins. 1965. "How to Choose a Burmese Numeral Classifier," in *Context and Meaning in Cultural Anthropology*, pp. 243–264.

———. 1970. *Man's Many Voices*. New York: Holt, Rinehart and Winston.

Burridge, K. O. L. 1960. *Mambu: A Melanesian Millennium*. London: Methuen.

———. 1969a. *New Heaven New Earth*. Oxford: Basil Blackwell.

———. 1969b. *Tangu Traditions*. Oxford: Clarendon.

———. 1973. *Encountering Aborigines*. Pergamon Press.

Clastres, Pierre. 1974. *Le grand parler*. Paris: Seuil.

Conklin, Harold C. 1954. "An Ethno-ecological Approach to Shifting Agriculture," *Transactions NY Academy of Sciences*, Series 2, vol. 17:133–42.

———. 1955. "Hanunóo Color Categories," *SW Journal of Anthropology* 11:339–44.

———. 1969. "Ethnogenealogical Method," in Tyler 1969, pp. 92–122.

De Heusch, Luc. 1971. *Pourquoi l'épouser*. Paris: Gallimard.

———. 1972. *Le roi ivre ou l'origine de l'état?* Paris: Gallimard.

Douglas, Mary. 1966. *Purity and Danger*. London: Routledge and Kegan Paul.

———. 1973. *Rules and Meanings*. Penguin Education.

Dumont, F. 1974. *Les idéologies*. Paris: P.U.F.

Eco, Umberto. 1968. *La struttura assente*. Milano. Traduction française: *La structure absente*, 1972.

———. 1975. *A Theory of Semiotics*. Bloomington: Indiana University Press.

Evans Pritchard, E. E. 1940. *The Nuer*. Oxford: Clarendon.

———. 1949. *The Sanusi of Cyrenaica*. Oxford: Clarendon.

———. 1956. *Nuer Religion*. London: Oxford University Press.

———. 1967. *The Azande Trickster*. Oxford: Clarendon.

Firth, Raymond. 1967. *Tikopia Ritual and Belief*. London: Allen and Unwin.

———. 1973. *Symbols: Public and Private*. Ithaca: Cornell University Press.

Fortes, Meyer. 1959. *Oedipus and Job in West African Religion*. Cambridge University Press.

———. 1970. *Time and Social Structure and Other Essays*. London: Athlone.

Frake, Charles O. 1961. "The Diagnosis of Disease Among the Subanun of Mindanao," *American Anthropologist* 63:113–32.

Geertz, Clifford. 1957. "Ritual and Social Change: A Javanese Example," *American Anthropologist* 59:22–54.

———. 1963. *Agricultural Involution*. Berkeley: University of California Press.

———. 1965a. *Peddlers and Princes*. Chicago: University of Chicago Press.

———. 1964b. "Internal Conversion in Contemporary Bali," in *Malayan and Indonesian Studies*, J. Bastin and R. Roolvink, eds., pp. 282–302. Oxford: Clarendon.

———. 1966. "Person Time and Conduct in Bali," Yale University, Southeast Asia Studies, *Cultural Report Series*, no. 14.

———. 1973. *The Interpretation of Cultures*. New York: Basic Books.

Godelier, Maurice. 1968. *Rationalité et irrationalité en économie*. Paris: Maspéro.

———. 1973. *Horizon: trajets marxistes en anthropologie*. Paris: Maspéro.

Goodenough, Ward H. 1956. "Componential Analysis and the Study of Meaning," *Language* 32:195–216.

———. 1965. "Personal Names and Modes of Address in Two Oceanic Societies," in *Context and Meaning*, M. Spiro, ed., pp. 265–276.

———. 1970. *Description and Comparison in Cultural Anthropology*. Chicago: Aldine.

Goody, J. 1969. *Comparative Studies in Kinship*. London: Routledge and Kegan Paul.

Greimas, A. J. 1970. *Du sens*. Paris: Seuil.

Griaule, Marcel. 1948. *Dieu d'Eau*. Paris: Fayard.

Hastrup, Kirsten et al. 1975. *Den ny antropologi*. Borgen/Basis.

Herskovits, M. J. and F. S. 1958. *Dahomean Narrative*. Evanston: Northwestern University Press.

Hjelmslev, L. 1963. *Prolegomena to a Theory of Language*. Madison: University of Wisconsin Press.

Hymes, Dell. 1971. "The Wife Who Goes Out Like a Man," in Maranda and Maranda, eds., 1971.

Jensen, Knud-Erik. 1975. "Britiske Symbolstudier," in: Hastrup 1975, pp. 130–149.

Keesing, Roger M. 1967. "Statistical Models and Decision Models of Social Structure: A Kwaio Case," *Ethnology* 6:1–16.

———. 1968. "Step-Kin, In-Laws and Ethnoscience," *Ethnology* 7:59–70.

———. 1969. "On Quibblings over Squabblings of Siblings: New Perspectives on Kin Terms and Role Behavior," *SW Journal of Anthropology* 25:207–27.

———. 1970a. "Kwaio Fosterage," *American Anthropologist* 72:991–1019.

———. 1970b. "Towards a Model of Role Analysis," in *A Handbook of Method in Cultural Anthropology*, Raoul Narroll and Ronald Cohen, eds. New York: Natural History Press.

———. 1971. "Formalization and the Construction of Ethnographies," in *Explorations in Mathematical Anthropology*. Cambridge: M.I.T. Press.

Leach, Edmund R. 1964. "Anthropological Aspects of Language: Animal Categories and Verbal Abuse," in *New Directions in the Study of Language*. Cambridge: M.I.T. Press.

———. 1969. *Genesis as Myth and Other Essays*. London: Cape.

———. 1971. "Kimil: A Category of Andamanese Thought," in Maranda and Maranda, eds., 1971, pp. 22–48.

———. 1972. "The Structure of Symbolism," in *The Interpretation of Ritual*, J. S. La Fontaine, ed., pp. 239–276.

Lévi-Strauss, Claude. 1958. *Anthropologie structurale*. Paris: Plon.

———. 1960. In *Anthropologie structurale deux*, Chapter 1.

———. 1962a. *Le totémisme aujourd'hui*. Paris: P.U.F.

———. 1962b. *La pensée sauvage*. Paris: Plon.

———. 1964. 1966. 1968. 1971. *Mythologiques* I–IV. Paris: Plon.

———. 1973. *Anthropologie structurale deux*. Paris: Plon.

———. 1975. "Anthropologie," *Diogène* 90:3–30.

Lienhardt, R. Godfrey. 1961. *Divinity and Experience: The Religion of the Dinka*. Oxford: Clarendon.

———. 1975. "Getting Your Own Back: Themes in Nilotic Myth," in *Studies in Social Anthropology*, J. H. M. Beattie and R. G. Lienhardt, eds., pp. 213–233. Oxford: Clarendon.

Lounsbury, Floyd G. 1956. "A Semantic Analysis of the Pawnee Kinship Usage," *Language* 32:158–94.

———. 1965a. "The Structural Analysis of Kinship Semantics," in *Proceedings 9th Intern. Congr. Linguists*, Horace G. Lunt, ed., pp. 1073–1090. Mouton.

———. 1964b. "A Formal Account of the Crow- and Omaha-Type Kinship Terminologies," in *Explorations in Cultural Anthropology*, W. H. Goodenough, ed. New York: McGraw-Hill.

Mabuchi, Toichi. 1967. "Toward the Reconstruction of Ryukyuan Cosmology," in: *Folk Religion and World View in the Southwestern Pacific,* N. Matsumoto and T. Mabuchi, eds. Tokyo: Keio Institute of Cultural and Linguistic Studies.

Maranda, Pierre and Elli Köngäs Maranda. 1971. *Structural Models in Folklore and Transformational Essays.* Mouton.

Mead, Margaret. 1964. "The Study of the Total Communication Process," in *Approaches to Semiotics,* Sebeok, Hayes, and Bateson. eds. Mouton.

Metzger, Duane and G. E. Williams. 1963a. "A Formal Ethnographic Study of Tenejapa Ladino Weddings," *American Anthropologist* 65:1076–1101.

———. 1963b. "Tenejapa Medicine I: The Curer," *SW Journal of Anthropology* 19:216–34.

———. 1966. "Procedures and Results in the Study of Native Categories: Tzeltal Firewood," *American Anthropologist* 68:389–407.

———. 1967. "Patterns of Primary Personal Reference in a Tzeltal Community," *Estudios de cultura maya* 6.

Middleton, John. 1960. *Lugbara Religion.* London: Oxford University Press.

Munn, Nancy, 1969. "The Effectiveness of Symbols in Murngin Rite and Myth," in *Forms of Symbolic Action,* R. Spender, ed.

———. 1973a. "Symbolism in a Ritual Context," in *Handbook of Social and Cultural Anthropology,* J. J. Honigman, ed., pp. 577–612. Chicago: Rand McNally.

———. 1973b. "The Spatial Representation of Cosmic Order in Walbiri Iconography," in *Primitive Art and Society,* Anthony Forge, ed. London: Oxford University Press.

Murphy, Robert F. 1971. *The Dialectics of Social Life.* New York: Basic Books.

Murra, John V. 1972. "El 'control vertical' de un maximo de pisos ecologicos en la economia de las sociedades andinas" in: *Visita de la Provincia de Leon de Huanuco* (1562) (Iñigo Ortiz de Zuñiga, visitador). Huanuco: Universidad Hermilio Valdizan.

———. 1974. "Débat," in Valensi, 1974, pp. 1158–1161.

Needham, Rodney. 1963. "Introduction," in *Primitive Classification* (Durkheim and Mauss, R. Needham, tr. and ed.). London: Cohen & West.

———. 1971. *Rethinking Kinship and Marriage.* London: Tavistock.

———. 1972. *Belief, Language and Experience.* Oxford: Blackwell.

Oppitz, Michael. 1974. "Shangri-la, le panneau de marque d'un flipper. Analyse sémiologique d'un mythe visuel," *L'Homme* XIV (3–4). 59–84.

Ortigues, Marie Cécile et Edmond. 1966. *Oedipe Africain.* Paris: Plon.

Parsons, Anne. 1964. "Is the Oedipus Complex Universal? The Jones-Malinowski Debate Revisited in a South Italian Nuclear Complex," in *The Psychoanalytic Study of Society,* W. Muensterberger and S. Axelrad, eds. New York: International University Press.

Peacock, James L. 1971. "Class Clown and Cosmology in Javanese Drama," in Maranda and Maranda, eds., 1971, pp. 139–68.

Peirce, Charles. 1965–66. *Collected Papers of Charles Sanders Peirce.* Cambridge: Harvard University Press.

Pike, Kenneth. 1966. "Etic and Emic Standpoints for the Description of Behavior," in *Communications and Culture,* A. G. Smith, ed., pp. 152–63.

Pouillon, Jean. 1975. *Fétiches sans Fétichisme.* Paris: Maspéro.

Pouwer, Jan. 1966a. "Towards a Configurational Approach to Society and Culture in New Guinea," *Journal of the Polynesian Society* 75:267–86.

———. 1966b. "Structure and Flexibility in a New Guinea Society," *Bijdragen tot de Taal-, Land- en Volkenkunde* 122:158–70.

Radcliffe-Brown, A. R. 1933. *The Andaman Islanders,* 2nd ed., Cambridge University Press.

Rappaport, R. A. 1967. *Pigs for the Ancestors.* Yale University Press.

Retel-Laurentin, A. 1974. "La force de la parole. Nazakura. Afrique," in *Divination et rationalité,* J. P. Vernant, ed., pp. 295–319. Paris: Seuil.

Rigby, P. 1968. "Some Gogo Rituals of Purification," in *Dialectic in Practical Religion,* Edmund Leach, ed. Cambridge University Press.

Robinson, Marguerite S. 1968. " 'The House of the Mighty Hero' or 'The House of Enough Paddy'." in *Dialectic in Practical Religion,* E. R. Leach, ed., pp. 122–52. Cambridge University Press.

Rosman, A. and P. G. Rubel. 1973. "Marriage Rules and the Structure of Relationships Between Groups in New Guinea Societies." Paper delivered at colloquium, "Ecology and Society in Melanesia," Paris.

Sahlins, Marshall. 1972. *Stone Age Economics.* Chicago: Aldine.

Saussure, F. de. 1916. *Cours de linguistique générale.*

Schneider, David M. 1967. "Descent and Filiation as Cultural Constructs," *SW Journal of Anthropology* 23:65–73.

———. 1968. *American Kinship: A Cultural Account.* Prentice-Hall.

———. 1972. "What is Kinship All About?" in *Kinship Studies in the Morgan Centennial Year,* P. Reining, ed., pp. 32–63.

Schwimmer, Erik G. 1973. *Exchange in the Social Structure of the Orokaiva.* London: Hurst.

———. 1975a. "Why did the mountain erupt?" in *Migrants and Exiles in Oceania,* M. Lieber, ed., University of Hawaii Press.

———. 1976. "Folkloristics and Anthropology," in *Semiotica* Vol. 17, No. 3, pp. 267–289.

Sebeok, Thomas A. 1976. "The Semiotic Web: A Chronicle of Prejudices," in *Contributions to the Doctrine of Signs,* Ch. 10 (pp. 149–188). Lisse: the Peter de Ridder Press.

Shands, Harley S. 1975. "Semiotics and Medicine." Paper read at North American Semiotics Colloquium, Tampa.

Sperber, D. 1974. *Le symbolisme en général.* Paris: Hermann.

Strathern, A. and M. 1968. "Marsupials and Magic," in *Dialectic in Practical Religion,* E. R. Leach, ed., Cambridge University Press.

Tambiah, S. 1968. "The Ideology of Merit," in *Dialectic in Practical Religion,* E. R. Leach, ed. Cambridge University Press.

Turner, Nancy. n.d. "Plant Taxonomic Systems in Ethnobotany of Three Contemporary Indian Groups of the Pacific Northwest." Unpublished thesis. Vancouver: University of British Columbia.

Turner, Victor. 1961. "Ndembu Divination: Its Symbolism and Techniques," *Rhodes Livingstone Papers,* No. 31.

———. 1964. "Witchcraft and Sorcery: Taxonomy versus Dynamics," *Africa* 34:314.

———. 1967a. "Aspects of Saora Ritual and Shamanism: An Approach to the Data of

Ritual," in *The Craft of Social Anthropology*, A. L. Epstein, ed. London: Tavistock.

————. 1967b. *A Forest of Symbols*. Ithaca: Cornell University Press.

————. 1968. *The Drums of Affliction*. Oxford: Clarendon.

————. 1969a. *The Ritual Process*. London: Routledge and Kegan Paul.

————. 1969b. "Introduction" in *Forms of Symbolic Action*, R. Spencer, ed.

————. 1971. "The Syntax of Symbolism in Ndembu Ritual," in Maranda and Maranda, eds., 1971, pp. 125–36.

————. 1973. "The Centre Out There: Pilgrim's Soul," *History of Religion*, 12 (3), 191–230.

Tyler, Stephen A. 1965. "Koya Language Morphology and Patterns of Kinship Behavior," *American Anthropologist* 67:1428–40.

————, ed. 1969. *Cognitive Anthropology*. New York: Holt, Rinehart and Winston.

Valensi, Lucette et al. 1974. "Anthropologie économique et Histoire: l'oeuvre de Karl Polanyi," *Annales Economies, Sociétes, Civilisations* 29:1311–80.

Valeri, Valerio. 1970. "Struttura, transformazione, 'esaustività': un'esposizione di alcuni concetti de Claude Lévi-Strauss," *Annali della Scuola Normale Superiore de Pisa* Ser. II, Vol. XXXIX: 347–75.

Veron, Eliseo. 1973. "Vers une logique naturelle des mondes sociaux," *Communications* 20:226–78.

————. 1974. "Dix remarques sur la sémiotique de l'idéologie," communiqué au premier congrès de l'Association Internationale de Sémiotique, Milan.

Vidal, Claudine. 1974. "De la contradiction sauvage," *L'Homme* XIV(3–4):5–58.

Vogt, E. Z. and C. 1970. "Lévi-Strauss Among the Maya," *Man* 5:379–92.

Watson, J. B. 1970. "Society as Organized Flow," *SW Journal of Anthropology* 26:107–24.

White, Douglas R. 1973. "Mathematical Anthropology," in *Handbook of Social and Cultural Anthropology*, J. J. Honigman, ed., pp. 369–446.

Willis, Roy J. 1967. "The Head and the Loins," *Man* 4:519–34.

————. 1975. *Man and Beast*. Paladin.

Zahan, Dominique. 1969. *La viande et la graine*. Paris: Présence africaine.

————. 1975. "Couleurs et peintures corporelles," *Diogène* 90:117–35.

Zimmermann, Francis. 1974. "Géométrie sociale traditionelle. Castes de main droite et castes de main gauche en Inde du Sud," *Annales Economies, Sociétés, Civilisations* 29:1381–1401.

Ecumenicalism in Semiotics

Thomas A. Sebeok

"[Catholics and Protestants] may and must talk to one another, but with a new approach; they should proceed from points on which they are united to discuss what separates them; and discuss what separates them with an eye to what unites them."—Karl Barth

"... c'est la sémiologie... qui prendrait en charge les *grandes unités signifiantes* du discours; de la sorte apparaîtrait l'unité des recherches qui se mènent actuellement en anthropologie, en sociologie, en psychanalyse et en stylistique autour du concept de signification."—Roland Barthes

"... it is clear that boundaries persist despite a flow of personnel across them. ... The critical focus of investigation from this point of view becomes the... boundary that defines the group, not the... stuff that it encloses."—Fredrik Barth

"End the Boundary Dispute!"—John Barth

The Organism as a Text

In what was assuredly one of his most stupefying lectures, titled "Consciousness and language" (7.579–596), delivered about one hundred and ten years ago, Peirce raised the question: "What is man?" His decisive answer was that man is a symbol. Peirce elaborated and deepened his argument by comparing man with some other symbol, to wit, the verbal sign *Six,* and showed that, "remote and dissimilar as the word and the man appear, it is exceedingly difficult to state any essential difference between them..." (7.588). Elsewhere, Peirce claimed that "my language is the sum total of myself" (5.314), a view tantamount to asserting that man is a string of signs, a process of communication (Fairbanks, 1976:20), or, in short, a text. Nor is man uniquely endowed with the property of life, "For every symbol is a living thing, in a very strict sense that is no mere figure of speech" (2.222). Furthermore, "the most marvellous faculty of humanity," one which we share with all other organisms, is "that of procreation" (7.590). Yet we have even that capacity in common with signs: "Symbols grow. They come into being by development out of other signs. . . . It is only out of symbols that a new symbol can grow. *Omne symbolum de symbolo*" (2.302). Chomsky (1972:90–93)— whose way of envisioning the acquisition of knowledge of language vividly recalls (as he is well aware) some of the ideas of Peirce on the logic of abduction—reconstituted, with the linguist's fruitful reformulation of "the creative aspect of language use" (1972:6), this notion and turned it to challenging problems of modern linguistics. Incidentally, Peirce's splendid manner of argumentation was very far from an instance of the Pathetic Fallacy. Indeed, his view that signs have an inherent measure of self-responsibility was developed much further a century later by René Thom.

Thom, especially in his neoclassical essay on a theory of symbolism (1974, Ch. xi), which adheres closely to the Peircean semiotic model (cf. Sebeok 1976b), has authoritatively delineated the fundamental identity of the processes of biological reproduction and semiosis, bracketed in the frame of his powerful catastrophe theory, or a kind of mathematics applicable to phenomena that are neither orderly nor linear, and hence relevant to the so-called inexact sciences, of which biology and semiotics are representative, each in its own ways. In the course of the former, a parent organism or "signified" emits a descendant, thereby engendering a "signifier" which, in an eternal and universal flux, reengenders a "signified" each time that the sign is interpreted. A signifier turns into a signified given only sufficient time, say, the lapse of a generation. By virtue of this subtle fluctuation between two morphologies, bound by the simultaneous exigencies of reversibility and irreversibility, "la dynamique du symbolisme," or, in Peircean terminology, semiosis, i.e., sign-action and sign-interpretation, "porte en elle . . . toutes les contradictions de la vision scientifique du monde, et qu'elle est l'image même de la vie" (Thom 1974:233; cf. Sebeok 1976a:69).

Two Traditions

The title for this summative essay was chosen less for its ecclesiastical connotations than to suggest that, in my view (Sebeok 1977a), the scope of

semiotics encompasses the whole of the *oikoumenē,* the entirety of our plane-
tary biosphere. The chronology of semiotic inquiry so far, viewed panorami-
cally, exhibits an oscillation between two seemingly antithetical tendencies: in
the major tradition (which I am tempted to christen a catholic heritage),
semiosis takes its place as a normal occurrence in nature, of which, to be sure,
language—that paramount known mode of terrestrial communication which is
Lamarckian in style, that is, embodies a learning process that becomes part of
the evolutionary legacy of the ensuing generations—forms an important if
relatively recent component. This accords with the view of the Stoics who
argued, *in nuce,* "that animals have 'expressive' reason, the power of speech,
by which they communicate with each other by means of signs" (Philodemus
1941:144), although they also drew a sharp distinction between the aforemen-
tioned properties, shared by animals with men, in opposition to synthetic and
combining reason, ascribed by them to men alone (cf. Simone 1972:6–7). It
was, however, St. Augustine (354–430), one of the greatest thinkers of all
times about sign functions, who, in his brief dialogue, *De Magistro,* first
wrestled with the perennial question whether it is feasible for an organism to
learn through signs at all and, if so, how.

The minor trend, which is parochially glottocentric, asserts, sometimes
with sophistication but at other times with embarrassing naïveté, that linguistics serves as the model for the rest of semiotics—Saussure's *le patron
général*—because of the allegedly arbitrary and conventional character of the
verbal sign. Much has been written within and about this tradition, which has
both a conservative and a radical wing. The orthodox line was quite succinctly
enunciated, in the weakest form, by Cassirer (1945:115): "Linguistics is a
part of semiotics...," but more emphatically so by Bloomfield (1939:55),
who averred that "Linguistics is the chief contributor to semiotic," then
Weinreich (1968:164), who declared natural language to be "the semiotic
phenomenon par excellence " (cf. Sebeok 1976a:11–12). The rallying cry of
the ultrarevisionists was perhaps most enticingly proclaimed by Barthes
(1964:81) in an often-repeated catchphrase: "... c'est la sémiologie qui est
une partie de la linguistique."

The distinction between what I have termed, although without elaboration
here (but see Sebeok 1977a), the major and the minor traditions has lost its
force, since it is amply clear that Darwinian and Lamarckian (i.e., sociogenet-
ic) evolution coexist in subtle interaction in the human animal (Bateson 1968)
(or, as Morris [1976:39] marveled about him in his delightful poem, "Animal
Symbolicum," "What a remarkable animal: physiological and symbolical./
Kin of every other animal, but symbol-haunted and dramatical"). Human
evolution is thus not only a reconfirmation of the evolutionary processes
which went on before man appeared on the scene, but continues as a dual

semiotic consecution that can scarcely be uncoupled in practice: one track language-free (or zoosemiotic), the other language-sensitive (or anthroposemiotic) (Sebeok 1972:163). Semiosis must be recognized as a pervasive fact of nature as well as of culture. In such matters, then, I declare myself not only a Peircean but a (René) Thomist, yet one who stands ready to obey Karl Barth's injunction as formulated at the outset.

The Distinctive Burden of Semiotics

Ecumenicalism in semiotics means, however, far more than a plea for attempting to capture global properties of sign systems in general and for unifying local variations that are criterial for heretofore unrelated information about the genetic (Marcus 1974), metabolic (in the sense used by Tomkins 1975), neural (Pribram 1971, Ch. 4, Rose 1973:100-110), intraspecific *vs.* interspecific (Sebeok 1972:79), nonverbal *vs.* verbal and nonvocal *vs.* vocal codes (Sebeok 1977b), beside a host of secondary modeling systems (Winner and Winner 1976:135-137). The term, which derives from the Greek *oikos,* designating "house," seems to be appropriate because it once again calls attention to the holistic force of semiotics, which many leading contributors to the discipline have marked as its distinctive burden. This perspective was perhaps best articulated by Morris who, working initially in the overall frame of the *International Encyclopedia of Unified Science* (the program of which was unfolded at the 1935 International Congress for the Unity of Science, plans for which were laid the year before, interestingly enough for those familiar with the classical period of the Prague School, at Charles University), conceived of semiotic as an instrument of all the sciences. An acute historian of the semiotic endeavor since 1865 recently remarked about this vista that "The foundations of the theory of signs were the foundations for the unification of the sciences" as well (cf. Fisch, in press, #13). "Semiotic has a double relation to the sciences: it is both a science among the sciences and an instrument of the sciences," Morris wrote in 1938 (1971:17-18), continuing: "The significance of semiotic as a science lies in the fact that it is a step in the unification of science, since it supplies the foundations for any special science of signs, such as linguistics, logic, mathematics, rhetoric, and . . . aesthetics. The concept of sign may prove to be of importance in the unification of the social, psychological, and humanistic sciences insofar as these are distinguished from the physical and biological sciences." Morris later provided for a still higher level of unification with the two last-mentioned groups of disciplines, having shown that signs are simply the objects studied by these branches of knowledge in certain complex functional processes.

A closely similar view was sanguinely expounded, in 1943, by the

Danish linguist Hjelmslev, whose glossematics professed to be grounded in Saussure's *Cours,* but who was also comfortably familiar with the work of such logical empiricists as Carnap, who, in turn, acknowledged his indebtedness to Morris's semiotic. Hjelmslev (1953:69) echoed: ". . . it seems fruitful and necessary to establish a common point of view for a large number of disciplines, from the study of literature, art, and music, and general history, all the way to logistics and mathematics. . . . Each will be able to contribute in its own way to the general science of semiotics. . . . Thus new light might perhaps be cast on these disciplines, and they might be led to a critical self-examination. In this way, through a mutually fructifying collaboration, it should be possible to produce a general encyclopedia of sign structures.'' French semiotic writings of the past decade seem often to have felt obligated to take a stance, whether pro or con, Hjelmslev's amplification of Saussure's outline of a prospective general science of signs; and Anglophone exegetes, like Whitfield (1969:258), who notes that glossematics views all sciences "as also being . . . semiotics," or like Lamb (cf. Lamb and Makkai 1976), are still endeavoring to reinterpret "the semiotics of culture" (Schwimmer, this book; Umiker-Sebeok 1977a) in various eclectic ways but seldom straying far from the broad if fragile framework erected by Hjelmslev. On the other hand, in his heroic but neglected attempt at a unification of the structure of human behavior, Pike (1967:63) has explicitly rejected both Saussure's theory of signs and Hjelmslev's version of it. Barthes, of course, as cited in the second epigraph, has persuasively and prestigiously rekindled the spark of coadunation.

The works of Morris, Hjelmslev, Barthes, and their numerous epigones on the holistic force of semiotics hardly exceed programmatic pronouncements. In truth, as Peirce came to recognize with increasing clarity after 1890, science is an ongoing quest that cannot be identified as a particular body of knowledge yet segments of which are delimitable in terms of particular social groupings of research scholars within a vaster community of investigators; as he wrote Lady Welby in 1908, "the only natural lines of demarcation between nearly related sciences are the divisions between the social groups of devotees of those sciences" (8.342). But Peirce also stressed that one of the first useful steps toward a science of *semeiotic,* "or the cenoscopic science of signs" (i.e., which does not depend upon new special observations), "must be the accurate definition, or logical analysis of the concepts of science" (8.343). Jakobson, in his masterful (though mistitled) essay, "Linguistics in relation to other sciences" (1971:655–696), has sketched out a way whereby the nomothetic sciences of man, and possibly some of the natural sciences alongside them as well, might be systematized to achieve a degree of logical filiation and hierarchical ordering exactly if linguistics—*alias* semiotics—is used as the point of departure for their tentative serial arrangement. However, Thom's outline of a general theory seems to me to provide the first rigorously monistic model of the living being endowed with the *facultas signatrix,* and to offer one pure topological continuum in which causality and finality are combined. Assuredly it is no accident that his dynamical topology was influenced by Peirce on the one hand (Thom 1974:229–230), and von Uexküll on the other (Thom 1975:xxiii, and passim).

The kinship of semiotically based programs, such as those mentioned, to the movement known as General System Theory (Bertalanffy 1968), or GST, is seldom underlined yet their common denominator is rather obvious. As a "natural philosophy," both these variants of a single metatheory can be traced back to Leibniz (ibid., 11; Dascal 1972) and his program for a *mathesis universalis,* and it was certainly not a coincidence that the founder of GST first presented his ideas, in 1937, in Morris's semiotic seminar at the University of Chicago (Bertalanffy 1968:90). Although the two different sorts of mobilization toward synthesis continued to develop and flourish independently one from the other, their proponents have not infrequently crossed paths here and there; for example, both Morris and I were occasional participants in discussion groups of scientists assembled, from the most various traditional disciplines, in the 1950s, "for the purpose of approaching a unified theory of behavior," or, as was sometimes grandiosely claimed, human nature (e.g., Grinker 1956:v). The San Francisco psychiatrist Jurgen Ruesch was an animating spirit in this striving for integration, drawing "from theories that derive from social anthropology, sociology, philology, linguistics, and related disciplines," all of which, he explicitly acknowledged much later, "are concerned with semiotics" (1972:11–12; cf. 127). Recently, the two main preoccupations of system theorists appear to have settled on *action,* or the movement of matter-energy over space, and *communication,* or the "change of information from one state to another or its movement from one point to another over space" (Miller 1975:346), but the two naturally flow together since information is always borne on a marker (id. 1976:299). The distinction immediately calls to mind Peirce's alterity of dyadic or dynamical action vs. triadic or sign-action (5.473), which, again, brings us back to his "doctrine of the essential nature and fundamental varieties of possible semiosis" (5.488). If the writings of Peirce had been available to von Uexküll, who also inspired von Bertalanffy (1968:288) (although the latter's avowed knowledge of semiotics seems to have been confined to some writings of Cassirer), GST would very likely have taken a radically different turn. The approach of von Bertalanffy consisted of treating sets of related events collectively as systems manifesting functions and properties of the specific level of the whole. This presumptively enables the recognition of isomorphies across ascending levels of organization—variously dubbed, e.g., org (Gerard 1957), holon (Koestler 1967:341), integron (Jacob 1974:299–324), or, processually, shred out (Miller 1976:226–227)—from which can be developed general principles or sometimes fundamental laws that operate commonly at all levels of organization in contrast with those which are unique to each. Semiotic ideas pervade GST, but are seldom anchored in a comprehensive doctrine of signs. For instance, Miller (1976:227) writes: "... the evolutionary shred out of the channel and net subsystem is from slow, inefficient, chemical transmission by diffusion at the cell level up to increasingly rapid and cost-effective symbolic linguistic transmission over complicated networks at the higher levels of living systems." However, as critics have justly pointed out—among other strictures (Phillips 1976:48–67)—GST suffers from an aura of vagueness over what is meant to be encompassed within it. The missing ingredient, the addition of which, I suggest, is most likely to dispel the fog, can only be supplied by way of a judicious linkage with a semiotic which must be firmly based upon the empirical facts of current biological thought as foreshadowed by Peirce, developed by Morris, independently furthered, in his own lambent fashion, by von Uexküll, and recently restated in the language of Thom's catastrophe theory (which, *pace* its detractors in some American mathematical circles [Kolata 1977], has already vastly enlarged the horizons of semiotic inquiry [Sebeok 1976b]). I emphasize the historical and logical associations between holism and semiotics because these are nowadays often overlooked: for instance, although Phillips devotes a section of his exploratory essay to the holistic connotations of structuralism (1976, Ch. 6), including its embodiment in Prague-style linguistics (pp. 83–84, 88), he ignores the more patently tenable and much more fundamental connections with semiotics. Precisely how semiotics can function as "an organon" (Morris 1971:67) of all the sciences, and the wide humanistic implications of the assumption that semiotics "provides a basis for understanding the main forms of human activity and their interrelationship" (ibid., 69), since all such activities and relations are mediated exclusively by signs, pose a host of further questions that need to be widely as well as urgently debated since, among other consequences, their satisfactory reformulation might well lead to badly needed improvement of the chaotic curricula which still inform students of the human sciences worldwide.

Communication and Manipulation

The Tampa Colloquium coincided with the heyday of an era in international relations epitomized by the fashionable slogan *détente,* which an interim President of the United States later tried to declare taboo. In the global pursuit of semiotics, we have no need for such artifices of labelling to characterize a relaxation of tensions. Wherever our workshops happen to be located—from Bloomington to Moscow, as the newest introductory manual would have it in the perhaps exaggerated heading of one of its principal chapters (Voigt 1977, Ch. 8)—the semiotic network amicably binds us together, to our immense profit, with only sporadic intrusions of that stain of darkness in the fabric that both mars the otherwise seamless web and invites ridicule upon the preposterous advocates of the intrusion of politics into our affairs (e.g., Sebeok 1976a:166). I do not mean to suggest that the practitioner of semiotics is more enlightened than the practitioner of politics, but only that the two trades are right to be uneasy with each other. Margaret Mead (1972:286) expressed the distinction between cooperative and manipulative behavior (Sebeok 1976a:80) with great delicacy and her customary vatical flair when she said that in inaugurating the new science of semiotics it "is of the utmost importance that continuing work . . . should take place not in a context of power," but that "we must affirm the acquisition of this greater systematic insight as part of man's scientific knowledge *on behalf of man.* Otherwise we may expect to encounter continual blocking resistance, misunderstanding, and downright fear and hostility both from outsiders and from members of disciplines included in the new science. . . ."

Indeed, the sign expert can supply the policy maker with pointers on how to sharpen his tools designed to exploit resources in certain very important areas of human activity, such as strategic conflict, say, in the transnational arena. Game theory, in particular that subclass to which two-actor zerosum games belong, clearly articulates, in yet another kind of holistic construct (Bertalanffy 1968:90), communication with manipulation, or, if you will excuse the reiteration, sign-action with dynamical action. The book of Jervis (1970), although held to the descriptive level and without the imposition of formal game models, serves as one outstanding illustration of a creative projection of semiotic theory and techniques to the level of diplomacy in international relations. Beyond this sort of service, entailing a heightened level of awareness about games in general and about the pervasively institutionalized human con-games (Goffman 1952) in particular, an insistent exertion of the semiotic point of view may merely embarrass politician and administrator alike. It is perfectly all right for our masters to be wary of what we know, do, and might yet uncover, but is it too much to ask for their trust?

The Contribution of Adnormal, Denormal, and Abnormal Semiotics

Most of the papers delivered at our conference can be pigeonholed as multifarious examples of work touching upon the semiotics of culture (Winner and Winner 1976, Umiker-Sebeok 1977a), broadly defined, in the sense of imperative language involvement. None dealt with the necessarily language-independent semiotics of nature (Sebeok 1977a), a marked/unmarked opposition the many consequences of which I do not want to pursue here. Instead, I should like to allude to another set of emergent distinctions that I think must rapidly be assimilated to a unitary pansemiotic (cf. Sebeok 1977b, Section 7). Sign processes in everyday life, or the semiotics of the *normal,* need to be closely reexamined in the light of their ontogenetic formation, or the semiotics of the *adnormal*; their dissolution in the course of a human life, or the semiotics of the *denormal*; and their modifications when caused by injury or disease, or the semiotics of the *abnormal.* In brief, two polar oppositions intersect here: one between the semiotics of ripening childhood and the semiotics of retrograde second childhood; the other, which Kleinpaul tried to make much of (1888:103–111) in a pertinent frame, between the semiotics of the "normalen . . . Formen der Gesundheit" and the semiotics of "Krankheiten."

The study of adnormal semiotics is shared with neurology and several branches of psychology; of denormal semiotics with social gerontology; and of abnormal semiotics with different medical specialties. As an example of distinguished consolidating work rooted in adnormal semiotics, let me single out McNeill's (1975) demonstration of the intimate connection between the production of speech by adults and the representation of conceptual structures on a sensory-motor level. His apt expression "semiotic extension" makes double reference to the basis of contact between "normal" adult conceptualization with the development of speech production in children and spontaneous gesticulations during speech that, "far from being mere embellishments," can also "be seen to arise directly from the operation of the speech mechanisms themselves" (ibid., 373), viewed, that is, as an external dynamic trace of the internal speech program. It is good news that McNeill is finishing a book on his fruitful notion of "semiotic extension," a kind of meaning relationship, and especially encouraging that for his underlying theory of signs he builds upon the strongest yet available—Peirce's.

The development of human communicative competence, including the unfolding of man's repertory of prelinguistic signs, "those which occur in the child's behavior before it speaks, or which later, even in the adult, are independent of language signs," according to the fruitful formulation of Morris (1964:58), involves a gradual increase in both nonverbal and verbal specializations and specificities that Eric Lenneberg has together termed "differentiation" (Lenneberg and Lenneberg 1975:1:32)—a label fittingly chosen, for it evokes, to my bent quite accurately, the proper embryological homology, or, rather, continuity. It has not yet been sufficiently realized that this amply documented process of semiotic differentiation in children not only perdures through adulthood but that it is an essential feature of senescence. While the aging and the aged shed, bit by bit, semiotic competencies "normal" adults take for granted, they also tend to acquire a new-sprung stock of message-types as a part of their adaptive reaction to the impact of their changing environment with which they must all learn to cope. Since it is one of the most dramatic and significant facts of demography that the number of people characterizable as elderly—i.e., 65 years of age and older—is increasing faster than that in any other age group, and that this population trend is likely to continue in the foreseeable future, the study of caducity and communication (Oyer and Oyer 1976) is becoming an ever more urgent research concern of our decade, just as adolescence and communication was—as it still is—a pressing preoccupation throughout this quarter of a century. The heterogeneous age-related alterations in the patterns of communication—which are more likely than not complicated by a host of other variables, notably by health-related impediments—in 11% of our population, or about 21 million Americans alone, a figure which is predicted to rise, for this country, to about 20% by the turn of the century, constitutes an unprecedented opportunity for the intensive semiotic quest whose time has come. The signs of old age, seen as adaptive strategies which are reasonable in particular semiotic environments, were studied by Stafford in a pioneering thesis (1977). He showed that many such signs are routinely "misread" in the community where he did his fieldwork as indices of physiological deterioration. He ascribes the embarrassment, alienation, and, eventually, the mental anguish of old people to the consistent misinterpretations of their messages on the part of their young interlocutors and interactants, or age mates, who don't share with them what I am here provisionally proposing to call their denormal code, resulting, according to Stafford, from a socially imposed decrease in responsibility coupled with a corresponding increase in dependence. "Old age," thus conceived, *is,* in fact, a system of signification, to which Peirce's notion of infinite semiosis is eminently applicable and which is fecundly analyzable within his trichotomous scheme of sign relations. In Stafford's favorite example, "repetitiousness" in the senescent is for them an index of old age, which, however, is regularly mistaken by others for an unwitting symptom of a physiological deficit, leading him to formulate the insightful maxim that "one man's index is another man's rheme," or, as I would prefer to phrase it in the vocabulary of cryptanalytic transformations, "one generation's cleartext is another generation's encicode." Nothing short of the armamentarium of cryptanalysis must be applied to appreciate the bracketing phases of man's full life cycle, from adnormal to denormal, perceived, at least within our own culture (cf. Umiker-Sebeok 1977b), as an essentially specular process.

    In their contribution to this book on some "Unexpected Semiotic Implications of Medical Inquiry," Shands and Meltzer discuss a fascinating array of semiotic observations characteristic of certain unskilled laborers following industrial accidents. At the same time, they emphasize that the "application of semiotic principles to the field of medicine is in its infancy, although it has long been clear that the physician's stock in trade is *interpretation.*" This protracted nonage of clinical semiotics is perplexing when one considers the Hippocratic roots of the doctrine of signs as a whole (Sebeok 1976a:125–126, 181–182, and 1977a), and particularly the explicit contributions of the immensely influential Galen (130–201 A.D.). It was Galen who classified semiotics as one of the six principal branches of medicine, and the strength of Galenism, according to Temkin's dependable account (1973:179), "reposed in no small measure in its having provided medical categories . . . for relating the individual to health and disease, [including] semeiology (the science of signs)." Galen subdivided the field into three abiding parts, inspection or diagnosis, cognition or anamnesis, and providence or prognosis. He regarded everything unnatural occurring in the body as a symptom, and a syndrome as an aggregation of symptoms *(athroisma ton symptomaton),* clearly recognizing that while both of the former directly reflect clinical observation, the formulation of a diagnosis requires causal thinking.

It is my layman's impression that semiotic ideas have, naturally enough, penetrated most pervasively into that area of medicine which is devoted to disturbances in signing function consequent to selective ravages of brain injury—the condition Steinthal termed *Asemie* in 1881, and Hamilton (later copied by Jackson) *asemasia* in 1878, but which is, of course, more commonly known, in specific reference to a variety of abnormal language functions, by the general label aphasia. But since all medicine, from the Corpus Hippocraticum to the present day, is in essence hermeneutic, the pertinence of semiotics, in a deep sense, to a universal theory of disease is not surprising. Note what one leading figure in cancer research told an interviewer: "I think the most important diseases amount to a problem of bad communication. . . . Cells and tissues respond to misinformation or misinterpretation from the environment and they do so in a certain way. They overreact. . . ." (Thomas 1976:114).

Children diagnosed as suffering from infantile autism, the descriptions of which are most often negatively stated as consisting of a minimal behavioral repertoire and almost no control at all by the social environment save, perhaps, for some elementary avoidance responses, offer one kind of a challenge to semiotic analysis, because this is a form of malady which is typically characterized by disinterest in interpersonal relationships (even within the family), let alone in looser forms of association. It is often asserted that the autistic child is indifferent to faces. One such boy was pictured as mute, and what activity there was consisted almost entirely of simple, stereotyped maneuvers, "such as moving his foot back and forth, flipping a shoe lace, rubbing a spot on the floor or flipping small objects pivoted between the fingers for many hours at a time" (Ferster 1964:317). Usually, the presence or absence of a potential interactant is reported to have hardly any effect on the patient's behavior, but it has occasionally proved feasible "to achieve an increasing level of social interaction and even considerable amounts of productive speech" (ibid., 326), as in the case in point by the interposition of a machine, i.e., by means of a form of operant conditioning. It is not at all clear whether infantile autism, variable as it is, is due to some genetic defect, personality disorder, or brain damage perhaps suffered at birth, or to a combination of such and still other "psychosomatic" conditions intuitively sensed to coexist in different measure (cf. Ingram, in Lenneberg and Lenneberg 1975:2:243).

Kanner's syndrome, or infantile autism in its classical form (ibid., Creak et al., 2:242), is recognized by an array of diagnostic features each of which represents some impoverished sign function, beginning with an underlying inability for sustained message coupling between source and destination, or, to phrase this in more positive fashion, its fundamental defining criterion limits the linkage between the child and any adult to mere symbiosis that approaches a zero degree of normal semiosis: while the child is indifferent to his caretaker's attention, the latter's frequency of responses decreases proportionately with the amount of stimulus aversiveness and may ultimately become extinguished. The autistic child is also apparently unaware of his personal identity, and may exhibit this anomic state, among other symptoms, by a confusion of personal pronouns. He will often be echolalic in the vocal mode and correspondingly imitative in the visual mode, as well as produce significantly more stereotyped utterances and contextually inappropriate remarks than a developmentally aphasic child. Autistic children are attested to "differ even in their cries from normal children and from other subnormal children" (Cromer 1974:251). Adding to these the bizarre postures and ritualistic mannerisms, such as spinning themselves or objects, it is small wonder that the Tinbergens—as "animal ethologists who have for years specialised on social encounters in higher animals, which are of course nonverbal"(1972:11)—have focused upon autism as a prime target for their ethological approach, noting "the considerable potential" residing in this method for the investigation of nonverbal communication in man and, of course, "in general." Since, in my view, the biological study of comportment and the semiotic study of communication and signification are largely overlapping disciplines (Sebeok 1976a, Ch. 5, and id. 1977a), I perceive here one common meeting ground where both methodologies could prove illuminating,

although we have contributed, so far, next to nothing to either theory or
rehabilitation. These brief remarks are meant to be read chiefly as a plea for
the reabsorption of clinical semiotics into the comprehensive doctrine of
signs, along with the signs of growing up and the signs of growing old.

Pavlov's Mice: Three Concluding Lessons

Before bringing these summary observations to an end, I would like to
address the issue of overarching principles guiding semiotic inquiry. I shall do
so briefly because I deal with it in substantially more detail in a separate
publication soon to appear (Sebeok 1978). Also, I prefer to approach the
question here obliquely, introducing it by way of an anecdote from the history
of physiology in the 1920s.

The episode, which is well authenticated (Gruenberg 1929:326–327,
Zirkle 1958:1476, Razran 1959:916–917), centers upon Ivan Pavlov, who has
justly been called "the 20th century's empiricist par excellence" (Razran
1959:916). It concerns experiments he caused to be conducted to demonstrate
the transmission of conditioned reflexes in mice from one generation to the
next. The experiments were actually carried out by an obscure research assistant of his, named Studentsov, whose published data showed 298, 114, 29,
11, and 6 conditioning trials for five successive generations of mice. Pavlov,
who had "shared the Lamarckian predisposition, common to Russian bio-
scientists" (Razran, ibid.) with his country's intelligentsia, accepted these
inheritance data initially or, at any rate, failed to repudiate the explanatory
hypothesis even after he obtained no evidence to support it. Not until 1929, in
an informal statement made during the Thirteenth International Physiological
Congress, in Boston, did Pavlov offer an alternative interpretation for the
amazing data: he explained that "in checking up these experiments it was
found that the apparent improvement in the ability to learn, on the part of
successive generations of mice, was really due to an improvement in the
ability to teach, on the part of the experimenter!" (Gruenberg 1929:327,
fn. 1.).

To me, this fascinating little story suggests three morals of particular
interest to our community of semioticians, the first of which is both the most
general and, at least at first blush, the most banal: that even the greatest
scientist can err. What is important for us is to distinguish between certain
major sources of error, and, notably, to recognize self-deception. Self-
deception is akin to the extremely widespread effect known as self-fulfilling
prophecy (Rosenthal and Jacobson 1968, Part 1), but will perhaps be best
recognized by scientists by an emblematic tag known as the "Clever Hans
phenomenon." Pavlov's gullibility was due to his wish, consonant with the

Fig. 1. Mr. von Osten with Clever Hans.

ambience of his times, to believe that acquired characters were inherited, just as, a few decades earlier, an unfortunate German high school mathematics teacher, Herr von Osten, very badly wanted his horse, Hans, to perform feats of arithmetic, spell and read, solve problems of musical harmony, and answer personal questions. "Pavlov, of course, was an honest scientist" (Zirkle 1958), and there is no evidence that von Osten ever had fraudulent intent; both simply fell victim to their passionate expectations.

Self-deception, then, must be sharply separated from deception of others, or deliberate fraud.[1] There are, alas, not a few cases of academic double-dealing, some British and U.S. perpetrators of which were exposed in recent issues of *Nature* and *Science*. I have followed with special attention the failed efforts of the 1960s to engage in complex communication with dolphins (Sebeok 1972:53–60), and parallel endeavors to unconvincingly (Limber 1977) attribute the use of human language to chimps and gorillas in the 1970s. Without impugning in any way the good faith of most investigators of the intellectual capacities of marine mammals and primates, I see the ever-present specter of Clever Hans, except in those instances where chicanery cannot be ruled out. After all, despite the innocence of von Osten, most of Hans's performing ancestors and descendants were operated for profit in confidence games, as for instance the famous "oat-eater" Morocco, "the dancing horse" mentioned by Shakespeare (in *Love's Labour's Lost* I.ii.51), exhibited by an Elizabethan rogue named John Banks, whose methods were exposed, in 1612, by one Samuel Rid in semiotic terms that are amazingly fresh: note, Rid wrote, in *The Art of Juggling,* that the horse can do nothing "but his master must first know, and then his master knowing, the horse is ruled by him by signs" (in Kinney 1973:290). It would surely have saved Oskar Pfungst (1965) a lot of time and effort had he known the case history of Morocco, a detailed account of which had been published (cf. Halliwell-Phillipps 1879), but which chanced to be reckoned in the field of literary exegesis instead of experimental psychology. Various other tricks enabling animals, horses as well as dogs, cats, pigs, and many kinds of birds, to say nothing of fleas, to perform such marvels of misdirection—as by a technique widely employed by mediums but known to only those in the trade as "pencil reading"—*pour épater le bourgeois* and, of course, for a modicum of profit, are illuminatingly and amusingly bared by the fine magician Christopher (1970:39–54).

The second lesson is a more palpably semiotic one, the essence of which was perfectly captured by the leader of the Hans-Commission, Carl Stumpf, and his brilliant investigator Pfungst, when they spoke of "looking for, in the horse, what should have been sought in the man" (cited by Rosenthal, in Pfungst 1965:xxx). As we saw, it took Pavlov a while to shift his attention from the mice to his overly zealous assistant, back from the event being

THE WONDERFUL HORSE OF AN. 1595.

Fig. 2. John Banks with Morocco, the wonderful horse of an. 1595.
In this woodcut, the steed is stomping out the numbers on a pair of
rolled dice.

scrutinized to the experimenter, from message destination to message source.
The role played by the observing subject in physics is fairly well understood
and respected: since the properties of the observer, especially with regard to
magnitude, are usually very different from those of the object observed, the
subject is likely to remain relatively outside the system that he is studying and
hence one may assume that his report will be reasonably unbiased. In the life
sciences, however, and *a fortiori* in the communication sciences of man, the
characteristics of the observer are likely to be similar to those of the observed
and must be supposed to influence the processes under scrutiny. The subject
himself will likewise be seriously affected by the stream of ongoing events

(cf. Ruesch 1972:54–55). In linguistic fieldwork, for example, hardly anybody has fully appreciated this, or, if so, conducted himself accordingly. A
sophisticated exception was Leonard Bloomfield, who, according to Voegelin
(1960:204), "preferred being corrected, when he made an error as a child-like
speaker of Menomini, to asking a direct question on how do you say so-and-so
to a bilingual Menomini—for fear of obtaining a false analogy. During the
three summers Bloomfield and I recorded Ojibwa texts together at Linguistic
Institutes, he never once asked a 'how do you say' question. . . ."

An area of special concern to us all is the art of healing, to wit, the
workings of the physician–patient dyad, and the so-called placebo effect,
which means the therapeutic sequel consequent to the patient's belief in the
efficacy of the treatment. This is a semiotic problem in its most crystalline
form: since a placebo is, by definition, a pharmacologically inert substance
that the doctor administers to a patient to relieve his distress when the use of
an active medication isn't called for, "its beneficial effects must lie in its
symbolic power. The most likely supposition is that it gains its potency
through being a tangible symbol of the physician's role as a healer" (Frank
1961:66). We learn from Shapiro's riveting sketch that, throughout the centuries from shaman to physician, this very coupling—this bond between the
healer and the troubled—"comprised all that the doctor had to offer the
patient" (1960:113–114); and he quotes other authorities who affirm that the
history of medicine is a history of "dynamic power" of the nexus between
doctor and patient (cf. once again Peirce's dynamical action and Thom's
"dynamique du symbolisme"). The placebo works best with those patients
who have favorable expectations from medicine and, "in general, accept and
respond to symbols of healing" (Frank 1961:70), but "the fact that one of the
best educated major religious groups in the United States is able to deny the
rational efficacy of any treatment or medicine and to assign all treatment
benefits to faith" (Shapiro 1960:114) strongly underlines the purity of the
semiotic import of the phenomenon, where faith itself acquires the essence of
a symbol and thus quite admirably meets Peirce's criterion of "an *imputed*
quality" (1.558), such that the two constituent sides of the sign, the signifier
and the signified, are bonded one to the other in "a relation which consists in
the fact that the mind associates the sign with its object" (1.372) regardless of
any factual connection. In passing, it should be noted that in medical history
as well as contemporary practice one may observe a gamut of procedures in
the administration of placebos from out-and-out quackery to their sensitively
controlled use by responsible physicians. What all have in common is the
confidence, the enthusiasm, and the ritual on the part of both interactants, and
it is therefore undoubtedly true "that the ability to respond favorably to a
placebo is not so much a sign of excessive gullibility, as one of easy ac-

ceptance of others in their socially defined roles" (Frank 1961:70). In other words, placebo-responsiveness assumes, so to speak, an indexical function in respect to the ability of patients to trust their fellow man as embodied by their physician or, to a lesser degree, his anointed surrogates (e.g., nurses).

The more or less synonymous sets of dyadic ties I have variously referred to in this section as source and destination of messages, observer and observed, subject and object, physician and patient, man and animal (horse or mouse, porpoise or primate), could be multiplied *ad nauseam* to encompass further particularized couplings, notably of parent and child. To my taste, the most suggestive pair of labels comes from the argot of the criminal world engagingly explicated by Maurer (1949; see also Goffman 1952): operator and mark. This consummate metaphor works something like this, to give only one example from an area of application that ought to pique the curiosity of all who would heed Pavlov's second lesson.

From time to time, claims are made that there are dogs that actually talk. There are records in the Académie Française of one such animal that, according to no less an authority than Leibniz, "had a vocabulary of thirty words, which was put to effective use when he wanted something specific to eat or drink" (Christopher 1970:51). The question is: how is such a con perpetrated, even on smart apples like Leibniz? Briefly (cynical data after Johnson 1912), a dog is conditioned, in the customary manner, to bark in response to certain verbal cues. Don, a seven-year-old German setter, who was reported by numerous observers to answer questions if food were held before him, replied to *"Was heisst du?"* (*"Don."*), *"Was hast du?"* (*"Hunger."*), and to other such queries, and was alleged moreover to answer categorical questions by *"Ja"* or *"Nein."* Don's behavior was thoroughly investigated by the same Oskar Pfungst who, in 1907, had unveiled the secret of Hans, and he concluded (1) that the dog does not use words with any consciousness of their meaning to the hearer, and (2) that he is not using words learned by imitation. Instead, he gave this comparatively simple explanation: the dog produced vocal sounds which induce "illusions in the hearer.... The uncritical do not make the effort to discriminate between what is actually given in perception and what is merely associated imagery, which otherwise gives to the perception a meaning wholly unwarranted; and they habitually ignore the important part which suggestion always plays in ordinary situations." In other words, "we may expect the majority of animal lovers to continue to read their own mental processes into the behavior of their pets. Nor need we be astonished if even scientists of a certain class continue at intervals to proclaim that they have completely demonstrated the presence in lower animals of 'intelligent imitation' and of other extremely complicated mental processes...." This is also precisely what happens in the circus, as Bouissac has emphasized when

Fig. 3. Blondie with Clever Daisy. © King Features Syndicate, Inc., 1977. Reprinted by permission.

he referred to inferences drawn from the humanization of animals: ''The most efficient training . . . evokes a behavior from the animal that, within the constructed situation, subtly creates the impression that the animal has humanlike motivations, emotions, and reasoning'' (1976:118), and when he drew attention to a characteristic feature of every circus act, namely, that it ''constructs its own situation, its own immediate context. . . .'' ''The circus act must be completed,'' he adds (in this volume), ''by the semantic operations which are performed in the process and account for the meaningfulness that such circus acts convey to their audience.''[2] The underlying principle, *that* we construct a context-based advance hypothesis about what the message will be to tune in our perceptual equipment to favor certain interpretations of the input and reject others, was elegantly demonstrated by Bruce over twenty years ago (1956), although *how* such contextual constraints actually work is still unknown. In sum, I read the second lesson of the Pavlov yarn as a strong injunction for us to look in the men and women (Lilly [1967] and Margaret Howe, Bernadette Chauvin-Muckensturm [1974], the Gardners, Premack, Rumbaugh, Francine Patterson, and their fellow trainers) for what has hitherto been assiduously sought for in Peter Dolphin, the Greater Spotted Woodpecker (claimed "to represent the phenomenon of man–animal communication analogous to that found in monkeys by the Gardners and Premack"), Washoe, Sara, Lana, Koko, and the rest.[3] This is not to deny the inherent interest of studies in animal intelligence. Quite the contrary; but I would like such studies additionally to take the crucial effects of man's participation into full account and, as in the Lana case, even the extremely subtle secondary effects of the computer used as the operator (Rumbaugh 1977, see esp. pp. 159 and 161; cf. Sebeok 1978). Incidentally, I concur with Hediger (1974:28–29) totally that the view held by some scientists that all contact between observer and observed must strictly cease in experimental (and, by extension, clinical) situations is basically untenable. There are two corollaries to this skeptical stance: first, that the source that generated the message has got to be at least as thoroughly investigated as the destination that is to interpret it; and second, that the properties of the channel(s) interconnecting the two organisms be probed with equal diligence—which brings us to the third implication of the Pavlov story.

No one, it seems, knows how Studentsov unintentionally instructed his mice. Rosenthal, as a part of his ingenious research on the generality of the effects of the experimenters' expectancy, employed rats, but had no idea how the animals came to differentially perform as they did: ". . . we cannot be sure of the sense modality by which the experimenter's expectancy is communicated to the subject" (1966:165), although these rodents are known to be sensitive to visual, auditory, olfactory, and tactile cues (for recent work on the surprisingly complex social interactions of rats, and especially the functions of their ultrasonic calls, cf. Lore and Flannelly 1977). Rosenthal thinks, however, that the specific cues by which an experimenter communicates with his animal subjects "probably varies with the type of animal, the type of experiment, and perhaps even the type of experimenter. With Clever Hans as subject, the cues were primarily visual, but auditory cues were also helpful. This seemed also to be true when the subjects were dogs rather than one unusual horse" (ibid., 177).

Detailed analysis of the carryings on in a laboratory shows that there are "sighs, groans, finger tapping, guttural exclamations or muted whispers" (Pilisuk et al. 1976:515) which are seldom discerned, not to mention "illicit communication" through all the other modalities that goes, if perceived, unreported. Pilisuk and his collaborators found that such signs "did, in fact,

have a significant effect upon the level of cooperative behavior,'' and advocated further studies of ''behavior that takes place 'on the sly' since human
interaction seems to be full of just such activity'' (ibid. 522).

The most prescient of animal psychologists, Hediger, rightly insists that
a wide-ranging, intensive program be launched to examine all known and
potential channels which are or might be sign-carriers, and thus to determine
what is really happening in the interaction between organisms. To this plea,
he immediately adds, ''Of considerable help in this endeavour is a new branch
of science known as semiotics: the study of all possible signals in technical as
well as biological and psychological fields'' (1974:29). He then enumerates a
few situations where reciprocal understanding between man and animal has
been achieved via media of communication that are out of the ordinary,
stressing not only that hitherto unknown channels are at work but ''that
familiar ones may already play a role even if outside our threshold of perception'' (ibid. 34). The Hess pupil response (which I recently discussed in
Sebeok 1977b, Section 5) furnishes one nice illustration of this kind of a
sign-process; the equally important eyebrow flash, ''discovered'' and described by Eibl-Eibesfeldt (1972:299–301), another. The pupil movement
and the eyebrow flash are both extremely common if mostly out-of-awareness
signs to which we respond strongly in defined contexts; they are used globally
by men, except where culture overrides nature (as in Japan, where the flash is
considered indecent).

A much more arcane illustration, from the underground literature of
semiotics, is furnished by the case history of Eugen de Rubini, the famous
Moravian ''muscle reader,'' who came to San Francisco shortly after World
War I. This young man had the uncanny ability to read the ''thoughts'' of
others from the patterns of their muscle tensions. Had he not been carefully
investigated by three of the most important contemporary psychologists, eminently including Edward C. Tolman, his feats might today be considered
fictional. The very careful experiments they conducted were reported in the
Psychological Review by Stratton, under the intriguing heading, ''The control
of another person by obscure signs'' (1921). Stratton and his colleagues
adopted Pfungst's paradigm for Clever Hans, but they never did succeed in
pinning down the precise cues employed by de Rubini, who modestly laid no
claim to mind reading. He was judged to depend ''to some appreciable extent,
even though subconsciously, upon visual cues . . . of a highly elusive kind''
(ibid., 309–310). Tremors of the floor, faint sounds of feet, of movements of
arms and clothing, together with those made by changes in breathing, were
diminished signs, but not excluded under the laboratory conditions imposed.
''The experimenters each and all assumed that [de Rubini's] successes de-
pended upon sensory cues of some sort, and not upon immediate influence of

mind upon mind'' (ibid., 310). This admirably cautious paper refrains from extrapolation beyond the evidence. Stratton believed that his subject ''caught, in the very periphery of his visual field'' (ibid., 309), postures or motions which assisted him, but couldn't prove so. It is instructive to contrast this with the plethora of early 1960s reports of observations of sight through the face (''dermooptical phenomena''): blindfolded subjects were said to read texts without using their eyes. Observations were accumulated, although no possible mechanism ever came to mind, until fraud was discovered. The last moral of Pavlov, then, is a simultaneous call for action, along lines set forth by Hediger, but foreshadowed by Jakob von Uexküll (Sebeok 1977a), yet tempered by a need for unceasing vigilance in the face of imposture. Clearly, we are all prisoners of our senses, which are imperfectly understood at best, and the weaknesses of which are exploited by con-artists, academic or laic, witting or unwitting.[4]

This book opened with Wells's ''fundamental message . . . of caution'' for semiotics. I do not disagree with his wise bidding that, ''whatever claims we make, we must be prepared to support,'' even though the theme of my closing chapter may have implied this, for I have taken the opposite tack here. My musings touched on many subjects which had in common what I have chosen to call ecumenicalism in semiotics—the pursuit of boundaries and of ways of transcending them. I believe that in semiotics, as in so many other areas of intellectual endeavor, the imaginative and sometimes intuitive search for invariance must go hand in hand with the empirical scrutiny of variation.

NOTES

1. Koestler's (1971) sparkling chronicle of the tangled Kammerer affair, which he dramatized as ''the case of the midwife toad,'' shows how painfully elusive the truth can be, and how difficult it is to decide among these two basic forms of deception, their intermixture, and still other alternatives. In the matter of Kammerer, the question will perhaps forever stand unresolved.

2. By the way, Hachet-Souplet (1897:85) has pointed out that ''Il n'y a, au point de vue théorique, aucune différence entre le dressage du singe et celui du chien. . . .'' In practice, however, circus trainers differentiate between the quadrupedal and the ''privileged'' quadrumanous species (viz., dogs *vs.* monkeys). Surprisingly enough, the excellent literature of dressage seems only very exceptionally to be utilized by psychologists who aim to impart language training to primates. It is a pity that the two traditions so seldom intersect.

3. A ''shill'' is an accomplice who plays a confidence game so that the mark sees him win (Maurer 1949:306). In reporting the unmasking of Don, Johnson (1912:749) makes a strong point of the fact that ''Extensive comment has been made in the German and even in the American daily press on [the dog's] reported conversational

ability. . . ." In the circus, posters (Bouissac 1976, Ch. 10) provide "the semiotic key" to the act, reinforced by carefully planted advance publicity. It would be easy to document the metaphorically shill-like role that popular magazines and other mass media, especially TV, as well as naive colleagues, unknowing shillabers, have played in the promotion of the dolphin mythology of the 1960s (Sebeok 1972:60) and the chimp mythology of the 1970s. As in any con, it is very difficult to "knock a mark," i.e., to convince him that he is being duped. Such diehard marks are called addicts. My experience has been that attempts to ameliorate academic addicts are met with resentment, even downright hostility; the reasons for this will, of course, be perfectly obvious to readers of Goffman (1952).

It took the dolphin craze about ten years to subside; the present chimp fad, which is as yet in the expansive stage, will take a little longer to ease off, since contemporary behaviorists are still in the firm grip of La Mettrie (Limber 1977:288). For a few notable exceptions besides Limber, see the prominent agnostic psychologists Brown and Herrnstein (1975:490–491) and Terrace and Bever (1976:583). A complication is that two delusions are almost inextricably entangled here: I already called attention to the Pathetic Fallacy in 1963 (Sebeok 1972:59); what I am after now are the background and broader implications of the Clever Hans Fallacy (id. 1978).

4. Some of the ideas incorporated in the last section were variously aired in lectures given at Brown University (November 15, 1976) and at the University of Hamburg (January 7, 1977). They were also presented, in condensed form and with different emphasis, at the 1977 meetings of the Central States Anthropological Society, held in Cincinnati last March, in the framework of a Symposium on Semiotic Perspectives in Human Relations (co-organized with the author by Dr. D. Jean Umiker-Sebeok).

REFERENCES

Barthes, Roland. 1964. *Eléments de sémiologie.* Paris: Editions Gonthier.

Bateson, Gregory. 1968. Redundancy and coding. In: *Animal Communication. Techniques of Study and Results of Research,* Thomas A. Sebeok, ed. Bloomington: Indiana University Press, pp. 614–626.

Bertalanffy, Ludwig von. 1968. *General System Theory: Foundations, Development, Applications.* New York: George Braziller.

Bloomfield, Leonard. 1939. Linguistic aspects of science. *International Encyclopedia of Unified Science,* 1, 4.

Bouissac, Paul. 1976. *Circus and Culture: A Semiotic Approach.* Bloomington: Indiana University Press.

Brown, Roger, and Herrnstein, Richard J. 1975. *Psychology.* Boston: Little, Brown.

Bruce, David J. 1956. Effects of context upon intelligibility of heard speech. In: *Information Theory,* Colin Cherry, ed. London: Butterworths Scientific Publications, pp. 245–252.

Cassirer, Ernst A. 1945. Structuralism in modern linguistics. *Word,* 1:99–120.

Chauvin-Muckensturm, Bernadette. 1974. Y a-t-il utilisation de signaux appris comme moyen de communication chez le pic epeiche? *Revue du Comportement Animal,* 9:185–207.

Chomsky, Noam. 1972. *Language and Mind.* New York: Harcourt Brace Jovanovich.

Christopher, Milbourne. 1970. *ESP, Seers & Psychics*. New York: Thomas Y. Crowell.

Cromer, Richard F. 1974. Receptive language in the mentally retarded: Processes and diagnostic distinctions. In: *Language Perspectives—Acquisition, Retardation and Intervention*, Richard L. Schiefelbush and Lyle L. Lloyd, eds. London: Macmillan, pp. 237–267.

Dascal, Marcelo. 1972. *Aspects de la sémiologie de Leibniz*. Jerusalem: Hebrew University.

Eibl-Eibesfeldt, Irenäus. 1972. Similarities and differences between cultures in expressive movements. In: *Nonverbal Communication*, Robert A. Hinde, ed. Cambridge: University Press, pp. 297–312.

Fairbanks, Matthew J. 1976. Peirce on man as a language: a textual interpretation. *Transactions of the Charles S. Peirce Society*, 12:18–32.

Ferster, Charles B. 1964. Psychotherapy by machine communication. In: *Disorders of Communication, Proceedings of the Association for Research in Nervous and Mental Disease*, 42:317–328.

Fisch, Max H. In press. Peirce's general theory of signs. In: *Sight, Sound, and Sense*, Thomas A. Sebeok, ed. Bloomington: Indiana University Press.

Frank, Jerome D. 1961. *Persuasion and Healing: A Comparative Study of Psychotherapy*. Baltimore: The Johns Hopkins Press.

Gerard, Ralph. 1957. Units and concepts of biology. *Science*, 125:429–433.

Goffman, Erving. 1952. On cooling the mark out. *Psychiatry*, 15:451–463.

Grinker, Roy R., ed. 1956. *Toward a Unified Theory of Human Behavior*. New York: Basic Books.

Gruenberg, Benjamin C. 1929. *The Story of Evolution: Facts and Theories on the Development of Life*. Garden City: Garden City Publishing Co.

Hachet-Souplet, Pierre. 1897. *Le dressage des animaux et les combats de bêtes, révélation des procédés employés par les professionels pour dresser le chien, le singe, le cheval, l'éléphant, les bêtes féroces, etc*. Paris: Firmin Didot.

Halliwell-Phillipps, James O. 1879. *Memoranda on Love's Labour's Lost, King John, Othello, and on Romeo and Juliet*. London: James Evan Adlard.

Hediger, Heini. 1974. Communication between man and animal. *Image*, 62:27–40.

Hjelmslev, Louis. 1953. *Prolegomena to a Theory of Language*. Baltimore: Waverly Press.

Jacob, François. 1974. *The Logic of Living Systems: A History of Heredity*. London: Allen Lane.

Jakobson, Roman. 1971. Word and language. *Selected Writings* 2. The Hague: Mouton.

Jervis, Robert. 1970. *The Logic of Images in International Relations*. Princeton: Princeton University Press.

Johnson, Harry Miles. 1912. The talking dog. *Science*, 35:749–751.

Kinney, Arthur E., ed. 1973. *Rogues, Vagabonds, & Sturdy Beggars*. Barre, Mass.: Imprint Society.

Kleinpaul, Rudolf. 1888. *Sprache ohne Worte: Idee einer allgemeinen Wissenschaft der Sprache*. Leipzig: Friedrich.

Koestler, Arthur. 1967. *The Ghost in the Machine*. New York: Macmillan.

———. 1971. *The Case of the Midwife Toad*. New York: Random House.

Kolata, Gina Bari. 1977. Catastrophe theory: the emperor has no clothes. *Science*, 196:287, 350–351.

Lamb, Sydney M., and Makkai, Adam. 1976. Semiotics of culture and language. *Current Anthropology,* 17:352–354.

Lenneberg, Eric H., and Lenneberg, Elizabeth, eds. 1975. *Foundations of Language Development: A Multidisciplinary Approach,* 2 vols. New York: Academic Press.

Lilly, John Cunningham. 1967. *The Mind of the Dolphin: A Nonhuman Intelligence.* Garden City: Doubleday.

Limber, John. 1977. Language in child and chimp? *American Psychologist,* 32: 280–295.

Lore, Richard, and Flannelly, Kevin. 1977. Rat societies. *Scientific American,* 236:106–116.

Marcus, Solomon. 1974. Linguistic structures and generative devices in molecular genetics. *Cahiers de linguistique théorique et appliquée,* 11:77–104.

Maurer, David W. 1949. *The Big Con.* New York: Pocket Books.

McNeill, David. 1975. Semiotic extension. In: *Information Processing and Cognition: The Loyola Symposium,* Robert L. Solso, ed. Hillsdale: Erlbaum Associates, Ch. 11.

Mead, Margaret. 1972. Vicissitudes of the study of the total communication process. In: *Approaches to Semiotics,* Thomas A. Sebeok, et al., eds. The Hague: Mouton, pp. 277–287.

Miller, James G. 1975–76. The nature of living systems. *Behavioral Science,* 20:343–535, 21:295–468.

———. 1976. Second annual Ludwig von Bertalanffy memorial lecture. *Behavioral Science,* 21:219–227.

Morris, Charles. 1964. *Signification and Significance: A Study of the Relations of Signs and Values.* Cambridge: The M.I.T. Press.

———. 1971. *Writings on the General Theory of Signs.* The Hague: Mouton.

———. 1976. *Image.* New York: Vantage Press.

Oyer, Herbert J., and Oyer, E. Jane, eds. 1976. *Aging and Communication.* Baltimore: University Park Press.

Peirce, Charles S. 1965–66. *Collected Papers of Charles Sanders Peirce,* Charles Hartshorne, Paul Weiss, and Arthur W. Burks, eds. Cambridge: Harvard University Press. [References are to volumes and paragraphs, not pages.]

Pfungst, Oskar. 1965. *Clever Hans (The Horse of Mr. von Osten),* Robert Rosenthal, ed. New York: Holt, Rinehart and Winston.

Phillips, D. C. 1976. *Holistic Thought in Social Science.* Stanford: Stanford University Press.

Philodemus. 1941. *On Methods of Inference: A Study in Ancient Empiricism,* Phillip Howard De Lacy and Estelle Allen De Lacy, eds. *Philological Monographs* 10 (Philadelphia: American Philological Association).

Pike, Kenneth L. 1972. *Language in Relation to a Unified Theory of the Structure of Human Behavior* (2d ed.). The Hague: Mouton.

Pilisuk, Mark, Brandes, Barbara, and van der Hove, Didier. 1976. Deceptive sounds: illicit communication in the laboratory. *Behavioral Science,* 21:515–523.

Pribram, Karl H. 1971. *Languages of the Brain.* Englewood Cliffs: Prentice-Hall.

Razran, Gregory. 1959. Pavlov the empiricist. *Science,* 130:916–917.

Rose, Steven. 1973. *The Conscious Brain.* New York: Alfred A. Knopf.

Rosenthal, Robert. 1966. *Experimenter Effects in Behavioral Research.* New York: Appleton-Century-Crofts.

Rosenthal, Robert, and Jacobson, Lenore. 1968. *Pygmalion in the Classroom: Teacher Expectation and Pupils' Intellectual Development.* New York: Holt, Rinehart and Winston.

Ruesch, Jurgen. 1972. *Semiotic Approaches to Human Relations.* The Hague: Mouton.

Rumbaugh, Duane M., ed. 1977. *Language Learning by a Chimpanzee: The Lana Project.* New York: Academic Press.

Sebeok, Thomas A. 1972. *Perspectives in Zoosemiotics.* The Hague: Mouton.

——. 1976a. *Contributions to the Doctrine of Signs.* Lisse: Peter de Ridder Press.

——. 1976b. Iconicity. *Modern Language Notes,* 91:1427–1456.

——. 1977a. *Semiosis in Nature and Culture.* Lisse: Peter de Ridder Press.

——. 1977b. Zoosemiotic components of human communication. In: *How Animals Communicate,* Thomas A. Sebeok, ed. Bloomington: Indiana University Press, Ch. 38.

——. 1978. "Clever Hans" in a semiotic frame. *Diogenes,* 28.

Shapiro, Arthur K. 1960. A contribution to a history of the placebo effect. *Behavioral Science,* 5:109–135.

Simone, Raffaele. 1972. Sémiologie augustinienne. *Semiotica,* 6:1–31.

Stafford, Philip B. 1977. The semiotics of old age in a small midwestern town: an interactionist approach, Ph.D. diss., Indiana University, Bloomington.

Stratton, G. M. 1921. The control of another person by obscure signs. *Psychological Review,* 28:301–314.

Temkin, Oswei. 1973. *Galenism: Rise and Decline of a Medical Philosophy.* Ithaca: Cornell University Press.

Terrace, H. S., and Bever, T. G. 1976. What might be learned from studying language in the chimpanzee? The importance of symbolizing oneself. In: *Origins and Evolution of Language and Speech,* Stevan R. Harnad, Horst B. Steklis, and Jane Lancaster, eds. *Annals of the New York Academy of Sciences,* 280:579–588.

Thom, René. 1974. *Modèles mathématiques de la morphogenèse.* Paris: Union Générale d'Editions.

——. 1975. *Structural Stability and Morphogenesis.* Reading: W. A. Benjamin.

Thomas, Lewis. 1976. Most things get better by themselves. *The New York Times Magazine,* July 4.

Tinbergen, E. A., and Tinbergen, N. 1972. Early Childhood Autism: An Ethological Approach. *Journal of Comparative Ethology,* Supplement 10. Berlin: Paul Parey.

Tomkins, Gordon M. 1975. The metabolic code. *Science,* 189:760–763.

Umiker-Sebeok, D. Jean. 1977a. Semiotics of culture: Great Britain and North America. *Annual Review of Anthropology* 6:121–135.

——. 1977b. Nature's way? Visual representations of American life cycles. Paper read at the Annual Meeting of the American Anthropological Association, Houston.

Voegelin, Carl F. 1960. Subsystem typology in linguistics. In: *Man and Cultures: Selected Papers,* Anthony F. C. Wallace, ed. Philadelphia: University of Pennsylvania Press, pp. 202–206.

Voigt, Vilmos. 1977. *Bevezetés a szemiotikába.* Budapest: Gondolat.

Weinreich, Uriel. 1968. Semantics and semiotics. *International Encyclopedia of the Social Sciences,* 14:164–169.

Whitfield, Francis. 1969. Glossematics. In: *Linguistics Today,* Archibald A. Hill, ed. New York: Basic Books, pp. 250–258.
Winner, Irene Portis, and Winner, Thomas G. 1976. The semiotics of cultural texts. *Semiotica,* 18:101–156.
Zirkle, Conway. 1958. Pavlov's beliefs. *Science,* 128:1476.

INDEX OF NAMES